Career Ladders

JUDY:

To AN OPEN-MINDED
TEAM BUILDER, AND
A COMMITTED ONE.

FORWARD 0

— Shep
4/30/08

CAREER LADDERS

Transition from High School to Adult Life

SECOND EDITION

Shepherd Siegel
Matt Robert
Karen Greener
Gary Meyer
William Halloran
Robert Gaylord-Ross

Foreword by Rob Riordan

pro·ed
An International Publisher

8700 Shoal Creek Boulevard
Austin, Texas 78757-6897
800/897-3202   Fax 800/397-7633
www.proedinc.com

© 1993, 2003 by PRO-ED, Inc.
8700 Shoal Creek Boulevard
Austin, Texas 78757-6897
800/897-3202   Fax 800/397-7633
www.proedinc.com

Library of Congress Cataloging-in-Publication Data

Career ladders : transition from high school to adult life / Shepherd Siegel . . . [et al.].—
2nd ed.
    p. cm.
   Includes bibliographical references and index.
   ISBN 0-89079-919-9
    1. Youth with social disabilities—Education (Secondary)—United States. 2. Youth
with social disabilities—Vocational guidance—United States. 3. Youth with mental
disabilities—Vocational guidance—United States. 4. Education, Cooperative—United
States. 5. School-to-work transition—United States. I. Siegel, Shepherd.

LC4091 .C34   2003
371.92—dc21
                                                     2002031928

This book is designed in Janson Text and Futura.

Printed in the United States of America

1 2 3 4 5 6 7 8 9 10   07 06 05 04 03

To Sylvia and Al

CONTENTS

Foreword ■ vii

Acknowledgments ■ ix

Introduction ■ xi

1 **Six Principles of Effective Transition Programming** ■ 1
Shepherd Siegel

2 **Community Classroom** ■ 9
Shepherd Siegel

3 **Employment Skills Workshop** ■ 57
Shepherd Siegel and Karen Greener

4 **Postsecondary Services for Youths in Transition** ■ 115
Matt Robert and Shepherd Siegel

5 **Job and Site Development for Community Classrooms** ■ 157
Gary Meyer and Shepherd Siegel

6 **Job Shadowing for Students in Grades 7 to 10** ■ 177
Shepherd Siegel

Afterword: Keeping the Change ■ 189
Shepherd Siegel, Robert Gaylord-Ross, and William Halloran

References ■ 195

Index ■ 197

About the Authors ■ 201

FOREWORD

At first glance, this volume appears to be a practical manual on helping disenfranchised youth find pathways into adult life. And indeed, it serves that function well. New and experienced educators alike will find wise counsel and hands-on materials by the bucketful, from development strategies to management tools to detailed lesson plans.

But there is much more to it than that. Shepherd Siegel and colleagues offer a visionary treatise that addresses two key failings of our education system: its tendency to isolate from the adult world of work and learning those who are about to enter it, and its implacable practice of labeling students in ways that limit their sense of themselves and their life chances. For this reason the book has applications far beyond any particular program or population. Due to the breadth and depth of the motivating vision, strategies originally aimed at meeting the needs of youth with disabilities turn out to be appropriate for all students, including even the highest achievers.

Underlying the structures and strategies laid out in this volume is a bold, generous vision of what young people understand and can do, along with an appreciation of their need to enhance their competencies through hands-on applications. The authors' understanding of integration is broad, going far beyond mainstreaming or inclusion and extending into the adult community. The authors provide compelling case illustrations for their argument that structural integration (e.g., constructing academically sound workplace internships) requires careful attention to the quality of life and human relationships if it is to lead to significant learning.

The six programmatic Career Ladders principles evoke other, more fundamental principles that, coincidentally, provide a sound basis for schools and youth programs in general. These principles are personalization, adult-world experience, and community engagement.

Personalization. Career Ladders offers a customized, holistic approach to learning. Students are intentionally invited to participate in determining the direction of their education. Where an "individualized" approach often benefits only those students who already have substantial personal resources, the Career Ladders approach addresses personal circumstances. Both in curriculum and structure, Career Ladders pays attention to students' affective needs. It recognizes the importance of the family as a critical influence in the student's world, for better or worse, and offers practical suggestions for helping students and families develop supportive relationships.

Adult-world experience. Siegel and colleagues rightly see work-based learning not as a track for some students, but as an essential part of the educational experience for all, extending over several years and deep into the world beyond school. The Career Ladders content goes far beyond simple "job skills," to encompass mentoring structures and reflective learning routines that serve all students well. In line with the needs of the new economy, this approach blurs the distinction between "career" and "college" preparation, addressing the concerns of both the employer who seeks applicants with "soft" skills like *following directions* and *punctuality*, and the engineering professor who complains that even top students demonstrate little sense of how to go about solving a real-world problem.

Community engagement. In Career Ladders, community engagement means more than partnerships. Well-managed work-based learning opportunities, such as job shadows and internships, not only extend learning into the community, but also build community itself. Critical to this approach is the belief that the educator's role in the community does not end with high school graduation. The Career Ladders structure lends itself to a case management approach that extends from middle school to beyond high school. It recognizes a programmatic responsibility to help students find mentors and develop support networks—to construct a "human ecosystem."

The "Career" in Career Ladders refers, in a John Deweyan sense, not to an outcome, but rather to a rich context for teaching and learning that puts students and their interests at the center. Career Ladders is inclusive, democratic, and pragmatic, inviting students to create their future within a community of learners.

In Minnesota some years back, I spoke with 10 students who were involved in career pathways programs in an inner city high school. The students spoke in glowing terms about their work placements and the high expectations they were experiencing, the new relevance they now saw in their schoolwork, and the inspiring relationships they were forming with adults. When I asked what one thing they would change about their high school, a student replied, "Some kids' attitudes." Others agreed in matter-of-fact tones. Finally, one student said, "You see, it's like this: If you're not in one of these programs, it's kind of hard to see your future." In that school, 400 students were in such programs—an extraordinarily high number, for any high school. But another 1,100 students were not.

We face an enormous task if we are to ensure a decent transition to adult life for adolescents. Our systems typically do not facilitate that transition; they assume it. As the authors themselves insist, there is no easy solution or single prescription for moving this work from the margins to the mainstream. What is important about this volume is that it offers a template, concrete strategies, and, most important, profound principles upon which educators may construct visible pathways to the future, not just for some students, but for all. In doing so, the authors offer educators a new look at their own possible future, too.

Rob Riordan

Rob Riordan, a long-time teacher, curriculum administrator, and trainer, is the former director of the U.S. Department of Education's New Urban High School project. He currently assists in the restructuring and reform of Rindge Latin High School in Boston, and in replicating and developing San Diego's High Tech High for the Bill and Melinda Gates Foundation.

ACKNOWLEDGMENTS

The original Career Ladders pilot was a small program, serving only 127 youths and their families. To them we offer our thanks; their belief in the program was the key ingredient to its success.

But the original Career Ladders could also be considered a large program, bringing together the resources of more than 100 local, state, and national organizations. To them we offer thanks; the program worked only to the extent that the people of these organizations respected and collaborated with each other. We gratefully acknowledge them.

To the memory of Robert Gaylord-Ross, who invented the community classroom. To Bill Halloran of the U.S. Department of Education, who always believed in the full potential of Career Ladders.

To the Career Ladders team in Seattle Public Schools: Catherine Unseth, Brian Lindquist, Joe Barrientos, P. J. Connell and Job Connection, Myrna Muto, Alison McCormick and Mainstay, Kathy Ackerman, Marcia Hitzman, David Kanetomi, Mick Moore, and Gayle Denys. And to the key employers who sponsor our students: Associated Grocers, King County International Airport, the Seattle Art Museum, A Contemporary Theater, the Seattle Symphony, the Westin Hotel, and the Seattle Public Schools Logistics Department.

To the King County school districts that have replicated Career Ladders: Lake Washington, with Marla Ingebrigtson, Dennis Meeks, and Becky Anderson; Renton, with Jay Leviton and the late Bob Dillman; Bellevue, with Kathy Montgomery, Ralph Allen, and Roberta Krause; and Northshore, with Dennis Milliken and Fred Row.

To the transition staff of the San Francisco Unified School District, especially the special education counselors of San Francisco's public high schools: Kofi Avoke, Jeff Bruno, Igen Chan, Will Cole, Yvette Fang, Eric Gidal, Mark Johnson, Susan Kwock, Dorian Laird, Mary Magee, Vic Milhoan, Susanna Praetzel, Joanne Prieur, Josephine Richau, Bill Schwalb, David States, Michelle Wagner, and Michele Waxman.

To the California State Department of Rehabilitation, especially Harry Brown, Lisa Eng, Keith Foster, Linda Gamble, Jim Kay, Phillip Magalong, Kate Moran, Susan Munoz, Rei Nishimura, and Kathy Shields.

To the employers of San Francisco, especially the California State Auto Association and its personnel department, the Marriott Corporation, the Photo & Sound Company, Saint Luke's Hospital, and the University of California Medical Center.

To San Francisco State University and the University of California at Berkeley, especially Ron Morrisette, Adriana Schuler, and John Sullivan.

To the other youth-serving agencies of San Francisco, especially Natalie Lopes and Beth Garvey of Arriba Juntos, Louise Nakamura of the City College of San Francisco, Coleman Advocates for Youth, Sherry Tennyson of the Department of Social Services, New Ways Workers, the Youth Employment Coalition, and Fred Hanson and Gary Fong of Youth for Service's Auto Tech Program.

To Eunice Elton of the Private Industry Council; Mark Donovan of Marriott's Bridges from School to Work program; Patrick Campbell, Pat Dougan, Lisa Hartman-Stie, Judy Hegenauer, and Bob Snowden of the California State Department of Education; and Selete Avoke and Edward T. Wilson, Sr., of the Office of Special Education Programs, U.S. Department of Education.

Personal thanks go to Dan Grazcyk, Sherman Anderson, Kristen Bachler, Linda Bourgaize, Deborah Brians, Bob Cipriano, Lyle Engeldinger, Desiree French, Cory Gaylord-Ross, John Greener, Ed Heller, Beth Iannazzi, Sandy Johnson, Sam Kaner, John Littel, Tom Long, Debbie Meyer, Cathy O'Connor, Pat Paul, Michelle Podell, Susan Portugal, Blair Roger, Suzanne Shaw, George Tilson, Steve Warren, Christine West, Pamela Wolfberg, Steve Zivolich, Joanne Patrick, Marcie Overbeek, Dale Brown, Roxanne Trees, Myrna Muto, Patsy Ethridge-Neal, Denise Fogleman, Linda Reidt, Bob Huven, and all the friends who helped to make Career Ladders a positive force in the community.

INTRODUCTION

A fuller integration of the nation's diverse groups will enhance our society. Along with the techniques for permitting that integration must come opportunities for enhancing the human relationships found at school, at work, and in our public places. Though the reader will find an emphasis in this book on the efficient management and documentation of a work-based learning program, the development of more caring relationships between all citizens—authentic community—is the underlying theme and purpose of the instructional program. The trend toward two-career families and the subsequent neglect of caring relationships with children drives this point home. We are so busy managing our fiscal survival that our spirits and the emotional nourishment of our children have suffered. If we have moved more of our time into the workplace, then that is where we must make our lives whole as well.

The way to a more whole society is a more complete integration of marginalized youth into the workplace. The overemployed probably have something to learn from the cultures and experiences of those who have been excluded from work. Although these two themes—the costs of two-career families and the contributions of cultural identity to the workplace—are relevant and need to be addressed, this book is about a third necessary piece of the puzzle: full integration in the workplace.

Much has been written and said about the value of work and employment. Those who have failed to achieve a gainful career are missing out on the richness of having an economic life, the self-respect that comes from being able to earn a livable wage, and the sense of community and personal growth that comes from being part of a work culture—the human relationships that can in fact be nourished in a work, service, or business setting.

We believe that, despite all its virtues, the current market system is one that does not naturally support meaningful relationships between people. When it prospers through hollow advertising and the promotion of false needs that substitute commodities for community, the quality of life and intimacy we instinctively seek suffers.

We believe that well-executed social and education services can support community, and that government can and should help create the conditions for the ongoing relationships that constitute true community, first with those in greatest need, and eventually with all its citizenry. First in the workplace, and eventually throughout the community. We propose that this include, but not be limited to, the realization of gainful careers, an end to welfare dependency, and full participation as citizens for the disabled, disenfranchised, and disenchanted young people of this nation. In fact, they need to be at or near the top of the list.

We support social service practices that attend first to the nature of the deliverer–citizen relationship, and then to the meeting of social and economic goals. We believe that this priority turns the tide of the economic imperatives that demean us as human beings and subsequently impoverish authentic community and culture.

The underemployment of youth is an issue that lends a concrete focus to this position. We cannot ignore the underemployment of our young people, whether they walk the streets without a high school diploma, with a master's degree, or with anything in between. Some of the effects are so tragic that they are themselves considered problems: substance abuse, crime, welfare dependency, homelessness, and suicide. These horrors would not completely disappear if our young people were more fully employed and engaged, but they would begin to. When we speak of employment, we know which indicators must be measured—percentage of time employed, wages, benefits, educational level, and so on—but in our value system *employment* is also a code word for a meaningful life and a fuller sense of citizenship. In our hearts, we all know that meaningfulness, with work as one critical element, is the only real solution to the social problems that afflict us.

The relationship of meaningfulness to work presents knotty philosophical issues, but these are not the immediate subject of this book. We write this manual under the temporal assumption that competitively paid employment, postsecondary education and training, and ascension up the career ladder are all a part of citizenship, an insufficient but critically necessary aspect of a legitimate, meaningful, and self-respecting life.

There is a serious mismatch between the needs and behaviors of the employment community and the groups who find themselves excluded from it. This is an issue not only of employment skills, but of values. Again, this conflict of values is not the main topic of this book, but it is the subtext that underlies every word. We seek to mollify and resolve that conflict through the teacher's and the service provider's commitment to a higher purpose and by proposing methods for bringing people who have been marginalized into the work world. In other words, rather than directly attacking a negative-outcome "social problem" like substance abuse or teen pregnancy, we propose the replacement of this type of effort with another one—an effective and cost-effective work experience and career development service that can function as a vehicle of empowerment and hope. So-called social problems are addressed, but always in the context of serving a positive career outcome. Graduates of Career Ladders commit themselves to legitimate lifestyles and make progress in the search for meaningfulness in their lives. We believe that a primary solution to the most debilitating of our problems is the enlargement of legitimate career opportunities. This means the inclusion of learning styles, abilities, skill levels, and cultures that are more diverse than those generally accommodated in the work world.

Flattening of organizational hierarchies and cooperative work groups are touted as a progressive innovation in the U.S. workplace. They are also a fantastic opportunity for the integration of people with fewer or different skills.

But the employment of marginalized youth is not simply a matter of creating job slots, nor does it mean "selling" the work world and having youth buy into it. Even if every young person exiting the educational system were to make an inviolable resolve to get and keep a decent job, even if every employer in the nation could afford to offer a decent job to every applicant who came to the door, we would still face the problems of helping these new workers succeed.

Youths who have come of age apart from the norms of the workplace bring with them diverse learning, emotional, social, and cultural styles. The workplace itself presents a social ecology, work demands, and a culture of its own. Discord is inevitable. A model for reducing that discord is the subject of this book. When recognition of the true nature of our problems is translated into programs that create real and meaningful career opportunities for underemployed people, when it is translated into counseling services and popular movements that inspire in underemployed people a passion to take responsibility and to venture into the risk of a career, we will still have to deal with job situations where mismatches between the worker and the task occur. In these pages, the reader will find a service delivery model—a technology, if you will—that enables professionals to effectively address these difficulties. The spirit of the civil rights movement, from the Civil Rights Act of 1964 to the Americans with Disabilities Act of 1990, will become a reality only when students exit school ready, willing, and enthusiastic about taking advantage of the accommodations employers are willing to provide.

Certainly, the activities that go on in the classroom are vital to the career prospects of youths and their development as good citizens. Every student must exit high school with the highest possible academic achievement and ready to continue their education. But the subject matter in this book is the learning that takes place in the community, specifically in the workplace. It is an approach of career exploration, training, placement, and ongoing development. Career-oriented activities in the high school years can be coordinated with classroom activities to mutual benefit. In fact, we offer a substantial classroom curriculum designed to complement the work experience. However, we have chosen to focus on community-based experiences. This book is a "how-to" manual: how to break down the barriers between school and community so that youths will feel included in the greater environment and be empowered to participate in it by the time they graduate.

The Career Ladders pilot was a special education program. But the critical strength of special education lies not in its designation of particular individuals as handicapped or disabled, but in the opportunities it affords educators to attend to student variance more intensively. The social implications of Public Law 94-142 (Education for All Handicapped Children Act of 1975) spawned a movement that brought a new respect for diversity, and an energetic quest to understand the wide array of behaviors we humans manifest. Even more important, special educators brought new levels of competence to systematic methods of instruction and accountability. The implications for improving the education of all children are obvious. Regardless of the future of special education, these advances are a contribution that should not be wasted. Consequently, this book dispenses with the language of disability whenever possible, and the program is presented as one that serves any student in need of special attention in order to adapt to the workplace. The model is viable with many special needs groups such as adjudicated, foster home, immigrant, teen parent, homeless, drug-involved, low-achieving, sexual minority, transient, and dropout populations.

The first chapter is an exposition of six principles that are key to Career Ladders success. In many ways, this chapter contains all the reader really needs to know because consensus on these principles can generate a successful program formatted quite differently from Career Ladders. These principles form the heart of the matter. We hope that they are convincing enough so that the reader will continue to read and take advantage of the materials that follow.

The rest of the book speaks to what educators can offer young people as they approach graduation. Chapter 2 is the central chapter addressing this endeavor. In it, the mechanics of managing a community classroom are elaborated. The community classroom is the core experience and the crux of the program, but using it is a calculated risk because if it is not properly managed, interns will actually damage their employability, and none of the other components of the program will be able to function properly. When it is well planned

and executed, the community classroom is a powerful introduction to the work world that truly gives the transition from school to work a tangible and meaningful expression.

Chapter 3 presents the curriculum that accompanies the community classroom experience. The beginning of the chapter outlines the posture that the teacher of the employment skills workshop must assume; this is followed by a series of lesson plans that cover an entire semester. The curriculum is designed to accompany a community-based work experience. In a self-contained classroom, these lessons will lose their context, and thus their effectiveness.

Our next chapter, Chapter 4, stakes out a lot of territory. In it, we describe the postsecondary services that fulfill the commitment first made to Career Ladders interns during their community classroom experience: ongoing availability of service. As with the other components, we build these services from young people outward, attending to their needs as they arise. The services described are thus a considerable expansion of what vocational rehabilitation professionals usually provide. However, they are always services that enhance and relate to career outcomes. In this chapter, the reader will also find our arguments for a reform of day-to-day service delivery, which we call *continuous cyclical triage*, and a dramatic challenge to the overall format of social service delivery, which we have dubbed the *cohort service delivery model*.

In Chapter 5 we begin to describe the activities that will enable a staff to develop a community-based career training program. Though plans for the previously described components must be in place, this chapter addresses their catalyst: the development of host sites where a community classroom will be allowed to establish itself and offer on-site training to a small group of interns. The techniques for developing working relationships with employers are detailed here. This chapter tries to answer the often-asked question: "Sounds like a great program, but how do you get the employer to agree to participate?"

Chapter 6, new to this edition, responds to the requests we have received over the past several years to detail appropriate career exploration activities for students too young for a full-fledged internship, but old enough to be disengaged from school and yearning for a relevant experience. For those students, in Grades 7 to 10, a rationale and methodology for a rich job shadowing program is provided. This type of program supersedes school-based career assessments and allows students to taste first-hand the excitements of the work world and the people whose distinct and differing passions give that world its character. If this book is your first introduction to the school-to-career pedagogy, you might want to read this chapter first.

The volume concludes with an Afterword outlining the reforms and social change that would enable the efforts of programs like Career Ladders to expand and flourish. The communities and schools that wisely commit to an innovative and effective program delegate the decision making to their frontline staff. Consistent with this approach, we voice a call for legislators and policy-makers to allow special dispensations to these administrators, so that the seeds sown by such a new service delivery model may take hold. We are proposing nothing less than a more intimate merger of educational, social service, and private-sector concerns with the community they serve.

Six Principles of Effective Transition Programming

Shepherd Siegel ■

When we visit different cities, towns, and school districts, the consensus on school-to-work transitions for youths who face risky circumstances is clear. Frontline practitioners want explicit and well-structured programs that they can use immediately. They will listen to esoteric theories, social rhetoric, and conceptual models, but they know the problems of the front line and the lack of adequate resources to deal with them. They may be tired of outsiders trying to give them the inside story, but if a good plan presents itself, they are ready and extremely eager to put it into action.

This is both good and bad news. The bad news is that the need for effective school-to-career programs is dire. The employability of youths, with and without disabilities, is still below acceptable standards. It is true that America is witnessing a new commitment to education, and American business is making statements of enthusiastic participation. But the crack that transitioning students fall into only widens as they leave decaying home lives and pass through schools that are displaced both from those home-life realities and from the work world into which they are supposed to be

graduating. And every 5 years, the educational field seems ready to scrap itself and start all over.

This continual renewal and reinvention of the education field is also the good news, for it is a misnomer to call education a social "science." In certain domains of learning and cognitive functioning, educational research does accumulate truths in a scientific manner, though at a grievously slow pace. But the field as a whole is a unique cultural activity. It is grouped with other scholarly fields, but perhaps inappropriately so. The harsh and bumpy rides created by the economy, immigration, the sexual and cultural habits of adolescents, and the myriad of unresolved social tensions create an immense demand on the educational system, which is somehow supposed to be a grounding and enabling force in this maelstrom. No mere science has ever been expected to accomplish so much.

Thus when educators[1] regularly commit to the renewal of their approaches and demonstrate zest for restarting educational programs, they are behaving with propriety and responsibility. Education is a field in constant flux. It realigns itself with rapidly changing economic and cultural norms and deviations. It nobly aims to serve the mainstream

---

[1]The broader term *educator* is used instead of *teacher* with the intent to include all professionals engaged in the educational process with youths, that is, the process of increasing literacy and citizenship. Thus, counselors, job coaches, Career Ladders personnel described herein, and even adult service providers in the rehabilitation and other adult service fields may fit this definition of the educator. Our deliberate intent is to emphasize the similarities among the endeavors of these various professionals.

by actuating it to include society's outliers without destroying them. This is not the immediate task of science but rather the task of citizenship.

Could it be done better? Certainly. There are many issues of training, financing, and positioning that cannot be addressed here. But when the failures and weaknesses of education are put up for public display, its urge to reinvent itself should not be counted among them. Only as new programs demonstrate success and the ability to revise themselves in response to changing conditions should they be more permanently installed.

This is why the program described in these pages cannot be limited to a simple manual. Make no mistake, this book will not disappoint the reader's dear request for a structured program. There are lesson plans, forms that can be duplicated, and step-by-step procedures, all of which can increase the employability and the career outcomes of youths. But the program only works if the implementation of procedures occurs with a clear understanding of the principles that brought them into being.

In this first chapter, we will define transition and discuss why it is an important activity. Next we explain the one overarching and six underlying principles that drive the Career Ladders program. These principles are key to the program's success. As practitioners review the other nuts-and-bolts components of the program in the subsequent chapters, they will find some parts useful and others superfluous; some activities compatible with their styles and others foreign; some procedures easy to implement and others impossible; and some practices that can be initiated without cost along with others that are prohibitively expensive.

If the replication of this program was defined as the use of only those aspects that were deemed useful, compatible, easy to implement, and inexpensive, no communities would benefit from the same success that Career Ladders experienced in San Francisco, where 92% of the participants, who all had disabilities, were employed or in college over a 5-year period (Siegel, Robert, Waxman, & Gaylord-Ross, 1992). By the same token, the rigid replication of the model without regard to expense or ease would carry no guarantee of success. But with a deeper understanding of the program's principles, the application of the structured methods explained herein will in fact result in their cost-effective, compatible, and practical regeneration.

Every community is unique, but we believe that there are universal qualities to these principles, and armed with them, practitioners can successfully adapt the Career Ladders model to most American communities. With activation of the program's principles in a community-based educational program, the educator can become an involved participant who is effective in the world of adolescents and in the world of work and adult life.

WHAT IS TRANSITION AND WHY SHOULD EDUCATORS PROVIDE TRANSITION SERVICES?

Life is full of transitions, and this book deals with only one, albeit a crucial one: the transition from secondary school to adult life. However, the program is doomed to either fail or oppress if it restricts itself to the chore of moving young citizens from one box (school) into another (employment). Employment *is* a critical aspect of citizenship, but by itself it is insufficient. In this program, the relationship formed between the *transition specialist* (discussed in Chapter 4) and the participating youth is critical, and often positive, even when it is confined to support for job success. We believe that to be necessary, but also insufficient.

The transition from school to adult life is the transition from lesser to greater participation in mainstream society. Restructured schools may someday change that fact by increasing participation in mainstream society throughout the school-age years. When they do, transition programs will become less critical and unstable. But presently, this definition of transition as increased participation in society is serviceable. A transition that does not increase the participation and citizenship of the youth involved may still qualify as a transition by some, but it is not the one of a noble educator.

In this broader context, then, the transition specialist engages the youth in a meaningful relationship and develops common goals with that youth to bring more power, meaning, participation, and responsibility into her or his life. When a trusting relationship is developed in that way, higher employment rates and greater participation in postsecondary training and college will result, *but as a byproduct* of the communal mission and contract entered into between the youth and the transition specialist. Work and college in and of themselves are insufficient motivators; they are representations of greater yearnings. It is the variously expressed desires for independence, belonging, self-sufficiency, enjoyment, meaning, and control of destiny that drive youths to succeed. To the extent that transition programs can resonate with and respond to those desires, they will engender measurable successes with youths. This, then, is the overarching principle at work in Career Ladders: *Services provided by Career Ladders are shaped by the lives of the youths served.*

For the present purposes, those services are directed toward enabling a successful career adjustment. But the principles of this program may apply to other types of success: educational, emotional, cultural, and social. They apply to many groups of special-needs youths—mildly to moderately disabled, group home, substance abusing, newcomer, adjudicated, dropout, low achieving, parenting, sexual minority, transient, and homeless.

When a transition specialist enters into a relationship with a youth, he or she must be ready to at least listen to and at most deliver services that attend to (seemingly) noncareer issues. The above list of youths with special needs implies the issues that many educators face. Thus, without losing focus on the career nature of the program, the transition specialist must be prepared and enthusiastic about expanding the relationship so that issues that are impeding a successful transition into adulthood can be addressed. Two features of the program exemplify this perspective: the affective curriculum that is integrated into the employment skills workshop (see Chapter 3) and the overall practice of the transition specialist (see Chapter 4).

Youths must understand and express their own needs. An educator cannot tell them that a job is their need; they have other needs that must be respected. If an educator limits what he or she provides to job placement and support, the success of the program will likewise be limited. Multiservice or one-stop centers and restructured schools may be able to bring a more comprehensive array of services under one roof, making the work of the transition specialist a little more convenient and efficient, but they will not diminish the necessity of seeking an understanding of the whole person when engaging a youth (hereafter referred to as an *intern*) in the program. With all these qualifiers

expressed, then, now comes the business of delivering career services.

THE SIX PRINCIPLES OF CAREER LADDERS

The following six principles are presented as two sets, each in the sequence of a context, a service, and a tool. A context is the setting that must be engineered to best deliver the service, a vessel. A service is the practice of the educator that initially fills the vessel and is always aimed at providing tools. A tool is a set of activities that enable interns to own the program, and to continue its principles without the aid or cost of the program providers (see Figure 1.1). The first three principles tend to apply to school-sponsored services during approximately the last 2 years of secondary school, and the last three principles emphasize services to youths who have recently exited the public school system, but all six principles have application throughout the transitional years.

Principle 1
Context: Individualized Responses to Personality and Learning Styles in a Real-World Environment

To successfully negotiate a career, adolescents need the best possible career and technical education, including, but not restricted to, supervised work experiences. Each individual presents a different profile of social, career, and emotional needs that must be assessed and addressed. Settling for a standardized approach would result in little more than the success of those who were going to succeed anyway, leaving behind those who have truly special needs. Such a program is actually a waste of taxpayer money. Only by respecting special needs and offering an individualized program that addresses them can a service make a significant impact on rates of success.

Inherent in this principle is the educator's ability to challenge and not underrate the potential of the intern. As a result, interns feel useful and the program brings meaningfulness, self-esteem,

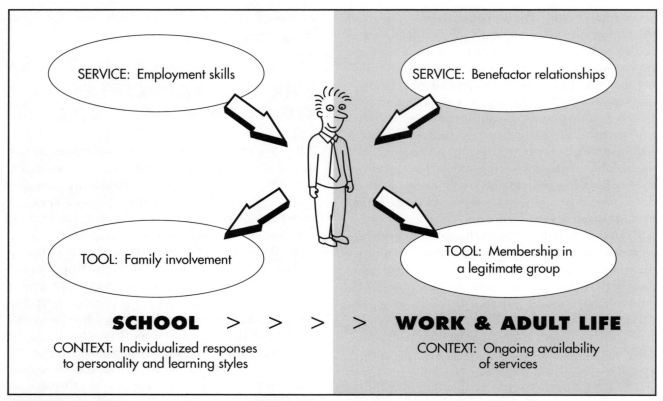

FIGURE 1.1. Services provided by Career Ladders are shaped by the needs of the youths served.

competence, and employability into their lives when it makes reasonable demands of them. In a career context, this means that job placement requires more than job development and occasional monitoring. Supported employment techniques must be used to analyze the job and the intern, and to ensure that challenge, learning, efficiency, and competency are part of the experience. In the actual delivery of on-the-job support, interns will perform better when systematic and data-based instructional methods are used to communicate objectively with them, and when means for improving job performance are devised. The tried-and-true special education techniques of writing objectives, varying behavioral interventions, self-monitoring, and social skills training are all good examples of this approach. Career programming can be further individualized through counseling techniques, life-space interviews (Redl & Wineman, 1951), team building, and other approaches to a rapport with the youth's personal culture. (See Chapters 2 and 3 for a full development of this approach.)

One young man serves as an example of Principle 1. John was an intern at an insurance company and processed policies 3 hours a day. He was capable of doing the job, but would wander off the task and begin doodling on scraps of paper. His instructor began measuring John's productivity rate and trained John's supervisor to do the same (after reassuring all nearby coworkers that he was not conducting time studies on them). John was intrigued by the measurement process and by the direction in which the data were moving. Soon he learned how to measure his own rate. Within 2 weeks, all doodling ceased, and John's rate approached that of his coworkers.

Principle 2
Service: Structured Opportunities To Practice Employment Skills

The skills most critical to developing an employment record are attendance, social skills, employer-pleasing behaviors, job skills, and job search skills. These can be taught through the systematic address of objectives, social skills training, counseling, job skills training, and job search skills training, respectively. Youths need these employment skills to develop careers.

One of the defining characteristics of the Career Ladders model is that employment skills are taught in an effort that is coordinated between the workplace and a weekly employment skills workshop (Chapter 3). By having 4 days a week to practice skills taught in the workshop in a real work setting, interns gain sophisticated generalization skills that will enable them to hold jobs, engage in lifelong learning, and have successful careers. Employers can also own the program by sharing responsibility for the careers of Career Ladders interns by participating in the selection, training, and evaluation of interns.

But when these skills are translated into staid career curriculum goals, educators run the risk of losing students the same way educators lose students to academic curriculum goals. To avoid this, interns must own the curriculum goals. They will do so and strive to become better and more independent job seekers and job holders when the curriculum is alive. They must use a process approach and integrate self-monitoring, cooperative learning, and peer counseling methods and principles. The educator's role is to effectively and objectively communicate the quality of the interns' performance.

Maria is a young woman whose experience illustrates Principle 2. Near the beginning of her internship, she insisted on being transferred to another department at the same insurance company. She said her supervisor was racist and "had it in for her." During the weekly employment skills workshop, she had a chance to vent her anger and to work on the problems in a group. With the whole group of about 15 youths and 3 adults supporting her, she moved through her feelings to a deeper understanding of the issues. She and the group generated a list of many actions she could take, and from these a strategy was devised: With her on-site instructor acting as facilitator, she would try to engage in this same problem-solving process with the supervisor who so troubled her. The two made peace. In fact, a robust friendship grew to the point that Maria was reluctant to move to another department when she was promoted.

Principle 3
Tool: Intern-Driven Career Planning

People do not live in isolation. An intern in transition needs to have the surrounding human ecosystem working in concert toward career development. For example, a family that does not support success for its members can easily sabotage and waste the efforts of a service provider. By the same token, it can offer support that critically empowers a troubled youth to mature and succeed.

Families share in the responsibility for the careers of our interns and can be key players in their development when they participate in the mandatory preprogram meeting and go on to sustain an ongoing relationship with program staff, emphasizing positive aspects and confronting areas in need of improvement (see Chapters 2 and 4). Career Ladders finds consistency with a Re-ED (Reeducation of Emotionally Disturbed Youth) approach that views a troubled and troubling youth as only the defining member of an intolerant system (Hobbs, 1982; Siegel, 1988). Transition specialists put this principle to work and bring the key players, usually in the family, onto the team that is developing career success. Practices described in Chapter 4, particularly Ecosystematic Intervention and the case study *Gloria* exemplify the Re-ED approach.

In instances where a family is not available, other key players, even in the workplace, must be engaged. Sometimes a school counselor can serve this function. Sometimes a spouse, boyfriend or girlfriend, clergy member, or community worker will rise to the challenge. Certainly, group-home or probation personnel must be involved along with Career Ladders staff. Ultimately, peer support can take over this support function (see Principle 6).

One young man, Enrique, though successful at work, had to leave his home when his mother moved out of the area. Only through the extra efforts of his school counselor was he able to maintain a roof over his head. Vo, a newcomer from Vietnam, was forbidden from participating in the program for fear of hurting his chances at college. The transition specialist went to Vo's home, drank tea with his family, and was able to convince them that Vo could work *and* go to school. With his father's blessings, Vo has gone on to be successful at both. Edgar is a young man who has held jobs successfully, but who, when he lost a job, would fall into drinking and despair. The consistent support of his parents helped reconnect Edgar to Career Ladders staff as he struggled through this floundering period.

When well coordinated, the operation of the above three principles can successfully launch a student through the initial transition from school to adult life. The next three principles support the continuing career development beyond high school.

Principle 4
Context: Ongoing Availability of Services

Many youths take a long time to develop trust. Thus when services are continuously available, youths can take the time they need to develop attachments that will ultimately benefit their career development. Some youths may only need to use the service once, but that one time could occur at any time after their high school graduation. Other youths have ambitions to ascend a career ladder, which means that even though they may be counted as a success now, they may want more education and a better job later and not know how to go about it; they have an intermittent need for service. A few youths have special needs so profound that they will require lifelong services to experience success in the work world. But any youth who knows that support is never more than a phone call away—even if that phone call is never made—gains the confidence and reassurance necessary to venture forth into a career. Continuous availability of services significantly alters the emotional tenor of the typical service provider–client relationship. The alternative is that youths will continue to fall between the cracks, or will be constantly passed from one social service agency to another, failing to find the right service in time. Thus there must be some constancy in the resources they are likely to seek.

One young man, Bill, worked for a "mom and pop" store on and off for 3 years after high school. His relationship with the owners was such that he would be fired or quit every few months and

would be rehired after a 2-week layoff, which was really a cooling-off period for whichever party had terminated the employment during their regular squabbles. For this young man, the process had a certain stability. His transition specialist realized that the relationship had its own life and dedicated his time to simply making regular visits, building trust by listening, and encouraging the young man to enter a training program where he could learn to tune up cars and change and balance tires because he had expressed such an interest. After about 2½ years of counseling, the young man finally enrolled in the course, quit the store job for good, and has been working for a national-brand tire outlet successfully ever since. His case, which required prolonged effort but never more than a few hours a month, demonstrates that the ongoing availability of services shaped to the lives and circumstances of the people served can make a significant difference to them. Chapter 4 offers a full discussion of practical ways to implement this principle.

Principle 5
Service: Benefactor Relationships

Youths need a benefactor whom they trust to believe in them (Edgerton, 1967). This benefactor must understand and be able to marshal the technical resources for engineering career opportunity and development, but must also be a counselor who can develop long-term, authentic, and committed adult relationships with graduates.

The benefactor never disqualifies a youth and fulfills the promise of continuous availability of service. This is the best way to develop the trust and reliability that allows the benefactor to participate in the empowering process. During their post–high school floundering period, youths need to know that someone else is watching over them. Graduates will keep their jobs and have the best chance to ascend a career ladder when they have the benefit of long-term follow-up services offered by one or two individuals with whom they can have an authentic adult peer relationship.

Karinn is a Career Ladders graduate who has moved in and out of several jobs since she graduated high school. She maintained contact with her

Career Ladders transition specialist, sometimes calling on him for a new job lead, but sometimes calling just to talk about boyfriends or the difficulty of still living at home with her parents. As she floundered about, the transition specialist helped her stabilize, counseling her away from bad decisions regarding the men in her life, enrolling her in a career and technical education program that would place her in a higher paying and more satisfying job, and helping her with her ultimate plan to move out of the area. Her reliance on him as a benefactor (not a rescuer) helped her steer a relatively safe course through her late adolescence and successfully start her adulthood.

Principle 6
Tool: Membership in a Legitimate Group

Youths and young adults need the reassurance of being members of a group of people who are engaged in a similar struggle to assume adulthood. They are no longer part of a school and often are not able to easily assume a new role as a working adult. Futhermore, competitive employment not only consists of applying learned skills, but also is an emotional and developmental process, the success of which can depend on a melding of affective and technical education. Members of a peer group in which that happens are more likely to act on socially beneficial decisions made in the group, and subsequently reduce their reliance on a social delivery system.

This is the ultimate natural support system, comprising not only coworkers and family, but also peers. It is not beyond the reach of the educational system to teach the tools of building true peer support among the youths it serves. There need be no fear that continuous availability of services will result in a costly safety net analogous to welfare dependency because the service itself is conscientiously defined as the empowerment of interns through the creation of self- and peer reliance. All of the other curricular and career goals of the program will be met more satisfactorily when the program is managed with time for interns to develop meaningful relationships among themselves.

For example, Bill was able to develop a job at the tire outlet for his buddy Jerome, another Ca-

reer Ladders graduate. Karinn also found a job for another graduate. Career Ladders graduates have been used as guest speakers for in-school interns. A Career Ladders transition specialist formed a support group for Career Ladders graduates who had become parents, generally young mothers. Ultimately, many Career Ladders graduates become integrated with the social groups at their workplace. But the surface has barely been scratched. The potential for support groups among transitioning students is untapped. That potential includes the possibility of peer group resistance to drugs and illicit careers, job networking, empowerment, and collective advocacy.

CONCLUSION

The beginning of this chapter may have skimmed over the critical second question, "Why provide transition services?" but posing that question is by no means a flip gesture. In fact, parts of that question must remain unanswered. If we substitute this chapter's definition of transition and ask, "Why provide services to increase the participation of youths in society?" the answer begins to emerge. The role of educators is to endow students with citizenship, and in a democracy, citizenship can be measured by the level of participation people exercise. A career is a fairly dependable indicator of participation. Thus, youths need careers because that is how people develop a legitimate identity and gain economic power, and because to assume citizenship depends in part upon having economic power. Services at the critical juncture between secondary and postsecondary school life will undoubtedly have a significant effect on the clients–citizens' adult life. That is why transition services must be provided.

How intensively and for how long the services are provided are more difficult questions that this book will only begin to answer. When are the supports removed and the forces of our economy and society allowed to play themselves out? It is our contention that the principle of ongoing availability of services dispensed in a manner that empowers the young adult to survive and prosper and to develop natural supports is a true one. By this we mean that in a society actively working to accommodate diversity, a great majority of participants in a program like Career Ladders will have no need, or only intermittent need, of services 5 years after graduation.[2] The remaining 10% to 25% are more challenging individuals, and their progress will depend more on externally related factors in society, such as the future of the workplace, family and child rearing, how drug use is modulated, and how powerful the support of more successfully adapted peers is.

Perhaps the idea of community itself in a complex urban environment can be developed and enhanced by cohorts of up to 100 otherwise marginalized citizens who have one or two career managers working to sustain pockets of cohesion among the group and to provide the kind of liaison, counseling, and support services Career Ladders has begun to develop.

Whether or not a Career Ladders model is precisely replicated is not the important question. The critical need is for our course to be steered by shaping services to the needs of the youths served, and for educators to remember that education's mission is not employability, nor is it academic excellence per se. The purpose of education is to give students the tools of citizenship, those skills that will preserve and develop democracy and interdependence. When educators have learned how to perform that duty, full employment and intellectual excellence will follow from a youth population that cares about the future of its own society.

This means that educators have a lot of work ahead. It means that the need is still dire. But it also means that solutions are within reach.

---

[2] In a population of youths identified as having mild disabilities, the success rate of Career Ladders participants after 5 years was greater than 90% (Siegel, Avoke, Paul, Robert, & Gaylord-Ross, 1991). The model has not yet been tested in the same way on youths with more significant disabilities or youths who are clearly defined as adjudicated, teen parents, and so on, though all manners of risky circumstances entered the lives of Career Ladders graduates.

Community Classroom

CHAPTER

Shepherd Siegel

The core experience of Career Ladders is what we call the *community classroom*, a 3-hour, semester-long, daily work experience. A group of 7 to 15 interns work in various aspects of the business operations at a single work site, under the incrementally faded supervision of an on-site instructor (this position correlates well with what many programs call a job coach, or schools call a diversified occupations teacher). In other words, employers agree to open their doors and provide work experiences—paid, stipended, or unpaid—to a defined group of youths who will be dispersed and integrated throughout the work site. In most cases, a regular employee is paired with each intern. The first Career Ladders pilot program had six community classrooms. (Chapter 5 discusses how to convince an employer to commit to this kind of program.) Implementation of the postsecondary services offered by Career Ladders (described in Chapter 4) results in a significant level of success only when graduates have had the background of the community classroom experience, or some other career preparation program that truly prepares and poises them for success. The employment skills workshop that is described in the next chapter will seem irrelevant and lack import if students are not participating in a community classroom experience that gives the course a real-world context. In other words, the essence of Career Ladders lies in the monitored work experience we call the community classroom. All the other as-

pects of the program flow from this experience. It provides the basis, training, context, and human bond that nourish career growth.

This chapter describes many areas of concern and eventualities that must be anticipated and planned for by either an on-site instructor or a head teacher (we call this position the Career Ladders manager) who manages and supervises several sites. This is unlike any other job in that the behaviors of players in a wide-ranging mesosystem (Bronfenbrenner, 1979)—workplace (managers and coworkers), school, home, program management, payroll system, and so on—must be coordinated so that the intern has a positive experience and so that all key players also participate and perceive the program positively.

The community classroom experience has three phases: recruitment, orientation, and program. (See Appendix 2.1, Community Classroom Flowchart, for a delineation of these phases. To illustrate the ideal continuity of a strong transition program, Appendix 2.1 also shows the post–community classroom graduation/transition phase.) This chapter describes one approach that reconciled the best practices advocated by Career Ladders staff with the realities of the community that hosted it. Individual programs' features will vary depending on the programs' environments. The intent of this chapter is to communicate the principles that underlie Career Ladders so that future program developers will apply wisdom in devising solutions to implementation problems in a way that always orders excellence above expediency.

The guiding principles of Career Ladders can be summarized by two questions. Before, during, and after the community classroom experience is designed, the educator needs to face each critical decision by asking: How can I make this experience most closely resemble the expectations and values that prevail in the workplace? How can this event or the program's response to this behavior bring the intern closer to career independence?

Often, the creative and clever educator can design a response that is both efficient and educationally excellent. But the professional who truly brings change will frequently have to go above and beyond to devise an educationally excellent intervention. Usually, taking extra time at the beginning of the semester to establish and teach the program's rules and policies ultimately results in less work overall and a more effective program. By the end of the semester, all interns are able to either meet the demands of the program or have been terminated earlier when they tested the limits of what the program can deliver and tolerate.

Consider this example of the empowerment dynamic that avoids a dependent relationship but does not neglect a student's need for special attention: In the beginning of the semester, an on-site instructor may have to make an extra effort to consistently make wake-up calls to an intern with a punctuality problem. After a couple of weeks, the intern will either start coming to work on time, quit the program, or begin a probationary period. Although this seems like a lot of work, the problem will drag on if it is not dealt with assertively in the beginning of the semester. In addition, a slow response to such a problem will result in the following consequences:

1. The intern will not have learned an important lesson in attendance and will be less employable.

2. Program policy will have been flaunted and will have lost credibility with all interns.

3. The program will have lost credibility with the employer.

4. The problem will have resulted in more work and aggravation over the long haul.

5. The relationship between the instructor and intern will have become based on an unsatisfy-

ing tolerance of an unacceptable behavior and will have lost its potential for quality.

STAGE 1: RECRUITMENT
Outreach and Referral

Career Ladders can work in school districts with many different high schools and alternative public schools. In this situation, the knowledge of referring teachers and counselors about the program is critical. They must be aware of the nature of the service offered by Career Ladders and must be able to make the best referrals of students and give the Career Ladders staff useful information. Appendix 2.2, Initial Referral for Transition Services, is a form that asks for information we have found to be critical, such as expected date of graduation, reading and math levels, and time-of-day availability. Word of mouth can be a powerful advertiser, and over the years, siblings and younger friends of former interns have sought out Career Ladders services. One teacher at each participating school is designated as a liaison and attends an orientation training. These teachers take responsibility for coordinating referrals from their schools and disseminating information throughout their schools.

The community classrooms described in this chapter are intended to serve high school juniors or seniors. However, in an ideal situation, younger students will have opportunities for career field trips that serve to generate enthusiasm, help candidates make better choices later, and further advertise the program. Optimally, middle school youths will have job shadowing experiences, where they spend intensive half days in groups of three or fewer at various work sites. Freshmen and sophomores will have introductory mini-internships in community classrooms.

In our San Francisco and Seattle Career Ladders programs, students were generically referred from all schools to a centralized site, where they were interviewed and assigned to work sites around the city based on student interest and ability. Site development is discussed in detail in Chapter 5, but some perspective is offered here. The program model was developed in the context of an urban setting. Participating employers were necessarily large companies that could provide work opportunities for 7 to 15 youths without creating a segregated or enclave situation. However, this model could be adapted to a less urban or rural setting, as one of our experiences suggests. We were fortunate to develop work experience sites in the cafeterias of office buildings that all subcontracted with the same provider, Marriott Food Services. Because each cafeteria could only offer one to three internship assignments, we worked with five different office buildings, all within a few blocks of each other. In this way, the original model was adapted and one on-site instructor traveled from building to building, monitoring interns throughout the day. The program principle of never being more than 10 minutes away from each intern remained intact. Similarly, in a less metropolitan area, the community classroom could be adapted by restricting the supervisory area of each on-site instructor to a manageable radius (fewer than 10 minutes to each intern). This is a critical feature of the program. Programs that deploy job coaches over larger regions frequently reduce the teaching task to one of "putting out fires" instead of the more proactive and efficient approach of being available to instruct and train. As efficiency declines, such programs quickly take the place-and-pray approach. In a nonmetropolitan setting, this efficiency can be achieved by assigning frontline personnel to tightly defined regions or neighborhoods that they can easily manage.

Still other configurations are feasible. Conceivably, a city could develop a community classroom program at each school, or form partnerships of two or three schools, rather than mixing all schools together as we did in San Francisco. The advantage of complete mixing is that it increases the choices that can be offered to participating youths.

Interviews

To build credibility with employers and develop a structure that will be able to accommodate higher risk youths over time, certain requirements and screens have been set up, beginning with the referral phase. Like all phases, it is critical that this one be implemented in a manner consistent with the posture adopted throughout the rest of the program. That is, reasonable demands are made of the student, and policies begin to resemble the work world more and the school environment less. Also, making certain demands right from the first interview does not indicate a desire to exclude any students. Instead, it is set up as an incentive to referring teachers to make sure that all candidates can meet the following minimum requirements:

1. A good attendance record

2. A demonstrated desire to go to work

3. Family support for the youth to work

4. Previous career-oriented experiences

5. At least one demonstrable job skill (e.g., the ability to alphabetize)

It is not unreasonable to expect that within the near future virtually every high school senior in the United States will be able to meet four of these five criteria. We usually demand that a candidate meet three of them and recommend the setting of this criterion as one (but only one) way to communicate work world demands to the teachers of the 9th- and 10th-grade classes. By the same token, the challenge of planning employment beyond high school is large. By making demands of referring teachers, we have been able to, for example, increase the number of candidates who come to us with Social Security cards and motor vehicle department identification, which are necessary for employment. For Career Ladders staff, having to assist in the documentation process is a distraction from the already significant task of quality training. Candidates must have documentation completed before entering the program, but this will only happen when the requirement is made in the earlier grades. At the same time, the Referral Checklist (see Appendix 2.3) communicates to program organizers the strengths and needs of an intern candidate.

There is one initial interview of all students at their high school to establish the intern candidate pool for both the fall and spring semesters. Students are screened and recommended to the various community classroom site supervisors. The students are offered a choice of sites for which they may interview. Counselors and interviewers can also assist students in making appropriate choices based on the students' abilities.

Students then receive their First Interview Notification (see Appendix 2.4), and are scheduled to interview with the site supervisor at specific times at a central location. As part of the interview, relevant entry-level skills (e.g., software, sorting, lifting, writing) may be checked, and each student is given an application form to complete from the sponsoring employer. Interview questions focus on previous work experience and motivation to work. The job site, job duties, and employment skills workshop are explained in general terms. Virtually all students who arrive at their interview reasonably on time are accepted. Students who are extremely withdrawn, aggressive, or immature may be screened out at this time; they can be referred to a more intensive/supportive program if one is available. Or they can be deferred until they make appropriate behavior changes.

A second interview is scheduled at this time with the sponsoring manager at the job site and students receive an application from the sponsoring company (see Appendix 2.5, Second Interview Notification). Employers have the final say in the hiring process. Send the employer twice as many candidates as it has openings. This is a critical feature of the program. This process more realistically simulates the competition of the job market, teaching a real-world lesson to both those selected and those passed over, and it begins the process of the employer taking responsibility by having participated in the selection of candidates. Job programs that simply place youths in employment settings without a competitive interview process miss out on this crucial opportunity to teach the realities of the job market, and to have the employer become more involved and committed to the success of the interns. Once the effectiveness of the program is established, many employers will deliberately select students presenting more problems. Their altruism and belief that the program works and can make a difference inspires them to join in the educators' work.

Enough sites exist so that a youth who is rejected from one site can interview again at another, and we have always been able to find a placement for any youth who is ready and eager to participate in the program. Teachers and referring counselors are notified of selected interns through the mail. Acceptance and notification to the candidates and families comes through the mail a few days after the interview (see Appendix 2.6, Final Acceptance

and Notification of Family Meeting). The employer's relationship with the intern at the interview should follow all laws, in particular procedures and protections outlined by the Americans with Disabilities Act of 1990 (and respect the confidentiality required by the Individuals with Disabilities Education Act of 1990). For example, a disability should be discussed when it might interfere with essential job functions, and reasonable accommodations should be collaboratively planned between program personnel and employers. Issues of safety to others, for example, concerning intern candidates with arrest records, should be reconciled during the initial interview and screening process, so that these behaviors are not an issue at the employer interview. When the Career Ladders model is used for a population with disabilities, it can become a safe and harmonious training ground for the employer and program personnel. Even when the Career Ladders model is used with youths who do not have disabilities, the individualized procedures and respect for individual differences can and should transfer.

ORIENTATION
Family Meeting

The family meeting is one of the most critical events of the semester. It is during this meeting that the students, who are now referred to as *interns*, and one significant other person in their life will be deciding whether to take the program seriously. If the leader of this meeting can make the connection between what the program offers and what the interns and their families want from adult life, then an important alliance will have been initiated. The team that helps lead youths to success will begin to function.

A letter has gone out to the homes of the selected interns, congratulating them on acceptance into the program and telling them that this evening meeting must be attended by them and at least one other person, whoever cares the most about their success after graduation. Attendance is mandatory.

Any person who fits the basic criterion of caring qualifies for attendance at this meeting. It should be someone who is of majority age, but siblings, spouses, steady boyfriends or girlfriends, parents, aunts, uncles, friends, and so forth are all acceptable as a significant other, as long as he or she is stepping forward to assume responsibility. It is the intern's choice. With rare exception, the student *must* bring someone.

The main purpose of the meeting is to obtain demonstration of a commitment by one other person in the intern's life. At this point, the program transcends the school context; it becomes a team effort of the school and the community. Career Ladders staff now knows that there is at least one other person deserving of credit and praise for helping an intern make his or her transition. And, if there is a problem during the semester, at least one other person can be counted on to help. These are the people who really make the program work.

The second purpose of the meeting is to explain how the program operates. There are three main components, which can be explained and summarized: (1) the community classroom, a su-

pervised work experience where interns will work and meet objectives; (2) a weekly employment skills workshop, where a teacher will teach the curriculum that is summarized in the Career Ladders Pyramid of Transition Skills (Figure 2.1); and (3) an ongoing commitment to interns who successfully graduate from the community classroom phase, through the services of the transition specialist.

As the program is being explained, the staff members who fulfill each of the functions are introduced: on-site instructor for work site; a teacher/manager for work site and employment skills workshop; transition specialist for postsecondary services; a coordinator as ombudsman; and advocates or staff from partnering social service agencies (see Appendix 2.7 for job descriptions).

Now that the team has been introduced and the program summary has provided a context in which the team will operate, the leader can talk

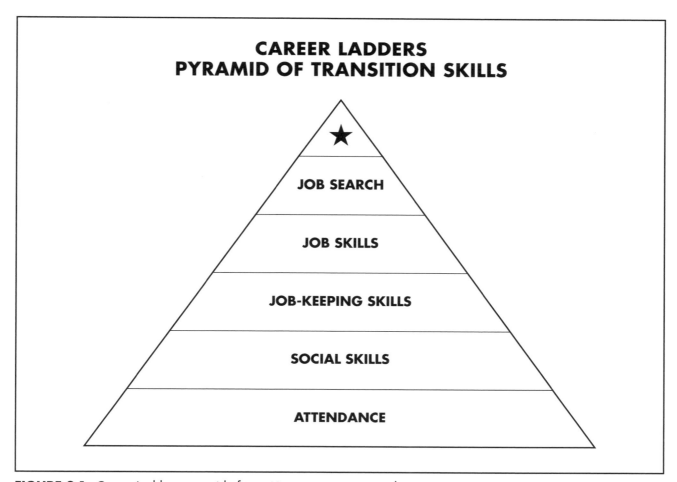

FIGURE 2.1. Career Ladders pyramid of transition to permanent employment.

about ways in which the family member can help the intern succeed: (a) by emphasizing at home, school, and work the absolute importance of good attendance and punctuality; (b) by getting the right clothes; (c) by reprioritizing medical and dental appointments and so on, so that they do not interfere with work; (d) by helping with attendance and punctuality problems; and most important, (e) by giving emotional support at home—no one has a good day at work every day, and now is the best time to face and accept that reality. Of course, family members must be encouraged to praise and be proud of the efforts of the interns.

The program staff will develop this relationship with the significant others through phone calls to them a minimum of once every 2 weeks, usually to report the successes and progress of the intern. The staff is trained to maintain a 7:3 ratio of positive-to-negative messages in phone calls home. When families perceive these phone calls as primarily a source of praise, the instructor can build authentic relationships with family members and enlist their support if there ever is a problem. If program staff call home only to report problems, they will not be able to build a team. Everyone, including families, needs positive reinforcement to make progress.

At the family meeting, the manager and other staff members explain in very clear terms, and repeat several times, the paid–unpaid terms of the program. For example, in the San Francisco Career Ladders pilot, the length of the unpaid trial period was 6 weeks, and was followed by pay only if the intern met assigned objectives (a California State Department of Education project, Work-Ability, provided funds for a stipended minimum wage). These are individually developed objectives, job practices, and procedures that interns must follow and criterion levels that they must meet. One of the objectives for all interns is the processing of necessary paperwork, without which paychecks cannot be issued. Staff members question the intern and significant other repeatedly, until understanding occurs: Are they paid at the beginning of the semester? Will just filling out the paperwork get them paid? What else do they have to do? If they meet all on-the-job requirements, will they be paid? What else do they have to do? and so on.

The nature of adult agency services is explained and the intake process begun. Jobs, tools, clothing, schooling, training, and college services are all part of what these various agencies can do for a person. It is best to clearly lay out and begin the intake and certifying process at this point. Interns should understand that they must, under current regulations, submit to physical and psychological examinations, unless they have a disability that is otherwise medically certifiable. At this point, having a case opened is a required part of the program. If other at-risk groups are being worked with, the criteria of cooperating adult service agencies, like those funded by the Workforce Investment Act of 1998 that support students from low-income families, should be explained at this time.

On-site instructors repeat for everyone the time and date when the interns should report to work or an employment skills workshop (see Chapter 3), and remind them to arrive a bit early. The instructors take questions and comments from the group. They reassure people that they have entered a top-notch program, but remind them that success hinges on the determination to achieve it. They then use the remaining time to let the groups from each work site meet with their on-site instructor informally and begin filling out paperwork (e.g., work permits, employment and Social Security forms, adult agency intake forms).

First Day on the Job

The Career Ladders philosophy is one of "throwing the students into the water" by putting them on the work site beginning on the first day. Some versions of the program instead provide a couple of weeks of workshop to prepare students. This is part judgment call, part philosophy, part a function of what exposure to the work world schools have provided students to this point, part a function of the local cultural landscape. We proceed with the model that puts interns to work on the very first day (under close supervision, of course).

Interns take a tour of the job site. They are introduced to the supervisors at the various workstations. The employee break rooms are pointed out, and interns are encouraged to take their breaks and lunches with other employees. The company's function and history are explained. Interns are asked to look up the phone numbers for their host company and the phone number for the location where the employment skills workshops will be taught (ideally in the conference room of an employer). The interns write down these numbers and are told the importance of calling in if they are going to be late, miss work, or miss the workshop. The rules of the program (see Appendix 2.8) are discussed and questions are answered. Interns may also be given some work tasks to assess their abilities in areas such as filing, software literacy, measuring, or customer service.

Depending on the nature of the work site and the new interns' class schedules, the interns' first day at the work site may be staggered over a period of 1 to 2 weeks. This can assist the on-site instructor in the management of the community classroom and in assignments to different departments.

Interns are finally introduced to their own supervisor and assigned to a department or station where they will report to work each day. The on-site instructor, in consultation with the employer, has made these decisions based on the interviews so far and the instructor's knowledge of the work ecology. For example, Career Ladders staff developed some special relationships with sponsoring employees over time, and interns were sometimes assigned to those employees known to be reliable benefactors. Some of our hosts are especially talented in dealing with certain attitude problems, or they may offer a cultural or ethnic identification opportunity that can maximize an intern's comfort and potential for growth on the job.

First Workshop

The employment skills workshop is described in the next chapter, but its close integration with the community classroom compels mention here. Because the community classroom is the core experience of the program, the first workshop is held after the interns have been going to work for at least 3 or 4 days and have real work experience to digest. Thus they are oriented to the no-nonsense work nature of the program, and the first workshop has a context. The trade-off, of course, is dependence on the on-site instructor, the family meeting, and previous career training to have sufficiently prompted acceptable behaviors on the job.

Workshops almost always begin with a job-related individual task activity that interns can begin as much as 10 minutes early. The first workshop also emphasizes peer-counseling activities that encourage the group to begin forming and to gain a sense of common purpose and camaraderie, and it offers exercises that build self-esteem. Then, first impressions of the workplace are discussed, which leads to lessons on how to make a good first impression on others. This provides time for the interns to reflect on the kind of impression they may have made their first days on the job. Finally, the exercise of Welcoming a Stranger recreates the dynamics that occur when a new person is introduced into an existing group—the interns gain a metaperspective on their own experience. Also, the exercise provides them with tools for making interns who will be new the next week more comfortable (see Chapter 3, Week 1, for a detailed lesson plan of the first workshop).

Anticipating Common Problems

Attendance is the most important requirement for getting an intern on the path to employability. On-site instructors need to be near-perfect role models, always arriving before the interns. Instructors must move aggressively and quickly when interns are late or absent without calling first. For example, if an intern claims that he or she cannot arrive on time due to the bus service, the instructor should take the bus route to check this out; if it is true, the instructor should work with the school counselor or employer to make a reasonable accommodation. Usually, an earlier dismissal from class can be arranged when transportation problems truly exist. If an intern is absent for a morning program, the on-site instructor should be on the phone within the first 30 minutes of work. A problem that persists can be solved by the instructor calling the intern's home every morning when he or she should be waking up. This is usually annoying enough to other family members that the intern will begin coming to work on time within 2 weeks. If the same problem occurs in an afternoon program, the solution must be similarly negotiated with the school counselor.

The Career Ladders attendance policy (see Appendix 2.8) should be implemented with consistency. In a worst-case scenario, one or perhaps two interns will be terminated for failing to meet the attendance policy. This has a deterrent effect on other interns who are flirting with an attendance problem; it will often solve their attendance issues before they become problems. If staff members do not enforce the policy, the quality of the training eventually declines to the point where interns will not be able to maintain employment after graduation (they have learned the wrong behavior) and the sponsoring employer will terminate participation in the program (the program has lost credibility).

As on-site instructors make assignments to stations, errors may occur, and instructors should be alert to a bad match (of either personalities or person-to-task) and not hesitate to make an early change. A bad match, however, should not be confused with the "growing pains" most people undergo as they enter the workforce. An intern who is acting out may need counseling and participation in a problem-solving process, rather than a transfer (see the Personal Growth section in the Week 4 lesson plan, Chapter 3), to address this situation. Appendix 2.9 is a counseling checklist that can help the on-site instructor develop a problem-solving approach.

Sometimes an on-the-job problem may be related to a school or family problem, and the on-site instructor needs to quickly investigate and offer appropriate counseling to help the intern develop and maintain some separation between her or his work and personal life. On-site instructors also can offer assistance, referral, or counseling to other members of the intern's ecosystem so that everyone is working together to reduce discord and encourage success on the job.

For many interns, early problems can arise from a misunderstanding of the rules, nature, or concept of Career Ladders, and they merely need to have the pay, attendance, or behavior policy repeated for them until they can articulate it themselves.

Referring counselors from the interns' home schools generally cooperate, but sometimes they need the program explained to them. Common issues include early dismissal from classes and independent arrival at work. A balanced arrangement might involve school support to obtain accommodating release from the school site, while stopping short of any overprotectiveness that maintains helpless behaviors (e.g., giving interns bus fare or a ride when they need to negotiate their transportation to work independently).

THE PROGRAM

Working with Employers and Families

On-site instructors have the delicate and complex task of understanding and supporting the social and work needs of the employers. On-site instructors also teach the performance of tasks and respect for the performance of tasks to their interns, many of whom may be getting their first serious exposure to the work world. In some instances, the intern may be the first member of the family in two or three generations to have a training and employment experience. Thus on-site instructors must have a chameleon-like ability to speak the languages of families, interns, school personnel, and, above all, the employer. Within one workplace, many different employer personalities must sometimes be accommodated. Power in the workplace is not always awarded to people who are well adjusted, and unless a situation is clearly intolerable, the intern must be taught the existence of unfairness and shown how to adapt if such learning is within the intern's reach. As an example, Appendix 2.10 describes one work site and how the on-site instructor adapted the program to it. Philosophical explanations and a process for dealing with the sacrifices everyone makes to sustain employment are discussed in the weekly employment skills workshop.

The overriding objective of the on-site instructor is to develop an adult relationship with interns in which the instructor can give feedback that will be accepted and that teaches interns to meet the criteria of behavior—social and career—established in the ecology of the workplace. Regular coworkers may perceive that the on-site instructor is there to accommodate the interns' needs, but she or he must continually emphasize that interns are to be treated like any other employee, and that they are not there to do make-believe work or to perform tasks that are not marketable. While Career Ladders' offer of intern accommodation is maximal—to the point of doing the work for the intern if necessary—the goal is to make every intern independent of school-sponsored supervision by the end of the semester. Employers are encouraged to take over the supervision as soon as possible.

Usually, the on-site instructor has been able to go to the work site a few days before the interns arrive and learn the tasks that they will be assigned. Also, the instructor can make arrangements with sponsoring coworkers and managers and can brief them on the interns who will arrive. This preparation phase is especially crucial when the on-site instructor is new to the site; we have developed site-specific minimanuals to brief new instructors on the idiosyncrasies of each job site (see Appendix 2.10 for one example).

The on-site instructor is there to serve the intern, but does so by representing the employer's needs in such a way that the intern can meet them. The instructor provides additional support and guidance if the intern needs it. Interns may have a variety of needs: instructions to be repeated many times, a task to be broken down into smaller steps, directions to be written down, an accommodating device to be designed or purchased. The on-site instructor is there to be alert to these needs and to meet them. In the beginning of the semester, this means doing whatever is necessary. However, the instructor's job for the semester is to incrementally fade or transfer his or her support to the natural supervision of the work site.

One of the best examples of this principle working was a situation where a student who was deaf had an internship at a bank. The school district offered to pay for a sign-language interpreter to accompany the intern as a reasonable accommodation that would allow her to maximize her working potential. The employer refused this service, requesting instead that the interpreter come and teach sign language to the intern's coworkers so that they could communicate with her independently. This is the way the program is supposed to work.

The instructor teaches interns to identify and articulate their own needs in a mature fashion, such as asking coworkers for help on a task. If there is a serious gap between the intern's behavior and the employer's expectations, the on-site instructor attempts to bridge the gap immediately and then creates interventions that will close it without external support. Often, a situation calls for a task analysis and a systematic approach to instructing the intern on a task. In other situations, a focused and intensive social skills training program may be needed, in which the intern models and rehearses the appropriate behavior.

On-site instructors represent the interns' needs by developing challenging job tasks for them throughout the company, recognizing and eliciting their competence in doing their tasks, and advocating for them in situations where they are unable to adequately represent themselves. In instances where a disability or cultural difference best explains an inability to perform according to the employer's standards, the on-site instructor will need to educate the employer. Such mediations are discussed in more depth in Chapter 4.

On-site instructors should frequently call the significant others who came to the family meeting. A minimum of 70% of these calls should be to praise the interns for work well done, and for making progress toward career independence. When the positive aspects are emphasized, the family member can be an enthusiastic and cooperative key player in devising an intervention if a problem should arise. If there are no serious problems, a positive momentum toward postsecondary success can be built up through the ongoing communication with the home. On more than one occasion, a parent has responded to one of these calls with tears: In 12 years of public schooling, no one had ever called home to report something his or her child had done right.

Academic Standards: What Students Need To Learn and Be Able To Do

Many states and local school districts throughout the U.S. have rewritten and made more demanding commitments to uniform academic standards and intensified graduation requirements. Almost as often, there has been the rudimentary error of assuming a return to drill, lecture, teaching to the test, and reducing the number of elective classes available to students will cause students to reach these requirements. But stringent academic standards in fact compel instructors to diligently seek out more diverse ways for students to reach and exceed those goals, such as more, not fewer, elective choices. The alternative is that schools will only work for one type of student, and society will become more stratified. Career Ladders provides a framework for community-based learning that connects students to the world of work and that makes their academic studies come alive with relevance and meaning.

A review of Seattle Public Schools' Profile of the Graduate (Rimmer, 2001, p. 1) demonstrates that community-based learning, like that coordinated in Career Ladders, can help a student attain many, and sometimes all, of the attributes expected by graduation (those specifically taught in the Career Ladders curriculum are marked):

Graduation Standards Taught in Career Ladders

- ☒ Master the foundational skills of reading, writing, mathematics, and science, and have the capacity for change
- ☒ Communicate effectively
- ☒ Be a critical consumer of information and be able to utilize changing technology
- ☒ Think analytically and solve problems
- ☒ Understand and value self and others
- ☒ Work respectfully and productively in teams
- ☒ Value democracy, diversity, and community stewardship
- ☐ Appreciate the arts
- ☒ Be prepared for careers and lifelong learning

Like many states and local school districts, Seattle Public Schools has instituted academic standards. Reproduced here are those in reading, writing, communication, and mathematics. As they compare learning on the job to mastering academic standards, competent instructors will see a high degree of overlap. Academic standards also act as a warning system in the Career Ladders program. If a student is not addressing academic standards and learning more in order to meet them, then it must be considered that the internship is not at that time in the best interest of the intern's development. The exception would be in the case of an intern with a significant disability where the Individualized Education Program supersedes district and state standards. The complete list of standards and benchmarks for Seattle Public Schools can be found at www.seattleschools.org/area/acastan/index.xml. Figure 2.2 shows how most 10th-grade academic standards are specifi-

cally taught in Career Ladders, or any quality community-based learning program.

Data Collection and Intervention

Data collection serves a variety of functions: cross-referencing with academic standards, staff accountability, counseling, nonjudgmental feedback, intern involvement, fair grading procedures, appropriate input on Individualized Transition Plans, and documentation for future programming. Data collection plays a crucial part in good instruction. This section will emphasize those aspects of data collection that directly affect the intern at the training site. In the beginning weeks of the semester, the on-site instructor develops objectives for all interns, usually two skills objectives and one social objective. Data collection and interventions are the tools that help interns meet these objectives.

Well-written objectives are a cornerstone of good instruction. Most special educators have training and expertise in the skill, but it bears some review. With well-written objectives, the instructor is focused on the task at hand, and the student or intern understands what is expected and can focus as well. When appropriate, employers, families, and program managers can have insight into and documentation of the on-the-job instructional process.

Objectives must (a) describe the task (i.e., what is to be done, its frequency, duration, and rate), (b) set a target date or time for mastery of that task or an incremental benchmark, and (c) describe the conditions under which the task is to be performed. For example, *By November 3 (target), Millie will file 35 personnel files with 100% accuracy within 1 hour (task). Her supervisor will give her the files and leave her undisturbed for the full hour (conditions).* This objective could have multiple steps leading to its final mastery in which Millie works her way up to 100% accuracy and to the 35 files per hour goal.

For another example, *Within the next month (target), Bill will ask two co-workers what they did for fun and recreation the previous weekend and will report these conversations to his instructor (task). The task will be measured only on a day when at least 4 of Bill's 6 favorite co-workers are at work (conditions).*

(text continues on p. 22)

TENTH-GRADE READING STANDARDS

Taught in Career Ladders

READING STANDARD 1.
The student understands and uses different skills and strategies to read.

☒	1.1	Uses word recognition and word meaning skills to read and comprehend text.
☒	1.2	Builds vocabulary through reading.
☒	1.3	Reads fluently, adjusting reading for purpose and material.
☐	1.4	Understands elements of literature.
☒	1.5	Uses features of nonfiction text and computer software.

READING STANDARD 2.
The student understands the meaning of what is read.

☒	2.1	Comprehends important ideas and details.
☒	2.2	Expands comprehension by analyzing, interpreting, and synthesizing information and ideas.
☐	2.3	Thinks critically and analyzes authors' use of language, style, purpose, and perspective.

READING STANDARD 3.
The student reads different materials for a variety of purposes.

☒	3.1	Reads to learn new information.
☒	3.2	Reads to perform a task.
☐	3.3	Reads for literary experience in a variety of forms.
☒	3.4	Reads for career applications.

READING STANDARD 4.
The student sets goals and evaluates progress to improve reading.

☒	4.1	Assesses strengths and need for improvement.
☒	4.2	Seeks and offers feedback to improve reading.
☐	4.3	Develops interests and shares reading experiences.

TENTH-GRADE WRITING STANDARDS

Taught in Career Ladders

WRITING STANDARD 1.
The student writes clearly and effectively.

☐	1.1	Develops concept and design.
☒	1.2	Uses style appropriate to the audience and purpose.
☐	1.3	Applies writing conventions.

FIGURE 2.2. Academic standards for 10th-grade students in Seattle Public Schools. From "Seattle Public Schools Academic Standards," by Seattle Public Schools, n.d. Retrieved from http://www.seattleschools.org/area/acastan/index.xml

**Taught in
Career Ladders**

WRITING STANDARD 2.
The student writes in a variety of forms for different audiences and purposes.

☒	2.1	Writes for different audiences.
☒	2.2	Writes for different purposes.
☒	2.3	Writes in a variety of forms.
☒	2.4	Writes for career applications.

WRITING STANDARD 3.
The student understands and uses the steps of the writing process.

☐	3.1	Prewrites: generates ideas and gathers information.
☐	3.2	Drafts: elaborates on a topic and supporting ideas.
☒	3.3	Revises: collects input and enhances text and style.
☒	3.4	Edits: uses resources to correct spelling, punctuation, grammar, and usage.
☒	3.5	Publishes: selects a publishing form and produces a completed writing project to share with chosen audience.

WRITING STANDARD 4.
The student analyzes and evaluates the effectiveness of written work.

☒	4.1	Assesses own strengths and need for improvement.
☒	4.2	Seeks and offers feedback.

TENTH-GRADE COMMUNICATION STANDARDS

**Taught in
Career Ladders**

COMMUNICATION STANDARD 1.
The student uses listening and observation skills to gain understanding.

☒	1.1	Focuses attention.
☒	1.2	Listens and observes to gain and interpret information.
☒	1.3	Checks for understanding by asking questions and paraphrasing.

COMMUNICATION STANDARD 2.
The student communicates ideas clearly and effectively.

☒	2.1	Communicates clearly to a range of audiences for different purposes.
☒	2.2	Develops content and ideas.
☒	2.3	Uses effective delivery.
☒	2.4	Uses effective language and style.
☒	2.5	Effectively uses action, sound, and/or images to support presentations.

FIGURE 2.2. *Continued.*

Taught in Career Ladders	**COMMUNICATION STANDARD 3.** The student uses communication strategies and skills to work effectively with others.
☒	3.1　Uses language to interact effectively and responsibly with others.
☒	3.2　Works cooperatively as a member of a group.
☒	3.3　Seeks agreement and solutions through discussion.

Taught in Career Ladders	**COMMUNICATION STANDARD 4.** The student analyzes and evaluates the effectiveness of formal and informal communication.
☒	4.1　Assesses strengths and need for improvement; assesses own and others' communication strengths and needs and sets goals for improvement.
☒	4.2　Seeks and offers feedback; seeks and uses feedback to improve communication; offers suggestions and comments to others.
☐	4.3　Analyzes mass communication.
☒	4.4　Analyzes how communication is used in career settings.

TENTH-GRADE MATHEMATICS STANDARDS

Taught in Career Ladders	**MATH STANDARD 1.** The student understands and applies the concepts and procedures of mathematics.
☒	1.1　Number sense
☒	1.2　Measurement
☐	1.3　Geometric sense
☒	1.4　Probability and statistics
☐	1.5　Algebraic sense

Taught in Career Ladders	**MATH STANDARD 2.** The student uses mathematics to define and solve problems.
☒	2.1　Investigates situations.
☒	2.2　Formulates questions and defines problems.
☒	2.3　Constructs solutions.

Taught in Career Ladders	**MATH STANDARD 3.** The student uses mathematical reasoning.
☒	3.1　Analyzes information.
☒	3.2　Predicts results and makes inferences.
☒	3.3　Draws conclusions and verifies results.

FIGURE 2.2. *Continued.*

Taught in Career Ladders	MATH STANDARD 4. The student communicates knowledge and understanding in both everyday and mathematical language.	
☒	4.1	Gathers information.
☒	4.2	Organizes and interprets information.
☒	4.3	Represents and shares information.
	MATH STANDARD 5. The student understands how mathematical ideas connect within mathematics, to other subject areas, and to real-life situations.	
☒	5.1	Relates concepts and procedures within mathematics.
☒	5.2	Relates mathematical concepts and procedures to other disciplines.
☒	5.3	Relates mathematical concepts and procedures to real-life situations.

FIGURE 2.2. *Continued.*

Artful instructors are able to understand and recognize important objectives to surviving and thriving in the adult world, describe mastery, and establish incremental steps by which interns achieve that mastery. Using forms found in the Career Ladders Data Collection Handbook (Appendix 2.11), instructors can document objectives written to address social skills (Quick On-the-Job Social Skills Assessment), document the six main objectives for an intern's semester (Work Performance Record), and track incremental progress on a single objective or a series of objectives (charts for Rate, Accuracy, and Quantity). Journal Entries provide raw materials for writing objectives, provide insight into deciding which objectives are important, and support the instructional team in helping a single instructor develop appropriate objectives. The Intern Recording Sheet and the On-the-Job Performance Summary Graph provide an abbreviated summary and "snapshot" of intern progress on a series of objectives. These summaries can quickly communicate a full profile of student progress when the instructor has organized teaching around well-chosen and well-written objectives.

Attendance and punctuality are the first and foremost areas where data collection serves an important function. If an intern is not meeting the standards set by the program and must be put on probation or terminated, accurate data are essen-tial for making the case to the intern, teacher, and administrator who must handle the transition back to school. Charting attendance and punctuality in a jeopardized situation may help the intern rectify the problem. Many job sites have time cards and time clocks, so these data are self-collected and are done so in a manner appropriate to the workplace.

Social skills comprise a domain of behaviors that is subtler and sometimes difficult to describe. However, research and our experience have identified some social skills problems that typically occur. The Quick On-the-Job Social Skills Assessment (see Appendix 2.11) is a tool the on-site instructor can use to report back to the Career Ladders manager, who can then develop and adapt the curriculum of the weekly employment skills workshop to the social skills needs of the interns. The assessment lists the following social skills: Conversing with Employees, Ordering Job Duties, Asking for Help or Instructions, Following Instructions, Giving Instructions, Accepting Positive Feedback, Accepting Negative Feedback, and Giving Negative Feedback. Certainly, some interns will have social skills needs beyond this short list.

For interns needing particular attention, the on-site instructor should include behaviors that can be precisely defined, observed, and finally counted, by either the intern, a coworker, or the instructor. These can then be recorded so that the effectiveness of any intervention is quickly noted or a lack of effectiveness eventually detected, in which case the intervention should be modified. For training to generalize social skills that have been taught and rehearsed in the employment skills workshop, the same rating forms used in the workshops (see Appendix 3.10) can be used by the on-site instructor, and performance of each skill on the job is conveyed as a final exam. When co-workers, instructors, and interns all complete rating sheets (from Appendix 3.10) on the same performance, interns and instructors can learn much by triangulating, analyzing, and comparing the three perspectives.

Like social skills, other job-keeping skills such as handling authority, being honest, leaving personal problems at home, and taking pride in your work can be the focus of objectives. If there are persistent problems, we strongly recommend that a key aspect (e.g., chronic negative complaining) be counted and charted in a nonjudgmental way so that the instructor can give feedback that will empower a youth to take responsibility for the problem and its solution.

The job tasks themselves, if they are routine, frequently require a combination of accuracy and speed. To help an intern meet the standards set for an entry-level employee, accuracy and speed can be charted and ultimately self-charted, with criteria goals set at the top of the chart. If an intern does not reach a criterion level of employability, these kinds of data are crucial in helping to decide whether the intern should persevere in the assigned task or move to another department. To leave interns in a position for a semester learning parts of a job that they would never fully qualify for is usually a waste of their time and a disservice to their career development.

In job situations where the assigned tasks vary from day to day, other approaches to data collection can train competency goals. If the intern has the objective of increasing general accuracy, the percentage of correct responses from a number of different tasks can be recorded on the same chart. If rate is an issue, the number of minutes beyond the expected time of completion can be recorded regardless of the task. If the intern's performance varies from task to task, supervisors can rate the quality of the work on checklists. This can help to identify areas in need of training, or provide data

that can play a role in helping the intern make career decisions. In one instance, an intern was able to stop his distracting behaviors and increase his rate on a clerical sorting task when he was given the opportunity to time himself and chart his performance. More complex jobs that demand problem solving and independent thinking can sometimes be quantified with decision trees, or addressed with correction and feedback strategies.

Evaluations of intern performance are conducted three times (every 6 weeks) during the semester, corresponding to the grading periods of the school. The on-site instructor uses the Intern Recording Sheet (Appendix 2.11), but the merit review forms of the host company are also used. The Work Performance Record (Appendix 2.11) can guide comments on the Intern Recording Sheet; employers should know the objectives on which the student is working. The first evaluation is usually conducted by the on-site instructor but is based largely on interviews with the sponsoring employer. The employer conducts the second evaluation, and the third is based on self-evaluation by the intern, using the same form. The concept guiding evaluations is to treat the intern just like any new employee at the company, and to request that employers maintain their usual standards. There is no point in saying that an intern is "doing well for a high school student" if that intern is about to become another young adult in the job marketplace, subject to the same standards and conditions as everyone else. Finally, the intern can learn the prevailing standards and apply them in the self-evaluation. This is probably the single most valuable counseling tool to see whether an intern is aware of and has internalized when he or she is not meeting employer expectations.

The Intern Recording Sheet can be used for multiple and frequent measures of intern progress. By converting scores to percentages, a master profile can be recorded on the Summary Graph (Appendix 2.11), which is really five graphs consolidated on one page. For example, a perfect score on the General Work Behaviors section of the Intern Recording Sheet yields a score of 24. Dividing 24 into 100 obtains a multiplier of 4.17. So an intern score in General Work Behaviors of 19 is equal to 79% of a perfect score (4.17×19). On the Summary Graph, under General Work Behaviors, the instructor or intern would record a 79 for this specific session. The Overall score on the Summary Graph is the average of Job Tasks, General Work Behaviors, Social Skills, and Problem Behaviors (note that the scale is reversed on Problem Behaviors; declines in such behavior earn higher scores) for that session. If an intern can be engaged in this data collection and recording process, she or he can be engaged in the overall development of good employability skills.

Data are pieces of information and can take many forms. A journal that is precise and avoids judgmental language can be as useful a source of data as charts and diagrams. The on-site instructor cannot balk at the task of configuring and counting behaviors and should be comfortable in the role of data taker. When designing interventions, the on-site instructor asks: Is the description precise, objective, and nonjudgmental? Is it in a form that is useful to the intern and to other instructors? Does it indicate strengths as well as areas in need of improvement? Are the data measuring behaviors that are relevant to the career independence of the intern?

Finally, data collection during the training period can teach an intern habits that will help when she or he embarks on a job search. Keeping track of the number of job leads, job interviews, and so forth can help maintain morale in this often frustrating process. If an intern knows ahead of time that it usually is necessary to follow up on 15 job leads before a job is obtained, that intern will take pleasure in beating those odds; collecting data during the process will help keep the intern organized and build in satisfaction. Some students will exceed academic standards or employer standards during their internship; they should get the maximum possible satisfaction from such accomplishments. Many excellent resources on developing data-based applied behavioral interventions are available elsewhere and are not described here. However, Appendix 2.11 contains the data-collection tools developed for Career Ladders on-site instructors.

PHASES OF THE TRAINING SEMESTER

The semester is divided into three phases—initial, middle, and ending weeks; this section of the manual is designed to help on-site instructors and managers anticipate the moods and events that typically characterize each phase. A timeline that the manager gives to the on-site instructors (see Appendix 2.12) serves as a summary of their duties and also corresponds to the chronology this section describes.

Initial Weeks

In the beginning of the semester, the on-site instructor is assiduously conducting evaluations of the interns' abilities and instructional needs and shuffling placements. If it is at all possible, most if not all interns should be placed in one department for the first week or so and then their assignments should be gradually distributed to other departments according to the informal instructor assessment and observations of the interns' independence and ability to perform the tasks. Interns who need more supervision stay closer to the on-site instructor. Out of this assessment comes two individualized work and academic objectives and at least one social objective that address the job and social skills each intern will need to develop. Interns need to be reminded that they must meet academic goals as well as those expected at the workplace.

Attendance and punctuality are heavily emphasized, and the demand to meet high employability standards is made at this time. Sometimes interns will drop out or be terminated at this early stage if they cannot come to work consistently and on time. Good attendance and punctuality are emphatically the above-all focus at this point in the semester, and failure to meet these requirements is not tolerated. Many interns will go through a honeymoon period, getting through the initial weeks but developing attendance problems during the middle weeks. Though an intern will not go on probation until he or she has had eight absences, two or three absences in the very beginning weeks should serve as a red flag and the referring counselor and host teacher should be notified.

Within the first 2 weeks of the program, the on-site instructor telephones the family contact to give the first progress report—almost always a positive one—and to establish what will become a cooperative, ongoing relationship. The instructor should praise good attendance and reinforce the priority of work.

Interns can be paid a wage in Career Ladders, but it is recommended that they earn the right to a wage by demonstrating employability. Therefore, during the first 6 weeks, all interns are in an unpaid trial period.[1] This is why the objectives are so important. Graduation from the trial period into pay is based on the intern meeting objectives or making reasonable progress on them. This develops the concept of earning and ongoing learning. Also, the unpaid trial period is a time to teach and learn about the rewarding aspects of work other than pay. Interns who take pay for granted are learning the altogether wrong lesson. We contend that anyone who works only for pay will not fully experience job or life satisfaction, and so, in these first weeks, we consider pay a distraction. Clearly, we do not condone exploitation through a manipulation of the volunteerist ethic. But we sincerely believe that interns have much to gain from a period in which they cannot justify working simply as a way to get a paycheck. The trial period is a time for them to search, find, and express deeper and more satisfying reasons for wanting to participate in the work life of their community, such as pride, self-respect, participation, learning, community, friendships, contribution to society, and development of more lofty career goals.

Another aspect of Career Ladders' particular pay program is the extensive amount of paperwork getting on the payroll entails. The skill of filling out forms is valuable, and understanding that paychecks cannot be generated without the proper paperwork is an important reality lesson. Before entering the Career Ladders program, interns need to already have Social Security cards and motor vehicle department identification because Career Ladders staff members are already significantly affected by the organizational tasks of all the other paperwork demanded by the school district. Such preliminaries to working must be addressed in the earlier grades, which also provides an extremely positive way for Career Ladders to have an instructional bridge to the classrooms of the referring

teachers. Social Security cards and other appropriate identification should be part of the curriculum in those classrooms.

The end of this trial period signifies that the intern is actually making progress, is at least closer to if not at the level of a typical entry-level employee with the sponsoring company, and has earned the right to a wage.

Middle Weeks

The middle weeks comprise the time period when the interns will meet the challenges of dealing with routine. This is the time when stamina will be learned, when negative first impressions an intern may have made on the job can be reversed, and when positive first impressions can be reinforced. It is the time when a host employer may decide to hire an intern after graduation.

The first signs of work tedium may emerge at this point. If the on-site instructor determines that the assigned job is nonetheless a good match, then he or she needs to conduct an intervention that helps the intern address feelings and behaviors. If an intern's attendance starts to decline, breaks go on too long, or tardiness begins to occur, the on-site instructor should inform the Career Ladders manager immediately so that the two can consult to devise a strategy. Every intern is different, and there are many possible interventions: calling the family and asking for their support; enlisting the employer as a confederate to articulate the demands of the workplace and set limits; counseling the intern and devising a formal or informal contract; transferring the intern (rarely recommended); putting the intern on probation; increasing or restructuring the work load; and analyzing with the intern the broader social arrangements that make it necessary for the intern to excel in this job.

Interns have told us that their work is boring, that they are always given the dirty or most menial work, and that their work is not essential to the

[1]Unpaid work experience must be conducted in compliance with the Fair Labor and Standards Act of 1938. In essence, student interns may not contribute to profit and must be learning new behaviors throughout any unpaid period. Interns must not go into "production" to the point where the employer is obtaining free labor from the interns or other workers are being displaced from their jobs. Thus, the interns must be in either a learning or a training mode, in which they have not mastered the skill and the employer is expending resources to train them or the work that they do must be undone. We support the ongoing learning of new skills throughout this 6-week probationary period. Once the intern begins earning a wage, by either the employer or a subsidy (like California's WorkAbility program), he or she may go into production.

business operation. Sometimes these complaints have merit. In a training program such as this, the program staff are obliged to seek a challenging work opportunity that will advance the career potential of the interns, and the instructor must ensure this is happening. On the other hand, dealing with the tedium that many workers experience is one of the lessons the program offers, as is the fact that new or entry-level employees are often given the most menial tasks, intern or not. Each situation is different, and the on-site instructor must perform a delicate balancing act. The instructor's job is to protect interns from exploitation while teaching job-keeping skills.

During the middle weeks, job task rotation becomes a powerful instructional tool. In instances where an intern is in a situation beyond her or his abilities, a social difficulty has not been resolved, or an intervention has not helped an intern reach criteria, a transfer to another department may be appropriate. In instances where an intern has excelled but the likelihood of a hire is low, or where the intern has mastered all the objectives, a transfer to another department can function like a promotion and enrich the training experience. To maximize the likelihood of a hire after graduation, the very best-performing interns can be transferred to another company entirely—called a *satellite site*—with minimal supervision; even if the intern is not hired, maximum independence will have been achieved. Such a satellite site can serve as a mini–community classroom for an employer who may consider sponsoring a full-blown community classroom in the future.

Another educational aspect of transfer and promotion is that interns relearn how to enter a new situation. Many of them protest their transfers, but it is a lesson in an event that is likely to happen later in their careers and practice for the inevitable transfer out of the community classroom and into the competitive work world. So except in the case of emotionally withdrawn interns who need more time to acclimate, all interns experience one to two transfers during the semester.

Final Weeks

If an intern has not established a record of competence and dependability by the final weeks, it is usually too late to do so. Instructors should be ask-

ing themselves what justified keeping a poorly performing intern in the program; there is a danger that the wrong lessons have been taught.

Attendance and social problems may still occur if the pressures that lead to them have been building, but not expressed, until now. In these cases, however, the value of preserving a good track record can be very convincing and can help an intern face situations with more maturity.

If there are interns who clearly are not likely candidates for hiring at the host company (regardless of whether there are openings), the final weeks provide a last-chance but powerful opportunity to collect employer feedback and communicate to those interns the job-keeping skills they still need to develop. This is a difficult message to convey, but it is given at a time when an intern is open to hearing it by virtue of it being at the end of the semester, and thus represents an educational opportunity that should not be missed.

School activities frequently punctuate the final weeks of the semester, especially in the spring. On-site instructor supervision, in most cases, is nonetheless minimal, allowing the natural supervision of the workplace to take over. Some interns will, however, continue to need assistance and counseling. Because a top priority of the program is job placement, interns will be released from work to go to job interviews, conduct job searches, or meet with appropriate adult service agencies. In the fall semester, on-site instructors find out the high school completion status of each intern, to determine which interns could take part-time jobs without jeopardizing their graduation.

Interns can be released from their usual work schedule to conduct a job search, but employers should be given plenty of advance notice. An employer who complains about losing an intern should be encouraged to hire the youth. By this point in the semester, interns should have been trained in how to inquire about openings at the host site, or the on-site instructor should do this for interns with limited job search abilities. Interviews should be arranged for top candidates, by interns themselves if feasible, by Career Ladders staff if necessary. Those who are unlikely to be hired should be given the highest priority for developing a job search strategy.

Career Ladders was originally structured to serve high school seniors, so the final weeks of the spring semester have always been difficult due to the celebratory activities that accompany graduation. One solution to these inherent problems is to serve seniors in the fall semester only, and juniors in the spring. This permits "senioritis" to run its course and saves interns some of the conflicts that often arise between work and school activities in the spring. To preserve the good work attendance records of interns, the community classroom experience can be shortened in the spring.

Another advantage of serving seniors in the fall is that, following the community classroom experience, they can and should be ready to develop real jobs for themselves. They are offered a thrice-weekly job club in the spring through the transition specialist (see Chapter 4), in which they share tales of job searches, network among themselves, share and develop job leads, prepare resumes and applications, rehearse interviews, and go out on supported job searches.

Supported job searches are for those youths who are capable of seeking out a job lead and passing a job interview, but who need extra support to actually go out and do it. An on-site instructor will travel to a potential job with a youth and wait outside while the youth goes in to ask for an application or interview. The instructor also helps interns develop leads and make cold calls. Youths who are known to be good workers but who may be handicapped by their inability to do a job search or handle an interview may actually have a job developed for them. A curriculum for a job search is described in Chapter 3, and techniques of on-the-job support for those who obtain employment are discussed in Chapter 4. It is expected that a few, and perhaps many, community classroom interns will seek and find jobs *during* the training semester, thus graduating from the community classroom early, so these training and placement skills are definitely within the duties of the on-site instructor.

Postsecondary activities will be coordinated and monitored by the Career Ladders transition specialist. Having visited the community classroom and the employment skills workshop, the transition specialist has had a chance to initiate relationships with the interns. At this point, the on-site instructors brief the transition specialist, who can complete the case-opening procedures for the interns and begin working with those most in need, thus minimizing the trauma and risk of the "pass-off." Such a transition should be friendly and allow interns to see the on-site instructor, transition specialist, and manager as members of one team. As graduates, interns will continue to have access to that entire team. All staff have thus been identified as caring adults who are available to help the interns achieve career goals. The community classroom has introduced the interns to a real work experience and to valuable contacts in the work world. They now understand the concept of work in an abstract way that has become part of themselves, in a concrete way through the work experience, and in an interpersonal way through the coworkers and professionals they have gotten to know during the training process.

APPENDIX 2.1
Community Classroom Flowchart

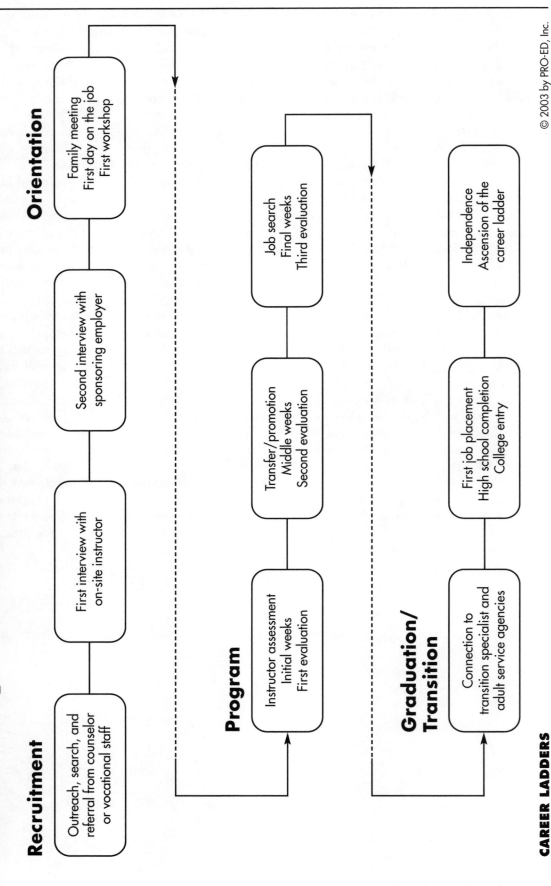

Recruitment

Outreach, search, and referral from counselor or vocational staff

First interview with on-site instructor

Second interview with sponsoring employer

Orientation

Family meeting
First day on the job
First workshop

Program

Instructor assessment
Initial weeks
First evaluation

Transfer/promotion
Middle weeks
Second evaluation

Job search
Final weeks
Third evaluation

Graduation/Transition

Connection to transition specialist and adult service agencies

First job placement
High school completion
College entry

Independence
Ascension of the career ladder

CAREER LADDERS

APPENDIX 2.2

Initial Referral for Transition Services

The following is an initial referral for the Career Ladders program. Our goal is to offer a work-based experience for students. The Career Ladders staff will contact you for additional information to assist in student placement. Through this initial referral, students 16 years old or older could be accepted into Career Ladders.

Student: _____ Birth date: _____

Parent: _____ Home phone: _____

Counselor: _____ Phone: _____

Expected graduation date: _____ Grade: _____

School: _____ Reading level: _____ Math level: _____

Previous job training or experience and goals: _____

_____

_____

_____

Reason for referral and transition goal: _____

_____

Will the student be able to work during the school day? _____

What are the best times for Career Ladders staff to contact you for additional information

about the referred student? _____

Please return this form by _____ to: The Transition Center
2120 S. Jackson
San Francisco, CA 94112

Additional comments: _____

_____

APPENDIX 2.3

Referral Checklist

The referred student is particularly strong or in need of assistance in the following areas:

	Is very strong	Is competent	Needs some support	Needs close attention
SOCIAL SKILLS				
Dealing with the public congenially				
Handling pressure				
Clear speech and language				
Eye contact				
Making friends				
Working with others				
Accepting criticism				
Resisting peer pressure				
Willingness to try new things				
Asking for help when needed				
EMPLOYABILITY				
Attendance				
Punctuality				
Awareness of safety				
Ability to make decisions				
Attention to task >5 minutes				
Attention to task >20 minutes				
Performing tasks at a consistent rate				
Attention to detail				
Working without supervision				
Performing repetitive or unpleasant tasks				
JOB SKILLS				
Memory of a motor task				
Memory of a rule (work or behavior)				
Ability to follow 1-step direction				
Ability to follow 2-step direction				
Ability to follow 3-step direction				
Ability to control hyperactivity				
Ability to screen out distractions				
Consistent behavior day to day				
Comprehension of spoken instructions				
Comprehension of written instructions				
Comprehension of modeled instructions				
Ability to alphabetize				
Ability to put in numerical order				
Ability to copy words and numbers accurately				
Ability to write down a spoken message accurately				
Ability to write legibly				
Coordination and dexterity				

APPENDIX 2.4

First Interview Notification

Ross Smithson
378 Oakmont Drive
Halloranville, MD 27398

November 2, 2004

Dear _____ Ross _____:

Congratulations! You have been selected to interview for Career Ladders.
Please come to the Transition Center at 1441 Gaylord Avenue, downstairs,
at ___3:10 P.M.___ on ___November 18___. We recommend that you arrive
5 to 10 minutes early. If you cannot make this time, call Marianne Jackson
at 555-4979 immediately. See you there!

Sincerely,

Carlos Hernandez   Marianne Jackson
Career Ladders Coordinator   Career Ladders Manager

APPENDIX 2.5

Second Interview Notification

Ross Smithson
378 Oakmont Drive
Halloranville, MD 27398

November 20, 2004

Dear _____ Ross _____ :

Congratulations! You have passed your first interview for Career Ladders.
The next step is a second interview with the business sponsor at the site
you have selected. Your interview is with this company:

_____ ACE Manufacturing Company _____

at this address: _____ 3232 Roberts Road _____

at this date and time: _____ December 7, 3:45 P.M. _____

Arrive 5 to 10 minutes early, and ask for

_____ Bill Frizell _____

    Bring your completed application with you. If you pass this interview,
we will invite you to participate in the program and will ask to meet with
you and one other person who is close to you. If there will be any problem
making your interview, please call us immediately at 555-4979 between
8:30 A.M. and 3:30 P.M. If we are not there, please leave a message. Thank
you and good luck!

Sincerely yours,

Carlos Hernandez   Marianne Jackson
Career Ladders Coordinator   Career Ladders Manager

APPENDIX 2.6

Final Acceptance and Notification of Family Meeting

Ross Smithson
378 Oakmont Drive
Halloranville, MD 27398

December 9, 2004

Dear _____Ross_____ :

Congratulations! You have been selected as a candidate for Career Ladders. If you are successful, you will have the chance to get job training for school credit. Even more important, the Career Ladders team will do everything it can to help you develop your career after you graduate.

    If you want to remain eligible, you must attend a meeting where you will receive an introduction to the program. Please bring with you the person who cares most about your success after high school. We would be happy to meet with a parent, brother or sister, aunt or uncle, or anyone over 18 who is close to you and will continue to be in your life after high school.

    The meeting will take place on Wednesday, December 16, at 7:30 P.M., in Room 107 at Abraham Lincoln High School, 2122 Cory Avenue. If you cannot make it, please leave a message for Ms. Jackson at 555-4979 or Mr. Hernandez at 555-1161 during business hours. If you do not come to the meeting or you do not call, we will have to disqualify you from Career Ladders, so please come to find out more. We are eager to meet you and your family, and we wish you the greatest success and fortune.

Sincerely yours,

Carlos Hernandez   Marianne Jackson
Career Ladders Coordinator   Career Ladders Manager

APPENDIX 2.7

Job Descriptions of Career Ladders Staff Members

On-Site Instructor

I. Conduct on-the-job education and training

    A. Prepare work site ahead of intern assignment by researching and planning

        1. Employer supervision

        2. Tasks and job analysis

        3. Your fading plan

    B. Instruct and fade

    C. Make written evaluations, objective and behaviorally stated

        1. Intern job and academic goals

        2. Intern social skills goals

        3. All other relevant factors

II. Work with entire ecosystem of intern

    A. Intern

    B. Intern's family

    C. Employer

    D. Peers

    E. Relevant agencies and other intern associations

III. Maintain positive images

    A. Self

    B. Student

    C. Program

IV. Facilitate job searches through coordination and role-playing with interns

V. Join the team

    A. Report to manager

    B. Work with transition specialist

    C. Work with coordinator

    D. Attend and participate in staff meetings

VI. Help in employment skills workshop as requested

VII. Process paperwork

Program Manager

  I. Supervise and orient on-site instructors

    A. Provide timeline; monitor

    B. Facilitate and consult about behavioral, career, and social skill intern objectives

    C. Consult about employee relationships

    D. Train in supported job search techniques

    E. Communicate information on meetings and other activities

 II. Teach employment skills workshop

    A. Prepare and develop curriculum; preview with project coordinator

    B. Outline workshop duties for on-site instructors

    C. Coordinate job searches

III. Supervise transitions

    A. Inform transition specialist

    B. Identify interns in need of more intensive support

    C. Coordinate postsecondary services: community college, one-stop service center, vocational rehabilitation, temporary employment, and so on

IV. Recruit new interns

    A. Solicit referrals from all high schools

    B. Conduct initial interviews; screen

    C. Set up employer interviews; consult and screen with employers

    D. Set up parent meeting, orientation

 V. Develop program

    A. Collaborate with project coordinator on presenior training

    B. Develop new sites

    C. Construct plans to increase success rate and number of students served

Transition Specialist

The transition specialist assumes responsibility for the career development of youths who are exiting school and have succeeded in Career Ladders community classroom as high school seniors. These duties are explained in detail in Chapter 4.

I. Visit sites

II. Visit employment skills workshop

III. Deliver transition services (see Chapter 4)

IV. Develop postsecondary plans

V. Follow up on former interns and maintain statistics

VI. Consult with current employers

VII. Facilitate job search or postsecondary education

VIII. Train, retrain, and mediate on-the-job problems

IX. Coordinate job club with program manager

X. Initiate contact with previous fall interns in late spring

XI. Coordinate case openings and closures with affiliated agencies

XII. Conduct job search with current interns

XIII. Prepare monthly reports

XIV. Attend staff meetings

XV. Collect assessment data

XVI. Perform other duties as assigned by adult agency caseworker and project coordinator

Project Coordinator

When Career Ladders is replicated by a school district or similar organization, the project coordinator's duties should be assumed by an administrator and adapted as needed.

I. Maintain liaisons between school district, host employers, and all affiliated partner agencies

    A. Inform school district administrators regularly; plan future of program collaboratively

    B. Conduct site visits with employers and host employees; obtain informal feedback on acceptance of program and attitudes toward it; consult before changing policies that will affect site; advocate for interns and for intern placement in permanent jobs; aid program manager in development of new sites and negotiations in current sites when necessary

    C. Provide ongoing services and appropriate research findings to staff, district, and employers; facilitate applied research efforts at sites; provide internships for university students

II. Provide leadership for Career Ladders staff

    A. Review program manager's performance and delegate responsibilities

    B. Recruit and hire new staff, terminate when necessary; facilitate orientation of new staff; maintain regular contact with staff, primarily through staff meetings; maintain close advisory relationship with program manager; review staff performance

    C. Advise staff on instructional methods, on-site problems, site development, job placement strategies, and intern assessment

III. Develop and manage program policy

    A. Communicate with interns and develop role model of executive; maintain worklike environment of program

    B. Develop philosophy and set Career Ladders policy: targeted populations, pay issues, school credit, liaison with other programs, parent and community policy, and so on

    C. Set guidelines for intern recruitment collaboratively with school district and program manager; advise on-site placement, movement, and termination of interns when necessary; review social and career objectives of interns, revise when necessary; provide guidance and instructional technology for training and attaining intern objectives; set objectives for employment skills workshop; advocate and direct strategies for job placement

APPENDIX 2.8

Career Ladders Rules and Attendance Policy

Rules

☐ Interns who are going to be absent must call the work site ahead of time.

☐ Interns must follow the dress code at work. Interns are requested to remove heavy coats and hats.

☐ Interns cannot borrow money from other employees or the on-site instructor.

☐ Interns are allowed a 15-minute break each day.

☐ No portable radios or tape players are allowed during the employment skills workshop.

☐ Use of portable radios and tape players is determined by supervisor at job site.

☐ Interns are advised not to bring valuables to work.

☐ No eating in the employment skills workshop or at work unless on break.

☐ Interns do not lose pay for visits related to their career plan or job search that are during work hours.

Attendance Policy

☐ 5 excused days absent in one semester allowed (interns must call in).

☐ Every 2 days over 5 days absent: one-half grade lowered.

☐ 8 days missed: intern is on probation.

☐ 10 days missed: intern is terminated.

☐ Parents and teachers must be contacted if intern has missed more than 3 days in less than 2 months.

☐ One unexcused absence: one grade lowered.

☐ Two unexcused absences: pay is docked.

☐ Three unexcused absences: probation.

☐ Four unexcused absences: intern is terminated.

APPENDIX 2.9
Counseling Checklist

Intern _____

On-site instructor _____

Date _____ Site _____

1. Did the intern apply suggestions from the last session?

2. Did the intern receive and understand current feedback? How did the intern express this?

3. Did the intern review self-monitoring data? Objectives? Recording sheets? Graphs?

4. Did the on-site instructor discuss strengths (reinforce)?

5. Did the on-site instructor address weaknesses or areas in need of improvement?

6. What specific advice did the on-site instructor provide?

7. How does the on-site instructor feel about the intern's overall job performance?

8. How does the intern perform relative to the regular employees?

9. Was a problem-solving approach used in the counseling session?

10. Was role playing used successfully in terms of performing behaviors and understanding?

11. What ecological interventions are being used in concert with the intern?

12. Have all the data been updated in the on-site instructor's records?

APPENDIX 2.10
Case Study

Eric Gidal

An on-site instructor must know more than the basic job description. He or she must also understand the larger qualities, the culture of work at that particular place. The following is written to assist a new instructor at sponsoring employer Lights and Action in getting to know the work site and its dynamics. As a new instructor myself this year, such a guide would have been extremely helpful and I hope any new instructor will take time to read this orientation information.

I recommend that the instructor take about 2 weeks before the start of the school year to become familiar with the company. Get to know the people who work here, understand the jobs required of the interns, and plan with supervisors possible long-term projects for the interns. The school district will allot the 2 weeks' pay to enable the instructor to do this.

This year, we had interns in three departments: Rental and Convention Services, Service, and Parts and Supplies. Each department works differently and the interns' duties and responsibilities in each vary. Accordingly, the instructor's role in each of the departments will differ in several respects.

 ## ORIENTATION TO LIGHTS AND ACTION

The Rental and Convention Services department has three internships, and its interns are given a wide variety of tasks. These include checking and cleaning equipment, organizing equipment on the shelves, taking inventory of parts and equipment, filling out paperwork, helping to load and unload equipment onto and from vans, assisting in deliveries of equipment, and performing general cleanup work. There is no daily routine. Things are done when they need to be done; some days are very busy and others are painfully slow. In terms of job task assignments, the atmosphere in the department is loosely organized, so interns need a good amount of initiative to stay busy and earn assignment to the more interesting job tasks.

This atmosphere requires the instructor to help supervisors develop job tasks for the interns and to keep on top of what needs to be done so that he or she can provide work for the interns when there is no supervisor present. Such an atmosphere also requires the instructor to act as a backup supervisor, particularly at the beginning of the semester, providing the necessary amount of structure that facilitates intern success. Once the interns can take initiative and keep busy, this role can be faded.

There were two internship positions in the Service department this year, a clerical assistant and a technical assistant. The clerical assistant is responsible for filling service reports, calling clients when services have been completed, answering the phone, directing calls, and entering data in the computer. Occasionally other tasks may be assigned but the duties remain relatively constant. This intern is given a good amount of one-on-one supervision from Marcia Palermo and therefore the instructor does not need to take a strong supervisory role. The on-site instructor can help, however, in reinforcing instructions. Marcia is busy and does not have time to repeat instructions or give extra training in the above-mentioned tasks. It worked well this year to keep in contact with Marcia and have her tell me when the intern was having difficulty in a certain area. I would then provide the repetition and extra training the intern needed, and arrange with the Career Ladders program manager for additional training (e.g., in answering phones and taking messages) during the employment skills workshop.

The second internship in the Service department is a jack-of-all-trades position. The duties range from organizing parts and labeling catalogs to helping disassemble computers and video equipment. The intern this year has also had opportunities to help set up computer hardware and software and salvage transistors from broken equipment. The job tasks range from menial to technically advanced. Ron Albright, the supervisor of the Service department, is also busy but willing to spend time with the intern when he can. When Ron does not have time to work with the intern, this role is delegated to various technicians who differ in the kinds of tasks they assign (i.e., some are more inclined than others to give interns challenging and interesting tasks). Like the Rental and Convention Services department, the Service department has slow days and busy ones, and the interns occasionally have little to do. It is more difficult for the Service department interns to find work for themselves than those in Rental and Convention Services. It is therefore necessary for the instructor to occasionally brainstorm ideas with the supervisors (Ron and Marcia) for new intern projects. The interns' lack of technical training puts some limitations on possible duties, but this year we have been able to develop a variety of semitechnical tasks.

The last department in which we have placed interns this year is the Parts and Supplies department. Although there were two available positions, we only placed one intern there each semester. The role of the intern changed in the spring from loosely defined to more specific in terms of duties and responsibilities due to policy changes in the department. As it stands at the end of this year, interns in the Parts and Supplies department are responsible for shipping equipment and parts to clients and other Lights and Action sites, which involves filling out shipping orders, looking up prices on the computer, and packaging equipment. Some of the skills this position helps develop include paying attention to detail and accuracy, maintaining a high production rate, and taking personal responsibility; the position also exposes interns to basic data entry and retrieval on the computer. However, the work is very repetitive from day to day and does not provide the variety of job duties found in some of the other positions.

The supervisors and regular workers in the Parts and Supplies department are very cooperative and try to make the interns' semester a good one. But they are less willing to take chances with interns and to make exceptions or accommodations to fit interns' specific needs. It is recommended, therefore, that the interns placed in Parts and Supplies show high degrees of responsibility and commitment, and be those whose special needs do not require as much attention. Because the work space is quite confined and busy, it is often difficult for the instructor to spend time with the interns in this department. Parts and Supplies has few slow days, although certain times of the day are less busy than others.

One of the major difficulties of working as an instructor in a work setting is dealing with the different perspectives between yourself and the supervisors. As an instructor, your primary goal is to teach the interns as much as possible while making the internship challenging and exciting. The supervisor's primary goal is to keep the department running smoothly and efficiently. These two goals do not always complement each other. As an outsider to the company, your only control over the job site is your ability to suggest and to persuade supervisors to go along with your ideas. This is not always possible. Often the interns are given menial duties or left with nothing to do, and much of the time there is little the instructor can do to resolve the situation. However, such experiences can be educational for the interns, because almost every job has uninteresting or unpleasant aspects; learning to accept this and understand the necessity of even the most routine job task is an important lesson.

I do not mean to present a scenario of confrontation or conflict between the supervisors and the instructor. This is not the case. The company is behind the program and the supervisors are all willing to help with the program and derive satisfaction from seeing interns succeed. Although I have actively met with supervisors and made many suggestions this year, I have also recognized and respected their needs and goals and have been willing to compromise in certain areas for the overall success of the program.

Certain supervisors and employees are particularly helpful to talk with and get suggestions from and who will make an extra effort for the interns. In Rental and Convention Services, A. J. Worthy has played an active role with the interns this year and is fully committed to helping them. Many of the technicians relate well to the interns and often play the role of counselor and instructor for them. In the Service department, both Ron and Marcia are committed to helping the interns but are busy and cannot always give them as much time as is needed. The Parts and Supplies department is in flux right now because John Cone, the old supervisor, left unexpectedly and no replacement has been found. Herbert Flanders, the second-in-command supervisor, has been helpful, but has not been willing to take as many chances with the interns.

Several times this year, I was told one thing by a supervisor and later discovered or realized that I was not being told the whole truth. I present these examples not to foster mistrust, but to make the point that, in the end, it is the instructor who is most concerned with the interns' welfare and that the ultimate responsibility for their success lies with the instructor and themselves.

During the first semester of this year, I asked Geoff Dunn, the manager, to give the interns in Rental and Convention Services more responsibility and initiative. He agreed with me and said that he would speak with the technicians about it. I also spoke with the technicians, who agreed but said they needed to be given the time to spend with the interns from Geoff and the other managers. After a few weeks there was no noticeable change in the interns' job assignments so I spoke with two of the technicians. They said, truthfully I believe, that Geoff had told them not to give the interns any real responsibility and to simply "babysit" them. There was obviously no real commitment to giving the interns a meaningful experience and by the end of the semester the interns in this department all but stopped attending, feeling unneeded and unchallenged.

This episode needs qualification, however. The interns in the Rental and Convention Services department that semester showed little initiative or responsibility almost from the start, creating a vicious cycle in which expectations were lowered by both the interns and the technicians. Also, after the fall semester, Geoff Dunn hired A. J. Worthy as a quality control specialist and gave him, as one of his stated duties, responsibility for making the intern program a success. A. J. has made a great effort to get the interns more involved in the department and the results have been fantastic—a complete turnaround from the fall semester.

A second episode worth mentioning also occurred during the fall semester in the Parts and Supplies department. We had brought in a new intern after the first grading period who was very articulate and showed a good degree of initiative. After his first week in Parts and Supplies, I met with John Cone, who said he was happy with this intern's performance; I had much the same impression. A week later, out of the blue, John announced that the intern had to leave the department because he was "belligerent and sloppy in his work." John was completely unwilling to let me work with the intern and, to keep the intern in the program, I was forced to move him to Rental and Convention Services. The intern did not want to work there and the move created a negative attitude that lasted throughout the semester. In fact, as I observed the intern more carefully, I, too, found him to be belligerent and sloppy at times. Yet these were problems that were to some degree being addressed and that I believe could have been resolved even better if the intern had been allowed to remain in Parts and Supplies.

Both of these episodes left a sour taste in my mouth for establishing a trusting working relationship with these two supervisors. John Cone is no longer with the company and Geoff has given this semester's interns more guidance, mostly indirectly through A. J. However, these incidents show that, in many ways, the on-site instructor is an outsider to the company and, when push comes to shove, the company's interests come first.

Finally, I want to emphasize the most important rule for helping the interns to succeed: Challenge them as much as possible. The more responsibility they are given and the more they are given tasks that require a real effort on their part, the more they will rise to the occasion. This may seem obvious, but it is important for the interns' success. They do have limitations and disabilities that make it harder for them to excel, but they all have the ability to succeed and to raise themselves up to the level of the other employees at Lights and Action. They only fail when they are put in situations where they are expected to fail. Given the proper supervision and understanding, they can, in time, succeed.

APPENDIX 2.11

Career Ladders Data Collection Handbook

Quick On-the-Job Social Skills Assessment

Interns	Conversing with Employees	Ordering Job Duties	Asking for Help or Instructions	Following Instructions	Giving Instructions	Accepting Positive Feedback	Accepting Negative Feedback	Giving Negative Feedback	Others

Key

++   Is excellent in this skill; needs no instruction.

 +   Is adequate in this skill; some feedback and training may help.

 •   Is apparently adequate.

 –   Has had some problems in this area that I have noticed.

 !   Has serious problems in this area.

 ?   I don't know.

 *   I need to explain what the student's difficulty is in this area.

→←   I have received peer (employee) feedback that confirms my rating.

Work Performance Record

Intern _____

Training Site _____ School _____

Counselor _____ Phone _____

Family Contact _____ Phone _____

Record dates on which the following events occurred.

Intern meetings to present and review objectives:

___/___ ___/___ ___/___ ___/___ ___/___ ___/___

___/___ ___/___ ___/___ ___/___ ___/___ ___/___

Phone calls home to report on intern progress and coordinate support:

___/___ ___/___ ___/___ ___/___ ___/___ ___/___

___/___ ___/___ ___/___ ___/___ ___/___ ___/___

Phone calls to school to report on intern progress and intern support:

___/___ ___/___ ___/___ ___/___ ___/___ ___/___

___/___ ___/___ ___/___ ___/___ ___/___ ___/___

Objectives (always include conditions, behavior, and criterion):

Weeks 1–6

1. _____
   _____
2. _____
   _____

Weeks 7–12

3. _____
   _____
4. _____
   _____

Weeks 13–18

5. _____
   _____
6. _____
   _____

Describe in a few sentences what program (including instruction, intervention, counseling, or transfer to coworker) you have designed for each intern objective.

Objective Number _____   Date ___/___

Program:

_____

_____

Objective Number _____   Date ___/___

Program:

_____

_____

Objective Number _____   Date ___/___

Program:

_____

_____

Objective Number _____   Date ___/___

Program:

_____

_____

Objective Number _____   Date ___/___

Program:

_____

_____

Recording the Data

If the intern will meet the objective by increasing

Rate . . . . use Chart 1,

Accuracy. . . . . use Chart 2,

Quantity (frequency, duration, or amount) . . . . use Chart 3,

None of the above. . . . . continue to next section.

SOCIAL SKILLS

Use the Quick On-the-Job Social Skills Assessment to discover any need for social skills objectives.

Discuss the results with the teacher at the home school. Write a measurable and non-judgmental objective.

For many social skills objectives, a recording sheet from the employment skills workshop can be used.

If the objective is not covered by one of the employment skills workshop recording sheets and cannot be easily charted by one of the charts, see Journal Entry below.

JOURNAL ENTRY

Keep dated notes on intern behavior. Always keep comments focused on the behavior(s) addressed in the objective. If observations reveal new issues, write new objectives. Avoid subjective or judgmental language. Report facts. If, for example, an intern behavior is provoking a negative response from the employer, describe the employer behavior: "John's supervisor was clearly distressed when John was 15 minutes late for the third time this week, but the supervisor did not say anything to John. I gave the information to John when he did arrive . . ." instead of "John screwed up again today. I told him to shape up when he finally got here . . ."

REPORTING THE DATA

After each 6-week period, complete an Intern Recording Sheet. It is recommended that the on-site instructor complete the first sheet, a coworker the second, and the intern self-evaluate for the third. More frequent data may be recorded on these sheets and charted on the Summary Graph. Copies of the 6-week interval sheets go to the teacher at the home school or directly to the school counselor and home. Arrange the reports with the supervising teacher, and make sure that the personal calls home to the family are consistent with what the data show.

Chart 1. Rate

Intern _____

Objective Number _____ Task _____

Units of measurement: Time increment _____ or Quantity _____

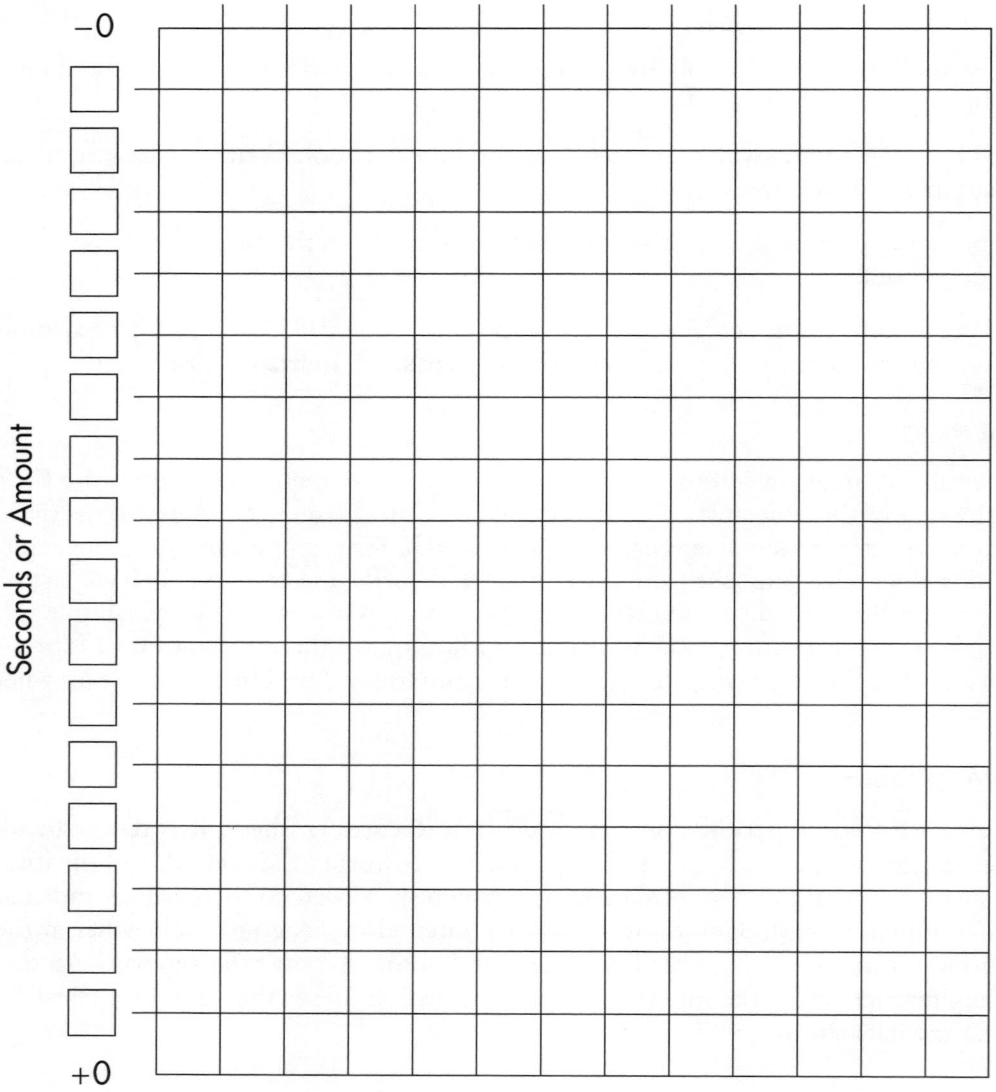

−0

Seconds or Amount

+0

Chart 2. Accuracy

Intern _____

Objective Number _____

Task _____

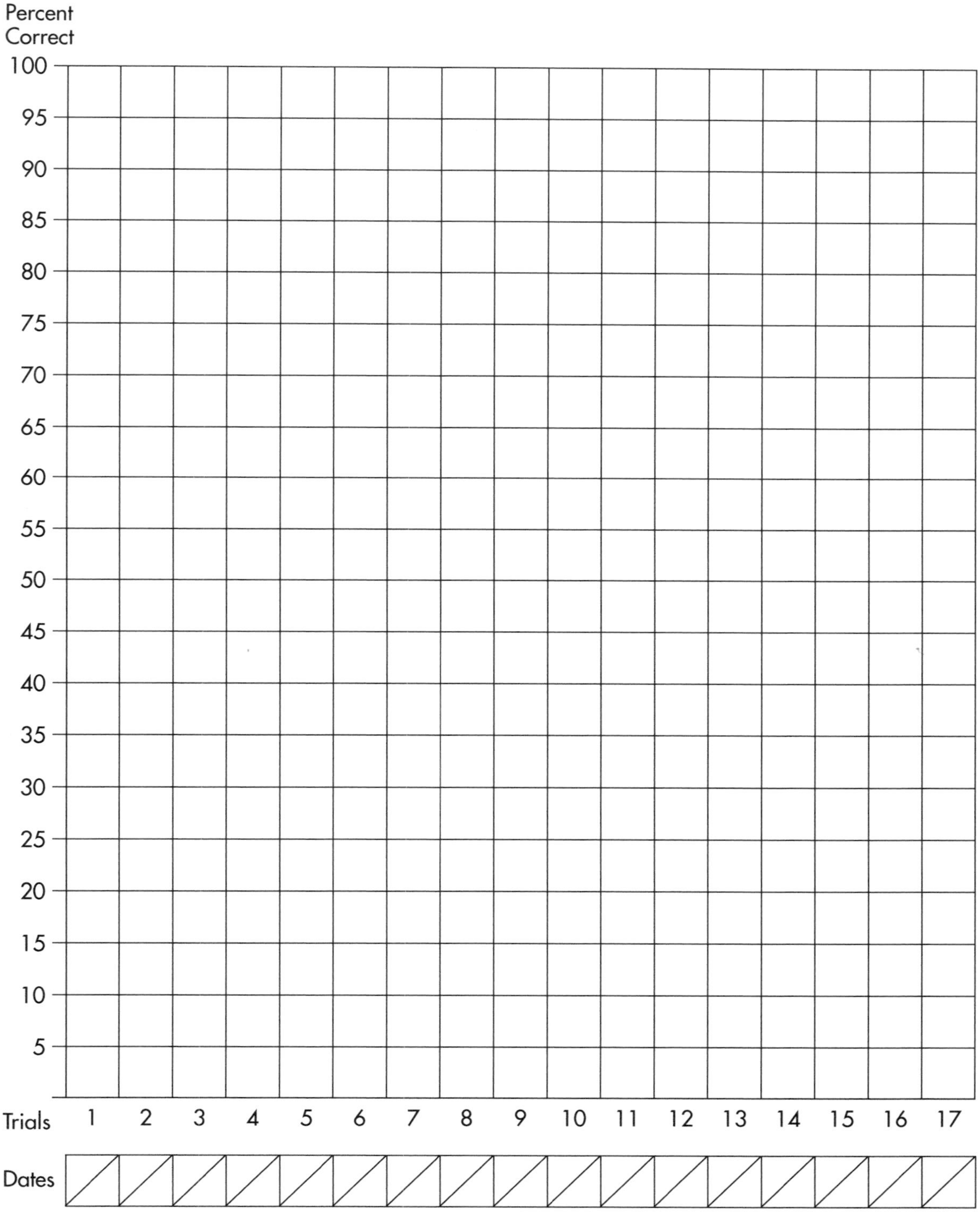

Percent
Correct

| Trials | 1 | 2 | 3 | 4 | 5 | 6 | 7 | 8 | 9 | 10 | 11 | 12 | 13 | 14 | 15 | 16 | 17 |

100
95
90
85
80
75
70
65
60
55
50
45
40
35
30
25
20
15
10
5

Dates

Chart 3. Quantity

Intern _____

Objective Number _____

Task _____

Circle one: Amount   Duration   Frequency

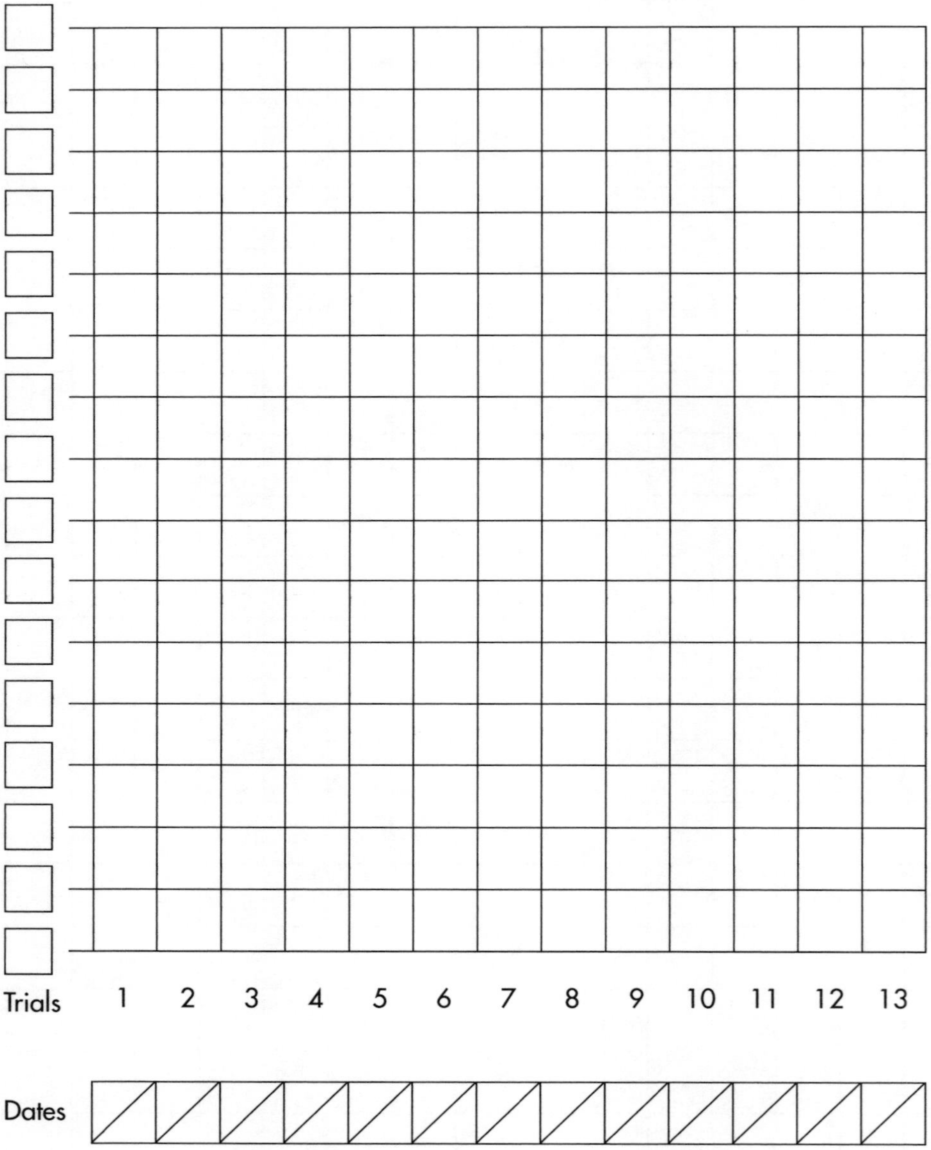

Trials   1   2   3   4   5   6   7   8   9   10   11   12   13

Dates

Journal Entry

Intern _____ Date _____ Objective Number _____

Notes _____

_____

_____

_____

_____

_____

_____

_____

_____

Intern _____ Date _____ Objective Number _____

Notes _____

_____

_____

_____

_____

_____

_____

_____

_____

Intern _____ Date _____ Objective Number _____

Notes _____

_____

_____

_____

_____

_____

_____

_____

_____

Intern Recording Sheet

Intern _____ Date _____

Recorder _____ Circle one: teacher intern coworker/employer

Job Tasks	Superior 4	Good 3	Improving 2	Poor 1	
1. _____	____	____	____	____	quality
	____	____	____	____	quantity
2. _____	____	____	____	____	quality
	____	____	____	____	quantity
3. _____	____	____	____	____	quality
	____	____	____	____	quantity
4. _____	____	____	____	____	quality
	____	____	____	____	quantity

Total ____

General Work Behaviors

5. Grooming	____	____	____	____
6. Punctuality/attendance	____	____	____	____
7. Follows directions	____	____	____	____
8. Seeks assistance	____	____	____	____
9. Production rate	____	____	____	____
10. Cooperative, team player	____	____	____	____

Total ____

Social Skills

11. Initiates interactions	____	____	____	____
12. Converses, responds, and takes turns in conversations	____	____	____	____
13. Terminates interactions	____	____	____	____
14. Maintains eye contact and body posture	____	____	____	____
15. Speaks clearly and loudly	____	____	____	____
16. Has pleasant demeanor and gives respect	____	____	____	____
17. Negotiates well and resists peer pressure	____	____	____	____

Total ____

Problem Behaviors	Never 4	Rarely 3	Sometimes 2	Often 1
18. Shows verbal or physical aggression	_____	_____	_____	_____
19. Temperament is moody or insulting	_____	_____	_____	_____
20. Manipulates and takes advantage of others	_____	_____	_____	_____
21. Breaks social rules (e.g., interrupts)	_____	_____	_____	_____

Total _____

Grand Total _____

Comments: _____

_____

_____

_____

_____

Comments by Career Ladders instructor: _____

_____

_____

_____

Skills to be addressed in employment skills workshop: _____

_____

_____

_____

On-the-Job Performance Summary Graph

Intern _____

Instructor _____ Date _____

Overall

100
80
60
40
20

Job Tasks

100
80
60
40
20

General Work Behaviors

100
80
60
40
20

Social Skills

100
80
60
40
20

Problem Behaviors

100
80
60
40
20

Date

APPENDIX 2.12

Timeline for Career Ladders On-Site Instructors

1 to 2 weeks before interns' start date: Visit job site, learn interns' job duties, and meet coworkers.

1 week before interns' start date: Attend the scheduled family meeting.

First instructional day of semester: Interns' first day on job.

Intern orientation.

Teacher/supervisor/on-site instructor begins evaluation of interns' abilities.

Weeks 1 and 2: Create a minimum of two work/academic objectives and one social objective for each intern (due by end of second week). Discuss objectives with each intern; remind interns that objectives must be met before pay starts.

Phone parents to report interns' progress (positive call).

Weeks 2 and 3: Fade supervision.

Develop alternative work sites for interns within the company (promotion for qualified interns).

End of second week: Prepare and distribute job duties for each intern.

Week 4: Phone family to report progress. Request that they help intern memorize his or her job duties.

Conference with interns; have objectives been met?

Week 5: Pay begins.

Complete evaluations of the interns' job performance; discuss evaluations with each intern. Make three copies: original to Career Ladders files, one copy to the intern's referring teacher, one copy to parents.

Phone parents to discuss evaluation.

Week 6: Grades due; turn in to Career Ladders manager.

Phone parents; report on progress.

Weeks 7 through 16:	Take a few interns out on job search each day as time permits. Continue to call family every 2 weeks.
Week 10:	Have supervisors complete intern evaluations.
Week 11:	Complete Career Ladders evaluations on each intern.
Week 12:	Turn in grades to Career Ladders manager.
Weeks 13 and 14:	Keep up the good work!
Week 15:	Have supervisors complete evaluations on each intern.
Week 16:	Complete Career Ladders evaluations on each intern. Grades are due.
Weeks 17 and 18:	Last day. Interns are dismissed.

Employment Skills Workshop

CHAPTER

Shepherd Siegel and Karen Greener ■

In Chapter 2, the core experience of Career Ladders, the community classroom, was explained and described. In fact, there are hundreds of similar work experience programs throughout the nation. The purpose of the previous chapter was to offer some tools that will enable teachers and supervisors of such programs to manage them efficiently so that interns will derive the maximum benefit from the experience. That is, they will have a "worklike" experience, where they respond to adult demands in an integrated adult environment; they learn real job skills; they learn to function well in an adult work environment; they focus on what their real career interests are; they develop a work ethic; and they are exposed to and make friends with legitimate and heroic role models. But the community classroom experience alone is no guarantee that interns will fully connect their own lives with the idea of a work life.

Going to work can be a shocking experience, and one that needs to be processed, reconciled, justified, and shared. The effectiveness of community classroom training can be greatly multiplied if interns are periodically able to meet in a safe environment with peers who are in the same program. In Career Ladders, interns meet for 3 hours weekly in a school classroom or employer conference room and learn a curriculum, called the *employment skills workshop*. Above, beyond, and underlying the curriculum itself, the weekly meeting is an opportunity for interns to solidify their career wills in a group of peers. They learn to give each other support, and they make their decisions to have a legitimate career in an atmosphere of shared reactions to the tumult of adolescence, leaving public school and entering the adult world of work. This chapter presents a curriculum intended to help an intern make the most of this experience and to make some sense of it.

THE CURRICULUM

Information for the Teacher

The purpose of the curriculum for this course is a simple one. Whatever will teach an exiting student to better make the transition from school to work and adult life is appropriate for the course. In many cases, this translates into asking whether the behaviors demanded of an intern by the course will help that person be poised and well directed to college or some other postsecondary training, and to get and keep a job that is satisfactory to all concerned parties. This is the priority of the program. Any curricular activities that do not serve this purpose should be discarded or given low priority.

For example, reading, writing, and math skills are critical, but during the last year of high school, it is difficult to effectively address them. Career Ladders is structured to work with whatever 12 years of public instruction have taught so far. Referral to a postsecondary institution that addresses these skills is usually more appropriate. When academic learning is a concern of the soon-to-be-adult graduate, referral to the community college system and procedures for enrollment are more appropriate than actual instruction. The intern must be prepared to meet the demands of the adult world and to use community resources; time in Career Ladders is better spent learning how to gain access to appropriate services. The Career Ladders Pyramid of Transition Skills (Figure 2.1), building from the bottom up, identifies the curricular components that are most critical at this point in the interns' lives.

All interns should have Social Security cards. Most should have driver's licenses. Clearly, this is one task that the family and school can complete before the interns' senior year. In the event that an intern does not have this documentation, a large part of his or her curriculum is probably going to consist of learning how to obtain this documentation. We live in a highly complex society, and the larger the gap between the skills a youth presents and the legal requirements for activating services, the more serious the struggle to survive will be. In one semester, a single intern may have to locate or obtain the following documentation: birth certificate, Social Security card, driver's license, I-9 form (proof of citizenship), psychological evaluation, medical examination, all other documentation to get on the school payroll (in a stipended program), all other documentation to have a case opened at an adult agency like a one-stop center[1] or vocational rehabilitation, all documentation to enroll in community college, two to four signed parental consent forms, and so forth. This "documenting" is a curriculum in and of itself. To the extent that these skills have not already been taught, Career Ladders staff work is necessarily reduced to the critical and regrettably clerical function of just getting the intern onto the career ladder. When these skills in conducting the paper chase are addressed in the earlier grades, Career Ladders staff

can put more effort into empowering interns to climb the career ladder.

Emotionally, Career Ladders interns are going through a transition as well. The exhilaration of independence and the burden of self-support can create a pressured situation. Interns react in a variety of ways: enthusiasm, withdrawal, aggression, immaturity, self-destruction, ambition, crime, boredom, truancy, and fantasy. All are growth responses, and all indicate some awareness of the magnitude of the imminent change in their lives. Thus the other critical task facing Career Ladders staff is to make a personal bond with the interns that reassures them that they are not alone during this time, and that Career Ladders will reward their efforts with an ongoing commitment. People are not used to having the assistance Career Ladders provides, and it takes consistent effort to connect with the intern, the intern's family, and the intern's employer and gain the trust that will encourage their best effort. Thus, affective or personal growth curricula such as peer counseling, counseling, parent or family contact and mediation will bring the intern emotionally into the transition process, while the functional curriculum makes the intern a legitimate player in the work world. Both of these domains must be addressed if Career Ladders is to enable success and empowerment.

All of the curriculum strands of the employment skills workshop follow a model that sequences three stages. First, lessons are keyed to heighten and develop an intern's sense of self. Next, the curriculum emphasizes sensitivity to others. Finally, interns have opportunities to develop and express values. Many of the peer counseling activities take the intern out of the career context temporarily, to ease the strain of transition and to build trust and bonding in the group. However, the purpose of the curriculum is for interns to be able to redefine themselves, improve and refine their sensitivity to others, and develop values that include career development and make it a priority. Regardless of the high success rate of the Career Ladders program, the real success occurs when every intern has taken the notion of career and of

---

[1]One-stop centers are a national initiative of the Employment and Training Administration of the U.S. Department of Labor, connecting employment, education, and training services into a coherent network. Part of the Workforce Investment Act of 1998, they bring multiple employment-related services, often including vocational rehabilitation, under one roof.

being respected to heart as a result of the experiences Career Ladders offers.

This curriculum does not stand alone. It reinforces and allows interns to maximize the core skills training—the community classroom—described in the previous chapter. It is a critical feature of Career Ladders that this workshop occurs concurrent to the community classroom, not before or after; this is one of the most powerful features of the program. Failing to integrate this curriculum with a community-based work experience and job search negates its purpose.

Finally, we realize that by themselves, social skills training, peer counseling, interview skills, and so forth are not new concepts; therefore, the curriculum borrows heavily from all of our best influences. The innovative and critical quality of Career Ladders curriculum is its holistic organization of these components in a way that integrates them with other services and with the transition phase of life for adolescents exiting secondary school. When it is well executed, the curriculum should ease and empower interns and enable them to best use available social services.

Information To Give the Intern

Interns: This course will provide you with the latest information and training on how to

- identify and express your feelings about leaving high school,
- know the importance of having a good attendance record,
- make friends on the job,
- be the type of worker an employer wants to hire,
- get the best education for your career,
- find a job opening,
- apply for a job,
- interview for a job,
- keep a job,
- make a career plan,

- get promoted and advanced in your job, and
- make friends with other interns facing the same challenges as you.

You will learn the most common reasons people are fired and how to avoid that situation. You will learn how to use the tools—from computers to shovels, from books to meetings—that help your employer to get the job done. You will learn how to be honest about your feelings and how to use this skill to your best advantage on the job. You will learn how to get along with coworkers, supervisors, customers, and people who work for you. During the second half of the semester, after you show that you understand what is expected from you on the job and that you have the skills to look for one, you will be given a chance to conduct a job search and prepare for college. If you get a job before the semester ends and have met all of your objectives, you will be released from the program so that you can go to work. You will still get credit for the course.

Course Objectives

By the end of the semester, all students with 95% attendance will be able to perform 90% of the following objectives:

- Use the equipment and tools relevant to their work site
- Recite their job title and job duties using correct job terminology
- Have a conversation with a coworker
- Formulate a job search strategy and begin to conduct a job search
- State the purpose of a personal data sheet and be able to use it in the application process
- Complete a resume
- Analyze the three most common reasons people get fired and identify how to avoid being fired
- Know how to contact appropriate adult service agencies (e.g., one-stop center, community college, temporary employment agencies,

Planned Parenthood, Department of Social Services, Social Security office, hospital, counseling services)

Methods, Strategies, Procedures, and Techniques

The course uses the following methods:

Role playing	Guest speakers
Lectures	Problem solving
Videotaping	Group process
Supported job search	Films
Drill and practice	Group discussion
Self-evaluation	Self-monitoring

Instructional Materials

The course uses the following instructional materials:

Slide shows	Internet
Films	Job announcements
Computers	Overhead projector
Calculators	Job applications
Agency brochures	Video cameras and monitors
Handouts	
Newspapers	Career workbooks
Employer materials	

Curriculum Note

Many curricular materials exist that are not directly recommended or included in the reference section of this book. This book uses those materials that have suited the teaching styles of Career Ladders staff in recent years, but instructors are encouraged to add other materials that serve the same purpose. The appendixes to this chapter include sample materials (e.g., interview questions, interview rating sheet) that can instead be generated (and therefore owned) by the interns' group process. In these cases, the appendix materials serve as guidelines. If the book has at least communicated what it means to make real career development a

priority in programming and instruction, then the use and adaptation of materials to that priority is encouraged and applauded. Some objectives, such as social skills, peer counseling, or specific job skills may require more depth and detail than is provided here, and instructors are encouraged to locate and use other materials as long as the overriding goal of career development is not compromised. It is especially recommended to use the job site itself as the raw material for curriculum.

Week 7 is a critical week for sustaining interest in the workshop for the second two thirds of the semester. It is packed with activities that will set a more serious and hardworking tone, and it presents procedures that will be used for the rest of the semester. Thorough preparation for Week 7's presentation is strongly recommended.

To implement this curriculum with greater rigor and ease, familiarity with the following materials is recommended. These books, or books covering the same curriculum areas (job-keeping skills, social skills training, and peer counseling/ cooperative learning), are especially critical to full implementation of the workshop.

- *Don't Get Fired! How To Keep a Job* (The Janus Employability Skills Program), by Durlynn Anema and William Lefkowitz (1996); Globe Fearon Pearson Learning Group, 135 South Mount Zion Road, P.O. Box 2500, Lebanon, IN 46052; www.pearsonlearning.com

- *Tribes: A New Way of Learning and Being Together*, by Jeanne Gibbs (2001); CenterSource Systems, 7975 Cameron Drive, Bldg. 500, Windsor, CA 95492-8567, 707/838-1061; www.tribes.com

- *Skillstreaming the Adolescent: New Strategies and Perspectives for Teaching Prosocial Skills*, revised edition by Arnold P. Goldstein and Ellen McGinnis (1997); Research Press, Dept. 22W, P.O. Box 9177, Champaign, IL 61826; 217/352-3273, 800/519-2702; www .researchpress.com

- *Values Clarification*, revised edition by Sidney B. Simon, Leland W. Howe, and Howard Kirschenbaum (1995); Warner Books, 1271 Avenue of the Americas, New York, NY 10020; www.twbookmark.com

- *CareerTalk, a special edition of SkillTalk*, by Ralph Allen, Roberta Krause, and Marty Hawkins

(2002); Performance Spectrum, 4041 West Lake Sammamish Parkway SE, Bellevue, WA 98008, 425/644-0086; www.mindtalking.com

- *Peer-to-Peer Asset Building*, by Barbara B. Varenhorst (in press); Search Institute, The Banks Building, 615 First Avenue NE, Suite 125, Minneapolis, MN 55413; www.search-institute.org

THE INSTRUCTOR'S STANCE

The relationship formed between staff and interns is critical. Staff members looking for a job that takes less than a serious, heartfelt commitment to the importance of the work will not be effective. Likewise, staff members who are looking for opportunities to make youths dependent upon them or who want to take care of helpless people will not be effective. The same delicate point of balance is sought for each intern, but for each intern the balance will be found in a different place.

That balance is the point where a youth is empowered; in other words, when an intern presents an authentic inability to perform what is normally expected at the workplace or other adult organization, the staff person is able to creatively invent an accommodation that is placed as much as possible within the control of the intern. When an intern presents an authentic ability to perform, the staff person is able to praise, and then leave the intern to function independently.

Staff members must be constantly alert to when they are crossing into a region of making an intern overly dependent or into a region of not being there to accommodate when assistance is needed. The point of balance will be unique to each intern; respecting the point of balance and making educational decisions based on it will truly support interns' growth into independence and self-sufficiency.

The relationship that critically involves the staff person, and then allows that person to fade out, moves in a progression from *telling* to *joining*. This progression takes place in a microcosmic form over every daily period of instruction, and in a larger arc extending over the course of the semester. It can be roughly described as follows, as if the instructor were talking to an intern.

Weeks 1 Through 4: Telling

You are now an intern in Career Ladders. This is part of your school course, and it is the beginning of your adult life independent of school. We will be making some demands of you, and if you want to remain in the program and succeed in it, you will meet those demands. They are not negotiable.

Weeks 5 Through 7: Selling

We believe that the skills we are teaching and the opportunities we are providing are essential to your success as a work- or college-bound individual, and that they will make you powerful, responsible, and successful. Career Ladders is a particularly good deal for you.

Weeks 8 Through 11: Testing

By now we expect that you have some idea of what this program is about: responsible and productive adult behavior in the work world. We are giving you some opportunities to show us that you have that understanding. We reserve the right to observe you, and to provide you with feedback and direction.

Weeks 12 Through 15: Consulting

You have proved that you understand what the work world and we expect of you, and you are pretty much on your own. We know that you will respect our opinions and advice. We appreciate being consulted when you are faced with a tough decision, or even when you need some help getting your career plan going.

Weeks 16 Through 18: Joining

You have really shown growth and you have learned what you need to do to succeed. You are in charge of your destiny, and we hope that you will use your power wisely and effectively. We are still here with you, but more as partners than as teachers or supervisors. We are always available if you need us, but we have so much faith in your abilities that this should hardly be necessary.

CURRICULUM STRANDS

The curricular content is divided into six strands: job skills, job-keeping skills, job search skills, personal growth, interpersonal growth, and timely topics.

Job Skills

Job skills are those that could be found in a job description. These are skills that are directly related to the performance of job tasks, from clerical to construction, from the lab to the office, from critical thinking to detailed procedures.

Job-Keeping Skills (or Employer-Pleasing Behaviors)

Job-keeping skills are those behaviors that please employers and that have been found by experience, employers, and educators to correlate highly with job retention, including handling authority, being on time, being responsible, keeping yourself busy, being honest, staying on the job, and asking for work when an assigned task is done.

Job Search Skills

Job search skills are those behaviors and strategies that increase the likelihood that an intern will be hired by an employer. These skills include using the self–family–friend network, filling out applications, preparing a resume, interviewing for a job, and using employment agencies.

Personal Growth

Personal growth refers to those activities whereby interns identify and express their feelings in an

honest and responsible fashion, create personal bonds and nonjudgmental postures, take control of their own group process, make wise decisions, own their problems, gain perspective on their own life continuum, and so on. Personal growth exercises demonstrate recognition that feelings are deeply interior, yet do not exist without the interaction of others. This curriculum includes tasks or activities that use role play, simulation games, and modeling to generate a flow of primary (e.g., feelings, emotions, fantasies, dreams, imagination) and secondary (e.g., reason, logic, intellect, thought) process data from the group, the results of which are totally within interns' control. This, combined with the interpersonal growth curriculum described below, comprises a movement from self-awareness, to sensitivity to others, to affirmation of values.

Interpersonal Growth

Often referred to as social skills training, interpersonal growth activities are a rehearsal of those behaviors that have been found by experience, employers, and educators to correlate highly with social acceptance on the job. These include having a conversation, giving and accepting negative feedback, giving and accepting positive feedback, following instructions, and giving instructions.

Timely Topics

Timely topics are special lessons, usually group discussions or lectures, that are best delivered at specific points during the semester. They are designed to reinforce other lessons and to anticipate and avert problems that frequently occur during the semester-long course. Topics include the following: Why work without pay? Why practice social skills? The Career Ladders pyramid; How does capitalism work? Job search strategies; Realities of the work world.

LESSON PLANS

Table 3.1 gives a week-by-week breakdown of the lesson plans. A matrix that summarizes the

TABLE 3.1
Lesson Plans for Employment Skills Workshop

Week	Job Skills	Job-Keeping Skills	Job Search Skills	Personal Growth	Interpersonal Growth	Timely Topics
1	Tasks from Community Classroom I	First Day on the Job, Part 1		Confidentiality		Warm-up and First Impressions
2	Tasks from Community Classroom I	First Day on the Job, Part 2		Introductions		Career Ladders Pyramid, Rules, and Agreements
3	Tasks from Community Classroom I	Be Aware of Time		Animal, Color, Water, White Room	Learning Your Job Duties	Pioneer, Warrior, Hero
4	Tasks from Community Classroom I	Be Responsible		Problem Solving	Ordering Job Duties	Why Work Without Pay? Why Be Supervised?
5	Tasks from Community Classroom I	Follow the Schedule		Making "I" Statements	Ordering Job Duties	Stamina and Determination
6	Tasks from Community Classroom I	Follow Directions	Job Interview Questions: Brainstorming for a Resume	Exchanging Positives	Ordering Job Duties	Tolerance and Terminations
7	Tasks from Community Classroom II	Be Helpful and Friendly to Everyone at Work	How To Conduct a Job Search; Learning How To Do a Job Interview	Asking Open-Ended Questions	First Session and Overall Session Format	Social Skills—Why Have a Workshop on Them?
8	Tasks from Community Classroom II	Don't Talk to Friends While Working	The Personal Data Sheet	Making Nonjudgmental Observations	Ordering Job Duties	Working with Adult Service Agencies
9	Tasks from Community Classroom II	Keep Yourself Busy	Complete a Personal Resume	Crocodile Creek	Asking for Help or Instructions	Beginning the Job Search
10	Tasks from Community Classroom II	Following Directions and Making an Extra Effort	Baseline Job Interviews	Decision Agent	Asking for Help or Instructions	Reevaluating Career Objectives
11	Tasks from Community Classroom II	Give Good Service	Mock Interviews	Values Ranking	Having a Conversation	Past Interns' Anecdotes
12	Tasks from Community Classroom II	Leave Your Personal Problems at Home	Mock Interviews		Giving Negative Feedback	Capitalism 101
13	Tasks from Community Classroom III	Get Along with Others	Mock Interviews		Giving Negative Feedback	Job Search Strategies
14	Tasks from Community Classroom III	Take Pride in Your Work	Mock Interviews		Giving Negative Feedback	Waiting for the Job You Want
15	Tasks from Community Classroom III	Don't Talk Back to Your Boss	Mock Interviews		Accepting Negative Feedback	Realities of the Work World
16	Tasks from Community Classroom III		Mock Interviews		Accepting Negative Feedback	What Is Postsecondary Life Like?
17	Continuing Development		"Real" Mock Interviews		Accepting Negative Feedback	Open Forum
18		Using an Appointment Calendar			Accepting Negative Feedback	Making Choices

TABLE 3.2
Matrix Defining Emphasis on Attendance and Curriculum Strands

Emphasis	Weeks				
	1–4 Telling	5–7 Selling	8–11 Testing	12–15 Consulting	16–18 Joining
Attendance	••••	••	•		
Personal Growth	•••	••••	••••	••	•
Interpersonal Growth	•	••	•••	•••	••••
Job-Keeping Skills	••	•••	••••	•••	••
Job Skills	•	••	••••	••••	••
Job Search Skills			•	••	••••

emphasis on attendance and five of the six curriculum strands is depicted in Table 3.2. Highest emphasis is represented by four dots and little to no emphasis by no dots. The chart divides the 18-week semester into five segments that roughly correlate with the progression of the instructor's stance from *telling* to *joining*. In the beginning, the "Telling" weeks, attendance has the highest priority. In the final weeks, "Joining," personal skills have the least emphasis, while interpersonal growth and job search skills have the most. Actual lesson plans for each week are discussed in detail in the following sections.

Week 1

Lessons In

☒ Job Skills
☒ Job-Keeping Skills
☐ Job Search Skills
☒ Personal Growth
☐ Interpersonal Growth
☒ Timely Topics

Job Skills: Tasks Imported from the Community Classroom

On-site instructors are familiar with the entry-level skills interns need at each work site and use this knowledge to structure the skill instruction in the employment skills workshop. By 10 minutes before class is scheduled to begin, instructors should be ready to teach interns individually on computers using software and other tools, such as Microsoft Word, Access, Works, PowerPoint, Excel; accounting software; cash registers; and so on. Interns want to learn and work, and those interns with attendance and punctuality problems will not devalue the experience of those with good attendance habits if individualized tasks are available 10 minutes before class. For example, have data entry exercises available and ready on interns' computers. Or for cash register training, have mock food products priced and available for checkout. In the first few weeks of cash register training, have interns work on accuracy of checkout, then accuracy of checkout and making change. Next, set up timings with rate charts (see Appendix 2.11) and work on speed. When using self-charting and data sheets, encourage interns to compete with their own personal best time. Or have lessons related to accounting or data entry. Emphasis on methodical sequences will make these activities more transferable to data entry and computer skills on the job. To train word processing skills, use standard manuals or tutorial software, emphasizing accuracy first and speed later. Interns with typing potential (i.e., those able to exceed 30 words per minute with a little practice) should be identified and allowed to practice typing during this period. After all interns have arrived, begin the following lesson, the purpose of which is to give students a sampling of what they will be learning, eventually or immediately, depending on their placement.

RATIONALE/WARM-UP/REVIEW

Explain one of the just-completed job skills lessons. Ask interns questions about why the lesson is important, and ask them to describe some of the details of the process, such as word processing, data entry, spreadsheets, and so on. Some job skills will be common among all interns, whereas other skills will be unique to each job site.

PRESENTATION

Write on the board the steps to becoming a good customer service worker: courtesy, speed, security, and accuracy. Define the terms. Lead a discussion on the different demands of a computer-based skill (person–thing–information) and customer service skills (person–person–information).

GUIDED PRACTICE

Have interns pair off and practice cashiering or another customer-service–related task. Pair experienced and inexperienced interns for peer tutoring. Have them purchase products from a cabinet that has priced food containers; or handle a five-step accounting procedure; or work in teams on a filing task; or time each other on a word processing assignment.

REAL-WORLD APPLICATION

Have interns work as cashiers, with the teacher being the customer. Rate their accuracy, courtesy, speed, and understanding of security.

Timely Topics: Warm-up and First Impressions

Expect that special circumstances will reduce the likelihood of a complete group on the first day. Perhaps the recruitment process from the previous semester was not complete, or some interns have not yet made it to the job site, or staff may be deliberately staggering the interns' first day of work to manage the flow of new people onto the work site. Therefore, a full orientation to program policies and expectations can and should be delayed until the second week to avoid incomplete communication. However, praise for making good first impressions on the job, basic concepts of employability, and expectations of attendance can and should be given. The contract nature of the commitment and services interns receive in exchange for satisfactory performance can be introduced and developed in detail in Week 2. Complete the paperwork process that was begun at the family meeting (see Chapter 2) and continue the same process for opening cases at any relevant adult service agencies.

Job-Keeping Skills: First Day on the Job, Part 1

The following lesson can be enriched by having interns observe and analyze the similarities between their first day on the job and behaviors that welcome a stranger.

RATIONALE/WARM-UP/REVIEW

Ask how many interns remember their first job. Ask them to remember back further to the first day on that job. Ask them to discuss what it felt like, what they had to know, how they found out what they needed to know, then ask them to discuss good and bad experiences in that job. Next, ask the interns to discuss the importance of first impressions, perhaps sharing stories from a past important first impression they made, positive or negative. Ask about the impressions the interns may have made so far on the job or with their fellow interns.

PRESENTATION

Watch any appropriate video or read text that addresses the first days on a new job.

GUIDED PRACTICE

Ask interns to name situations in which they might find themselves concerned with making a good first impression and where another intern might be helping them get acquainted. Responses might include first dates or blind dates, a new school, or a new neighborhood. What would an intern do to welcome a new person? Responses might include introducing himself or herself and others to the new person, showing the new person around, or showing the new person how to do something. Characteristics of making a good impression include friendliness, willingness to answer questions, clean and neat clothing, politeness, and so on. Pair or group interns to select a situation and role-play.

REAL-WORLD APPLICATION

Assign interns to practice what they have learned with a coworker on the job (not another intern) and give feedback at the next workshop. During the coming week, have on-site instructors give nonjudgmental feedback to interns regarding the impressions they are making on the job.

Personal Growth: Confidentiality

Briefly introduce the purpose of doing activities that concern feelings and group process, but delay a full introduction until Week 2. For this lesson, discuss the concept of confidentiality and explain the trust that can grow from it. Varenhorst's (in press) *Peer-to-Peer Asset Building* addresses this as does the *Tribes* curriculum (Gibbs, 2001). Because interns are experiencing the feeling of being a stranger, to each other and on the job, this is an excellent opportunity to demonstrate the usefulness of the deliberate self-consciousness, self-monitoring, and self-evaluation that makes the workshop powerful. The personal growth exercise, "Welcoming a Stranger," is integrated with the job-keeping skills lesson in Week 2, and the exercise can be prepared for this week by (a) doing the "Introduction to Session Topic" in *Peer-to-Peer Asset Building* (Varenhorst, in press); (b) evaluating what coworkers did to make the interns feel welcome during their first days on the job; and (c) assigning the interns the task of making new interns who will be on the job and at the workshop in Week 2 feel welcome by using the methods discussed and learned in the lesson. On-site instructors are responsible for prompting responses from interns during the coming week on the job, and during the Week 2 workshop.

Week 2

Lessons In

- ☒ Job Skills
- ☒ Job-Keeping Skills
- ☐ Job Search Skills
- ☒ Personal Growth
- ☐ Interpersonal Growth
- ☒ Timely Topics

Job Skills: Tasks Imported from the Community Classroom

Repeat the exercise from Week 1 this week. Emphasize the act of referring back to performance from the previous week, so that interns can see their progress and practice memory tasks related to the interns' job skills that the interns will need to be successful on the job.

Personal Growth: Introductions

Review concepts of confidentiality and trust from Week 1. Review the introductory concepts that were discussed last week from the "Welcoming a Stranger" exercise (in the *Peer-to-Peer Asset Building*, Varenhorst, in press), and have interns share observations and reports of welcoming behaviors on the job and at the workshop. Discuss how interns who attended the previous week's workshop welcomed the newcomers. Praise follow-through on this welcoming activity heavily. With what is now the complete group for the seminar, fully discuss the purpose of the peer counseling activities: to learn how to better share feelings, to learn how to support each other, and to get through the transition from school more successfully. Provide interns with the overall context of the activities, which is the transition from school to adult life. The power that comes from the communication skills learned in the peer counseling activities will certainly increase success on the job, but the group will be more effectively built if peer counseling is introduced as a set of activities that have their own merit and are not directly related to work and career. When the interns know there is a safe place for feelings and for building relationships, the overall power of the career-oriented curriculum will multiply. For today, interns can introduce themselves to each other by talking about their names, where they are from, and other autobiographical information that is safe to share and that will make them more memorable to other members of the group. Gibbs (2001) and Varenhorst (in press) both offer exercises that structure and facilitate the process of getting acquainted with other people.

Timely Topics: Career Ladders Pyramid, Rules, and Agreements

Explain the Career Ladders Pyramid of Transition Skills (see Figure 2.1). This figure illustrates the curriculum and shows how it must be built from the ground up. The purpose of the curriculum is not to make interns pass a class or get a grade. Rather, the purpose is for them to find a job, get into college, or both by the time they leave the program. Explain the ongoing commitment of Career Ladders staff, mention that the interns will be meeting their transition specialist the following week, and say that this is how the staff lives up to that commitment. Explain their right to challenge the curriculum and your right to justify it. At this point, you are not "selling," you are telling them what must be done.

Pass out and discuss Career Ladders rules (see Appendix 2.8). Make the presentation concise, clear, and direct.

Job-Keeping Skills: First Day on the Job, Part 2

Repeating this lesson is an excellent opportunity for those who attended last week to feel competent and confident, and for the newcomers not to feel that they are being left out or are lagging behind.

RATIONALE/WARM-UP/REVIEW

Ask who in the class knows everyone there (no one will know everyone). Explain that the group is going to do an exercise called "Welcoming a Stranger." Ask interns to guess what the exercise is about and what they might do in the exercise. Review the relevant points from Week 1's discussion of first impressions.

PRESENTATION AND GUIDED PRACTICE

Follow the "Welcoming a Stranger" lesson in *Peer-to-Peer Asset Building* (Varenhorst, in press). This exercise simulates the feelings of being an unoriented newcomer in a group. Interns are broken into small groups of six or fewer. A single intern is asked to leave the room and return. The group role-plays the Career Ladders community classroom, which gives interns a chance to imitate some of the behaviors they have observed, and the group members are left to their own devices after

being asked to act as they would in order to welcome a newcomer. Afterward, the participants are debriefed with questions that address how it felt to be treated as a stranger and what techniques were effective in making a person feel more comfortable.

REAL-WORLD APPLICATION

Ask the interns to decide where and how they will adapt and use what they have learned, preferably at the work site. Have them negotiate with their on-site instructors about how they will report the results of their efforts.

Week 3

Lessons In

- ☒ Job Skills
- ☒ Job-Keeping Skills
- ☐ Job Search Skills
- ☒ Personal Growth
- ☒ Interpersonal Growth
- ☒ Timely Topics

Job Skills: Tasks Imported from the Community Classroom

As in previous weeks, remember to have materials and instructors ready for the interns 10 minutes before class is scheduled to begin.

Review Week 1. Those interns who have gained some proficiency, speed, and accuracy in their initial tasks should move on to more challenging ones. Interns with word processing potential—able to exceed 30 words per minute with a little practice—should be identified and allowed to practice during this period.

Assign a small group of interns to the following lesson in taking phone messages and using voice mail. The goal is to teach interns how to identify an occupied line, an incoming call, and a call on hold by the rate of flashes; to learn how to use the intercom; and to learn the parts of a message notepad.

RATIONALE/WARM-UP/REVIEW

The interns generate a list of job skills that are helpful to learn. Write their answers on the board.

Possible responses include answering phones, typing, using e-mail, using voice mail, operating a cash register, and operating a calculator.

PRESENTATION

Demonstrate message taking to the interns. Using a transparency of a message pad on an overhead projector, teach the following steps: identify information that must be taken right away (the name of the person calling, the person the message is for, the phone number, and a short message); repeat back the information recorded on the message pad; hang up and finish completing the message, with the date and time of the call and the message taker's signature.

Teach interns tips to slow down a fast caller and how to take the message as quickly as possible. Demonstrate shortcuts.

GUIDED PRACTICE

Have interns form a triad. Using a telephone trainer, have one intern take a message, one intern call, and one intern operate the telephone trainer. Have the interns rotate in the roles.

REAL-WORLD APPLICATION

Have the interns answer the phone in the school office, with supervision as necessary. Request that supervisors at the work site allow the interns to answer phones.

Job-Keeping Skills: Be Aware of Time

Review the first step on the Career Ladders pyramid (Figure 2.1). Use the *Don't Get Fired!* lesson (Anema & Lefkowitz, 1996) and have a serious discussion about the importance of good attendance habits. Review the Career Ladders policy on attendance—rewards for good attendance such as good grades, pay, and future employment; warnings, probation, and termination for unexcused absences—and explain that Career Ladders is more tolerant than most employers, but different in quality from and stricter than schools. Make sure interns have the correct phone numbers and contact people for calling in when they cannot get to work, and remind them that there is never an excuse not to call. Role-play responses to hypo-

thetical situations. Ask interns what they would do if they were an employer with an employee who was late or absent frequently.

Personal Growth: Animal, Color, Water, White Room

The following activity helps interns begin to develop a sense of self. In this exercise, interns write adjectives describing their favorite animal, color, form of water, and reactions to being in a white, enclosed room. Have every intern seated with a pencil and piece of paper. Explain that this is an exploration apart from their job training, and it requires that they not talk at all in the first part. Review the definition of an adjective and give several examples. Ask the interns to write down their favorite animal and three to five adjectives that describe it and that explain why they like it. Keep the room quiet, and help the interns search for the best words without disturbing the peaceful ambiance. Then ask them to write their favorite color and list adjectives that explain why they like it. Follow the same for the interns' favorite form of water (e.g., lake, steam, ice, rain). Finally, ask the interns to imagine themselves in a white, enclosed room with no windows or doors. Then have them write adjectives that describe how that feels. Give the interns adequate time to respond.

Now find a volunteer willing to share her or his favorite animal and the accompanying adjectives. Ask for a few more volunteers to share their favorite animals and the associated adjectives. Share the idea that these answers are thought by some to reveal what people think of themselves. Keeping this in mind, the last volunteer to speak before you disclose this information should be one who has previously demonstrated high self-esteem. Ask for more volunteers. Draw in the ones who do not want to share.

Next, ask for volunteers to share their favorite color and accompanying adjectives. After a few, or perhaps all, have volunteered, tell the group that these answers are believed by some to tell how people would like to be perceived, or how they believe they are perceived. Repeat this process for water and its adjectives. This one reveals sexual self-image or perceptions of intimate relationships. Finally, the white room reveals feelings about death, transformation, or drastic change.

Let the information be shared, the feelings felt. Avoid coercion, lecturing, judging, or explaining.

Interpersonal Growth: Learning Your Job Duties (Ordering Job Duties)

Have the interns write down their job title and job duties. This will later be taught as a job search skill also. Before dismissing the interns, have them stand up tall—even in a line—and recite their name, job title, and at least three job duties. Always praise each intern for good voice, pleasant presence, good eye contact, precise recitation, sincere tone, or any combination of these qualities. Give some general feedback and modeling on how you would like to see this performed, but remarks to individuals should be generally positive. When interns meet the criteria, they may be seated. When interns do not meet the criteria, which has been clearly explained, have them remain standing, go through the rest of the line, and then come back to those who are still learning. Tell them how you want them to improve their performance, and give them another opportunity, until all interns are seated. Make sure all interns recite their job duties at least once before being dismissed. By practicing this as a rote exercise, interns attain a useful job interview tool, and also will be able to help you present the program to potential employers, sponsors, and supporters. Give each intern a copy of his or her job description. On-site instructors will ask interns to recite their job descriptions in the coming week at the community classroom sites.

Timely Topics: Pioneer, Warrior, Hero

Ask the interns to define *pioneer*, *warrior*, and *hero* and put their ideas on the board. Whatever they say is essentially correct. After each term is defined by the interns, offer your own definition, and explain that you are looking for those qualities in a work personality. Pioneers venture into unexplored territories (like work). Warriors are prepared to fight and struggle, but are wise in picking their battles and only fight when they absolutely have to. Heroes rescue others in need of help and can rise to a challenge and overcome odds. Clearly, in-

terns with serious learning, behavior, family, or neighborhood problems must develop these qualities if they are to succeed. This is an opportunity to praise them heavily for trying.

Ask for feedback on the curriculum so far, and write down what the interns say. Do not respond to the comments, or defend or "sell" the program. Just take in the feedback and let the interns see that their comments are being recorded. Let them know that they are free to say whatever they want.

Introduce the transition specialist, who visits today. His or her presentation should explain the following:

- How he or she keeps the Career Ladders promise of an ongoing commitment

- The benign nature of opening a case with an adult agency

- The advantages of adult career counseling services

- Anecdotes of several success stories

- Ways the transition specialist can be contacted, and ways a relationship can develop between transition specialist and intern

Week 4

Lessons In

☒	Job Skills
☒	Job-Keeping Skills
☐	Job Search Skills
☒	Personal Growth
☒	Interpersonal Growth
☒	Timely Topics

Job Skills: Tasks Imported from the Community Classroom

Repeat Week 3 activities this week.

Job-Keeping Skills: Be Responsible

This lesson can be found in *Don't Get Fired!* (Anema & Lefkowitz, 1996).

Use the *Don't Get Fired!* lesson. Have the class brainstorm what being responsible means, and then test and organize the concept.

PRESENTATION

Follow the *Don't Get Fired!* lesson, assigning interns to parts.

GUIDED PRACTICE

Lead a discussion based on the *Don't Get Fired!* questions (Decision Time and Discussion Questions) at the end of the lesson.

REAL-WORLD APPLICATION

During the coming week, have the on-site instructors give nonjudgmental feedback to the interns based on the points of this lesson.

Personal Growth: Problem Solving

Introduce problem-solving skills. Begin with a discussion of how the interns are feeling about their jobs. If any interns have had problems they want to share, make note of them, and return to these interns later to demonstrate the skill. Remember that this is not the place to lecture or to tell interns the solutions to on-the-job or other communication problems. It is the place to show them how they can generate strategies and experience satisfaction and competence. Teach and show the problem-solving process in the following way:

1. *Identify the feelings involved.* Introduce the List of Feelings in Appendix 3.1 and model "I" statements. Although "I" statements are taught in Week 5, they should be modeled and introduced here. Interns can become desensitized to the idea of "I" statements and can also grasp the first step in making an "I" statement, which is identifying and speaking the feeling.

2. *Identify the issues* around the problem. Show interns how to make an abstraction, form a concept, and get some distance from the problem, thereby taking control of it.

3. *Generate alternatives* in a free-for-all brainstorm. In this brainstorming session all suggestions are acceptable and put all of them on the board,

making sure that extreme solutions are included. Do not lecture or restrict the options.

4. *Test alternatives.* Let the interns set the standards of what are and are not reasonable courses of action.

5. *Make a strategic plan* to act on some of the better alternatives.

When the group understands these steps, return to the problems that were previously shared, or ask for other problems, and facilitate the group as it moves through this process at least two more times, using real on-the-job problems.

Complete the "Having a Conversation" exercise in *Peer-to-Peer Asset Building* (Varenhorst, in press) or various activities in *Tribes* (Gibbs, 2001). This is an opportunity for the interns to spend unstructured time in pairs and have conversations. Encourage interns to select partners whom they do not know. As with all personal growth exercises, this is an opportunity for on-site instructors to let go of their authoritarian role and let the employment skills workshop teacher lead the group. The on-site instructors should join the group and relate to the interns as peers.

Interpersonal Growth: Ordering Job Duties

Have interns practice the "Ordering Job Duties" exercise from Week 3.

Timely Topics: Why Work Without Pay? Why Be Supervised?

Begin to move from a "telling" to a "selling" stance with the group by asking the interns to brainstorm reasons they might ever be willing to work without pay. The idea is to tease out some of the other reasons for working, and to help the interns recognize some of the satisfactions of work beyond pay. The program fails when an intern views work or a job as merely a way to make some extra money. Career Ladders pays too little, and interns must understand that the real value of Career Ladders is that it will provide them with the tools to get and keep a better paying and more satisfying job.

One of the things Career Ladders offers is on-the-job supervision, and "selling" this to interns is one of the tricky tasks the staff faces. There must be open channels that allow the staff to give interns specific feedback, enabling them to improve performance. Staff must avoid humiliating interns by criticizing their lack of employability. At the same time, staff cannot let them believe that they are more competent and job-ready than they really are. Developing good on-the-job supervisory skills is one way the staff can achieve this delicate balance. Here, the employment skills workshop teacher can "sell" the idea of supervision. It is up to the on-site instructors to make good on the benevolence and educational merit of their presence on the job.

Reward and praise heavily interns who have completed and processed their paperwork. Use a posted chart to record their progress (see Appendix 3.2, The Paper Chase). Interns who have not kept pace with their paperwork should stay after the workshop. Make a contract with them, explaining the consequences clearly: By the time the work experience becomes paid employment, interns without completed paperwork will return to their schools until it is done. This situation will probably occur in the upcoming week. Legally, interns cannot continue to work when other interns at the same site are being paid. Ethically, they have earned the right to receive pay if they have been making progress. Educationally, they must experience real consequences for not processing paperwork in a timely fashion. Give a 3- to 5-day deadline, and return to school any interns who have not completed their paperwork at that time, with no exceptions.

Before the interns are dismissed, have them recite their name, job title, and at least three job duties again. On-site instructors will again prompt them to recite duties on the job during the coming week.

Week 5

Lessons In

☒	Job Skills
☒	Job-Keeping Skills
☐	Job Search Skills
☒	Personal Growth
☒	Interpersonal Growth
☒	Timely Topics

Job Skills: Tasks Imported from the Community Classroom

Repeat the activities from Week 3. Remind the interns that they will be rotating to new job skill activities in 2 weeks (beginning Week 7), and that this is an opportunity to really master the skills they are working on. If any interns have mastered the skills, either move them to more advanced activities or rotate them to new activities early.

Job-Keeping Skills: Follow the Schedule

This lesson can be found in *Don't Get Fired!* (Anema & Lefkowitz, 1996).

RATIONALE/WARM-UP/REVIEW

Follow the *Don't Get Fired!* lesson and use actual events that have happened during the semester, letting the group define and explain the concept and consequences of sticking to the schedule.

PRESENTATION

Use the *Don't Get Fired!* lesson.

GUIDED PRACTICE

Lead a discussion based on the questions at the end of the *Don't Get Fired!* lesson.

REAL-WORLD APPLICATION

On-site instructors should give nonjudgmental feedback during the week based on the points of this lesson.

Timely Topics: Stamina and Determination

The novelty of going to work is wearing off for some of the interns at this point, and the first cases of boredom are probably emerging. Thus, it is a good time to develop the concepts of stamina and determination. In this particular instance, examples of how athletes and popular celebrities needed stamina and determination to reach their goals are effective as reinforcers and are easily understood. Then return to the issue of the day, which is helping interns develop the skill of getting through the work week at a job that is good but less than ultimate in satisfaction.

If this lesson is going well, it can be extended to a general discussion of the line between tolerance and stamina on the job and more serious job dissatisfaction, which may lead to job change. Give examples. Despite this discussion, remember that in 99% of the cases, a Career Ladders internship should be an experience and lesson in following through, and only the most extreme cases of dissatisfaction or potential failure should result in an intern transferring, quitting, or being terminated. For interns who are less than satisfied with their Career Ladders placement, this is an important lesson in sticking it out for a semester and building a resume and a good reference that will ultimately get them to the job they want. It is crucial not to back down on this point. Explain various career pathways and how the entry-level experience can be the foundation of a lifelong career. The fundamentals of stamina, determination, and delayed gratification, as illustrated by example, are the key lessons here. This is an excellent opportunity to have interns brainstorm their very highest career goals. With stamina and determination, what could be achieved?

Before dismissing the interns, have them recite their name, job title, and at least three job duties. On-site instructors will prompt them to recite duties on the job during the coming week.

Personal Growth: Making "I" Statements

"I" statements are a key tool for building assertive social skills, problem-solving skills, self-awareness, job interview skills, and overall clear communication. On this day, "I" statements should be presented outside of a career context. Model "I" statements with several examples, using the List of Feelings (Appendix 3.1).

An "I" statement has three parts: the feeling, the conditions under which it is felt, and a self-disclosing statement that explains why it is felt: "I feel _____ when someone _____, because _____." For example: "I feel angry, betrayed, and mistrustful when someone steals from my purse at work, because I am poor and need the money, and because I want to feel safe and trust my coworkers." "I feel supported, cared about, and appreciated when someone tells me that I am doing good work, because I want to succeed, and

because sometimes I don't know when I'm doing well, and I never did well in school before."

Remember that interns can and should use examples that are not job related. Repeat the "Having a Conversation" exercise from Week 4, but encourage interns to incorporate "I" statements into the conversations. Tour the room and actively prompt interns into making the statements. This is an opportunity for interns to practice making these statements, without being in the high-pressure setting of actually resolving a crisis. The practice will prepare interns for those situations when they do arise. Include on-site instructors as participants.

During the debriefing of this activity, return to the problem-solving process taught last week, and show how "I" statements can help people identify problems on and off the job. Use a real-life example from the group if one is volunteered. Close by showing how an "I" statement can communicate a problem clearly to another person without antagonizing him or her, and how it is a powerful alternative to blame, resentment, and repression. In future lessons, making "I" statements can be tied to social skills training in relationships with superiors and coworkers, but that is not essential today.

Interpersonal Growth: Ordering Job Duties

Have interns practice the "Ordering Job Duties" exercise from Week 3.

Week 6

Lessons In

- ☒ Job Skills
- ☒ Job-Keeping Skills
- ☒ Job Search Skills
- ☒ Personal Growth
- ☒ Interpersonal Growth
- ☒ Timely Topics

Job Skills: Tasks Imported from the Community Classroom

Repeat Week 3 activities. Remind interns that they will be moving on to new tasks and new job stations at work in the next week. Encourage them to try for a personal best in accuracy and speed. At the end of the session, give each intern a piece of paper with the skill that has been achieved so far, written in the form in which it would be found on a resume.

Personal Growth: Exchanging Positives

Have the group sit in a circle. Each intern must go around the circle and tell every other person something he or she likes about that person. Avoid going first so that interns will generate and search for real feelings, and not simply mimic yours. However, you can go third or fourth to keep the pace going. When all interns have participated to the best of their ability, let the group sit for a long moment with the good feelings that have been generated. Explain how these feelings of praise and positiveness can be repeated in other areas of their life, including the job. Ask the interns to think of characteristics they like about their co-workers, and assign them the task of delivering that praise in the coming week. On-site instructors should prompt the interns to complete this assignment.

If there is time, prolong the good feelings by repeating the "Having a Conversation" lesson (see Personal Growth, Week 4).

Interpersonal Growth: Ordering Job Duties

Have interns practice the "Ordering Job Duties" exercise from Week 3.

Job Search Skills: Job Interview Questions

RATIONALE

Allow interns to discuss the importance of knowing how to conduct a job search. When they have articulated and reached a consensus about a desire to do so, offer them the services of the program. Present the Counselor–Job Seeker Agreement (see Appendix 3.3). Read and review it, and have each intern who wants to look for work sign it. This agreement will be offered again when graduation is more imminent. If an intern does *not* want to

embark on a job search at this point, that is fine, but explain that working and going to college are not mutually exclusive.

WARM-UP/REVIEW

Develop an intern-generated list of skills necessary to search for and find a job, and write the responses on the board. Possible responses include interview skills, resumes, job applications, and job leads.

PRESENTATION

Ask how many interns have gone on job interviews, how it felt, and what helped the most. If any interns have interviewed multiple times, ask what areas of improvement they noticed from interview to interview? Have they improved since their first interview, and if so how? What advice would they give other interns? Have the interns practice answering interview questions (see Appendix 3.4 for suggestions) to learn what information interviewers are seeking.

GUIDED PRACTICE

Have the interns break into two groups. Group 1 generates a list of possible interview questions, while Group 2 generates an interview rating sheet. The results of both activities are shared with the rest of the class. You can later type up the intern-produced work. Or use the Interview Rating Sheet (Appendix 3.5) and have both groups generate questions, exchanges, and answers.

REAL-WORLD APPLICATION

Interns will use the rating sheet and interview questions they generated to practice interviews in Week 10.

Job Search Skills: Brainstorming for a Resume

Take the sheet of paper listing an achieved job skill that was handed out in the Job Skills session this week, and ask interns to review their work experiences from as far back as possible. Have them write down more of their skills (e.g., supervise young children, enter data, assist carpenter, perform receptionist duties, file records), learning the writing style to use on a resume and translating volunteer, summer job, and school work–study experience into a respectable history of skills. Also ask interns to list their hobbies and interests. Make sure to save this document because interns will use it to generate resumes in Week 9.

Job-Keeping Skills: Following Directions

Ask for examples from the interns that show instances when they have needed to follow directions on the job. Poll the on-site instructors for examples of both excellent following-directions behaviors and problems. If an intern with a problem following directions is comfortable enough discussing it, use the problem-solving process (see Personal Growth, Week 4) to find a solution, such as asking for help when needed, asking for modeled instructions, or asking for instructions to be repeated. Remind interns that they will be doing a lot more work in this area because it is an important job-keeping skill.

Use the *Don't Get Fired!* (Anema & Lefkowitz, 1996) lesson about following directions, using the same format as previous weeks (for example, Week 5).

Timely Topics: Tolerance and Terminations

Illustrate the continuum from school to work and a successful postsecondary life. Career Ladders can be one possible route, for interns who make it through the program. Interns who are terminated (list the reasons why one might be terminated: attendance, disruption, dishonesty, poor effort, poor performance) may still succeed through the other paths. The role of Career Ladders is to be more tolerant than an employer in a real-world job situation, but more demanding than school; Career Ladders staff reserves the right to return to school any intern who is not succeeding, just as an employer has the right to fire an employee.

Introduce the positive role adult agencies can play and identify their services, including the Career Ladders transition specialist. Tell interns that getting a case opened is the next round of necessary paperwork to be covered, and remind them that it is also going to further test the skill of navigating adult service systems.

Before dismissing the interns, have them recite their name, job title, and at least three job duties. On-site instructors will prompt them to recite duties on the job during the coming week. (They should be getting pretty good at this by now!)

Note to Instructor: Week 7 is a critical week for sustaining interest in the workshop for the second two thirds of the semester. It is packed with activities that will set a more serious and hardworking tone, and it presents procedures that will be used for the rest of the semester. Thorough preparation for Week 7's presentation is strongly recommended.

Week 7

Lessons In

- ☒ Job Skills
- ☒ Job-Keeping Skills
- ☒ Job Search Skills
- ☒ Personal Growth
- ☒ Interpersonal Growth
- ☒ Timely Topics

Job Skills: Tasks Imported from the Community Classroom II

All interns should move to a new, more challenging and sophisticated activity imported from the job site. Exceptions might include an intern who is making very good progress in a specific skill, such as mastering a particular software program, and who wishes to continue working at it. The on-site instructors, in the normal course of interaction with the employer supervisors, should have a sense of what new skills interns need to be more competitive in that organization. On-site instructors should report whether they have observed interns having learning difficulties with any job skills, and you can address these if appropriate. This new job skills assignment can be planned in concert with any upcoming transfers to a new department within the job site.

Personal Growth: Asking Open-Ended Questions

Tell interns that today they will learn ways in which they can improve their ability to make friends by asking good questions. Use the lesson from *Peer-to-Peer Asset Building* (Varenhorst, in press) on asking open-ended questions. In this exercise, interns learn appropriate ways to ask personal questions that stimulate full conversation. The point of the exercise is to break students free of monosyllabic nonresponses to questions, and to let them know how it feels to be truly interested in someone else's favorite topic, or to have several people interested in theirs.

A second lesson for this day is on active listening. Use the corresponding lesson from *Peer-to-Peer Asset Building* (Varenhorst, in press). Working in pairs, the interns take turns engaging in active listening while their partner shares something personal and positive.

Timely Topics: Social Skills— Why Have a Workshop on Them?

Talk about why social skills on the job (i.e., getting along with others) are so important. Tell the story of past terminations and successes, such as the story of one graduate who was poorly matched to a job at a large business office, but whose social skills were so good that the employer found and redesigned a job so that she could do it. We have found that a decision to hire a person is a decision to like that person. Refer interns back to the Career Ladders pyramid (Figure 2.1). Show the interns how social skills are a foundation to the transition to a successful work life. At this point, all interns are attending work regularly (problem solved or intern terminated). Now that the interns are all going to work, are their coworkers happy to see them? Social skills training ensures that they will be.

Job-Keeping Skills: Be Helpful and Friendly to Everyone at Work

WARM-UP/REVIEW

Discuss what being friendly and helpful means, and why it is important.

PRESENTATION

Use the *Don't Get Fired!* (Anema & Lefkowitz, 1996) lesson and assign parts to interns.

GUIDED PRACTICE

Lead a discussion based on the questions at the end of the *Don't Get Fired!* lesson.

REAL-WORLD APPLICATION

During the coming week, have the on-site instructors give nonjudgmental feedback to the interns based on the points of this lesson.

Interpersonal Growth: First Session and Overall Session Format

Lead a discussion in which interns articulate and begin to understand the need for learning social skills.

Introduce the concept of social skills and the concepts of learning and teaching using the basketball analogy in *Skillstreaming the Adolescent* (Goldstein & McGinnis, 1997). When an intern has taught the basketball skill and the group can repeat the process (show, try, discuss, practice), demonstrate how it will be used by teaching "Ordering Job Duties" (see skill sheet, Appendix 3.10). This skill integrates a rote task that interns have been practicing and know from the past several weeks. Now they can put it into the social skills training format and experience mastery of the skill—enabling them to grasp the process—almost immediately. The process includes instructor modeling; letting an intern try it, with other interns rating the performance; having a quick discussion and using nonjudgmental feedback (introduce this concept—it will be taught with detail in the "Personal Growth" strand); and allowing the intern additional practice in it. Video is a powerful tool that can be used if it is available, both to record performances and to show taped demonstrations of social skills being performed. The advantage of video feedback is that "the camera doesn't lie," and interns are left to their own devices to modify their appearance and behavior (i.e., it is not coming from an adult, but from the videotaped evidence).

The session format can be outlined as follows:

1. Introductions:
   a. Name something you like doing in your spare time.
   b. Name something you like doing at work.

2. Overview:

   a. Purpose of the group—learning to get along, dealing with people, dealing with feelings, handling stressful situations, being liked so that you will get hired, feeling comfortable in situations.

   b. Examples—asking for help, starting a conversation, accepting negative feedback, ordering job duties.

   c. Procedures of learning—show, try, discuss, practice.

   d. Steps—listing the steps in teaching someone how to shoot a basketball.

3. Rules: The group is confidential. Be on time. Don't be afraid to perform.

4. First and subsequent sessions–overview of skill:

   a. Define the skill (trainer and interns).

   b. Give its rationale.

   c. Give examples where the skill would be used.

   d. Distribute skill sheets (Appendix 3.10).

5. Present videotaped models.

6. Give and get feedback on the models.

7. Present live trainer models—give and get feedback.

8. Organize intern role playing:

   a. The volunteer chooses a coactor who is most like the actual person in the role-played situation.

   b. Set the stage with a lot of verbal detail of the situation. Where is it? Are you standing or sitting? What is the time of day? What is the emotional atmosphere?

   c. Develop a script. What will you say for step A? What will the coactor say? Ask the same questions for step B.

   d. Develop contingencies—what will you do if . . . ?

   e. Give a pep talk and begin.

9. Perform trainee role playing:

   a. Place one trainer at the chalkboard.

   b. Ask one trainer to prompt.

   c. Interrupt if necessary.

10. Feedback:

    a. The main actor should wait until all comments have been heard.

    b. Ask for the coactor's reactions.

    c. Ask how well the steps were followed.

    d. Ask the main actor: How do you feel about your performance?

11. Practice:

    a. Repeat until the script is mastered.

    b. Expand feedback to adjunctive components following mastery.

    c. View the videotape before final feedback.

12. Homework:

    a. Ask the main actor how, when, where, and with whom the skill could be practiced.

    b. Trainees who didn't role-play can still do the homework.

    c. Remind the trainees that they will be approached and prompted on the job site, and given real-life opportunities to practice social skills on the job.

Job Search Skills: How To Conduct a Job Search

Show the entire group how to use a job search contact sheet (see Appendix 3.6 for an example) to help organize their efforts. Send two previously chosen interns out on a supported job search. These two interns are actually dismissed from class, and they will "pound the pavement" with an on-site instructor accompanying them. The on-site instructor role-plays with them, prompts the responses necessary to track job leads, and encourages them to walk into businesses.

If the previously chosen interns have not dressed well enough, send out two other interns who are better dressed. In other words, show that interns will lose out on opportunities if they do not prepare for them. The rest of the class, intrigued by the dismissal of two of their peers, will immediately engage in active preparations for their own job search.

BASIC SKILL OBJECTIVES

Interns will look for jobs through cold calls, walkins, employment agencies, school programs, and adult service agencies.

WARM-UP/REVIEW

Use an intern-generated list of job search skills necessary to find a job. Put responses on the board, including interview skills, resumes, job applications, and job leads.

PRESENTATION

Brainstorm ways people find jobs and write them on the board, defining terms as they come up: want ads, school, family and friends, walk-ins, cold calls, employment agencies. Have the interns write the names, addresses, and phone numbers of personal contacts who would be good for job leads *and* as references.

Ask each intern the number of jobs he or she has obtained through the various methods and make a group tally. Draw attention to the fact that school programs will probably top the list, but that interns will not have school programs after they graduate. The next most successful area is family and friends. Point out that these resources will remain after graduation, and that they are the easiest and most reliable method. Then rank the rest of the methods. Ask the interns why they think the methods fall in that order.

GUIDED PRACTICE

Have interns role-play walking into a business. Who will they ask to speak to? (The manager or the person in charge of hiring) Will they leave anything? (Yes, a resume, job application, or both) Will they call back? (Yes, approximately every 3 weeks to remind the employer that they are still interested) Where will they go? (Many places, especially those likely to hire at that time of the year) Next role-play cold calls. Who will they ask for? (The manager) What will they say? (Their name and the purpose of the call) What if there are no jobs available? (Ask the manager for other leads) Will they take notes? (Yes, on a job search contact sheet like the one in Appendix 3.6) Show the interns how to use a job search contact sheet to help organize their efforts.

REAL-WORLD APPLICATION

Have the two chosen interns conduct their own job search, with support and supervision from an on-site instructor. During this job search, interns should do walk-ins and pick up applications, prac-

tice cold calls, and talk to family and friends about job leads. Have them report back about the search every week, and praise their efforts heavily. Have them get two copies of applications (one for practice, one to submit), and praise them just for getting the applications. In later trips, make the goal getting an interview. Throughout the search, emphasize follow-up. Pick two other interns to be excused for a job search the next week, and tell them to dress appropriately (the on-site instructor should provide additional prompts). If the scheduled interns fail to do so, send better-dressed interns in their place for that day. In other words, they will lose the opportunity if they do not prepare for it.

Job Search Skills: Learning How To Do a Job Interview

Have interns make a poster together that lists all the things they should do for a good job interview, such as being 10 minutes early, being able to describe themselves in positive terms, talking about their experiences related to the job for which they are interviewing. Lead a large-group discussion on the following topics. Break the interns into dyads or small groups to give every intern an opportunity to engage in these activities:

1. Have the interns practice answering possible interview questions. Focus on taking one of an intern's problem areas, and turning the negative trait into a positive one (e.g., "I'm slow, but accurate"). Practice these statements until interns get the hang of it.

2. Ask the interns to list positive hobbies: team sports, reading novels (versus comic books), volunteering in the community, and so on.

3. Have the interns ask the interviewer questions, such as about company benefits. Show videos or use other materials that explain company benefits and union membership.

4. Have the interns state why they want the job and why the company should hire them.

WARM-UP/REVIEW

Use the intern-generated list of job search skills necessary to finding a job from earlier this session and put their responses on the board. Responses might include knowing who you are and what you really want to do, interview skills, resumes, job applications, and job leads.

PRESENTATION

Use an overhead projector to review the intern- and teacher-generated interview rating sheet created in Week 7 (or use Appendix 3.5). Discuss the different areas on which the interviewee will be rated.

GUIDED PRACTICE

Show interns a video of a brief part of a former intern's interview and ask them to rate it using the rating sheet.

REAL-WORLD APPLICATION

Have interns form triads to practice interviewing: one intern is interviewer, one is interviewee, and one is rater. The interns should take a turn playing each role. Demonstrate the skill of nonjudgmental observation (directly addressed in Week 8) to help interns rate each other. Have the interns observe other interns' interviews and record strengths and weaknesses. Heighten the interns' awareness of language: voice tone, amplitude, clarity, sentence structure.

Week 8

Lessons In

☒	Job Skills
☒	Job-Keeping Skills
☒	Job Search Skills
☒	Personal Growth
☒	Interpersonal Growth
☒	Timely Topics

Job Skills: Tasks Imported from the Community Classroom II

See Week 7. Have interns stay with the new activity begun last week.

Personal Growth: Making Nonjudgmental Observations

Review last week's lesson, "Asking Open-Ended Questions," and lesson in active listening. Today interns will learn how to make nonjudgmental but helpful observations. In so doing, they will develop questioning and listening skills and help each other in social skills training. In this lesson from *Peer-to-Peer Asset Building* (Varenhorst, in press), a third person is added to a pair to observe the interactions of listener and speaker, and to give feedback that objectively mirrors but does not judge. Use the items from the appendix in *Peer-to-Peer Asset Building* on active listening and observations to achieve comfort and familiarity with this skill.

Timely Topics: Working with Adult Service Agencies

Ask the transition specialist or a staff person from a partnering agency to address or conduct case opening procedures, general medical exams, psychological testing, paperwork, job club, or other appropriate topics. Interns should perceive the transition specialist as part of the same team as the on-site instructors and program manager, and use the familiarity, comfort, and security of the workshop setting to make a bridge from school to adult life.

Job-Keeping Skills: Do Not Talk to Friends While Working

Use the *Don't Get Fired!* (Anema & Lefkowitz, 1996) lesson on this topic.

WARM-UP/REVIEW

Discuss why not talking to friends while working may or may not be a good rule of thumb on the job.

PRESENTATION

Follow the *Don't Get Fired!* lesson and assign parts to the interns.

GUIDED PRACTICE

Lead a discussion based on the questions at the end of the lesson.

REAL-WORLD APPLICATION

Have on-site instructors or supervising employees give nonjudgmental feedback to the interns based on the points of this lesson during the coming week.

Interpersonal Growth: Ordering Job Duties

Continue practicing the "Ordering Job Duties" exercise. Everyone should get through it and should be able to master it, but do take enough time to give repeated practice to those interns who need it. This session should complete learning and mastery of this skill, as well as orientation to the social skills training format introduced in Week 7. Tell the interns that they will be prompted on the job by staff and visitors (e.g., prospective employers, interested educators) on this skill—remind on-site instructors to prompt it daily—and that it also will be integrated into their job interview skills.

Job Search Skills: The Personal Data Sheet

At the end of this lesson, interns will be able to explain how a personal data sheet can be used to assist in completing job applications.

WARM-UP/REVIEW

Have interns generate a list of skills that are necessary to finding a job and write their responses on the board. Possible responses include interview skills, resumes, job applications, and job leads.

PRESENTATION

Break interns into small groups of four to five. Pass out various sets of two completed job applications, both from the same person. One has obvious misspellings, incomplete answers, obvious wrong dates, poor choices of personal references, and poor reasons for quitting a job. The other has no misspellings, complete answers, every box completed, professional language, smart answers, and accurate dates. Have the interns compare the two applications and ask one person from each group to point out errors in the first application to the class. Discuss the tools necessary to complete a good application. Possible responses include a dictionary, phone book, friend, and personal records, also known as a "cheat sheet" or personal data sheet (see example in Appendix 3.7).

GUIDED PRACTICE

Brainstorm possible work experiences that would help build a job history. Many students neglect to realize that they have been doing volunteer work for their families (e.g., child care, housecleaning, landscaping) that is appropriate to put on their resumes as work experience. Have interns complete personal data sheets in small groups, providing a dictionary, telephone books, and instructor assistance.

REAL-WORLD APPLICATION

Have interns first role-play and then actually go out on their own asking for job applications. Interns who have demonstrated capability can conduct independent job searches during the workshop. They should bring in and show different blank applications, then use their personal data sheets to complete them. If there are questions on an application that are not covered on the data sheet, tell the interns to add the information to the back of their sheets. Interns should take their personal data sheets on every job search. Review the interview questions generated by the group in Week 6. Ask whether any of the job seekers have been asked these questions. How did they answer?

Send a new set of two previously chosen interns out on a supported job search with an on-site instructor.

Week 9

Lessons In

- [x] Job Skills
- [x] Job-Keeping Skills
- [x] Job Search Skills
- [x] Personal Growth
- [x] Interpersonal Growth
- [x] Timely Topics

Job Skills: Tasks Imported from the Community Classroom II

Repeat activity from Week 7.

Job-Keeping Skills: Keep Yourself Busy

Use the *Don't Get Fired!* (Anema & Lefkowitz, 1996) lesson on this topic.

Role-play an employer who has one opening and two candidates who appear to be equally qualified. The employer can afford to hire them both for a 2-week probation period, but does not tell the candidates that one of them will be retained and the other let go. Then role-play one candidate who does everything she is asked to do and finishes her assigned tasks, but then lights up a cigarette and takes a break. Then role-play a second candidate who finishes his tasks and then looks for more work to do or assists coworkers. Ask the class who they would hire if they were the employer.

Address this topic in lecture form as one of the realities of the workplace, briefly mentioning the necessity to *appear* busy at times—especially when facing the public. Focus the lecture on situations where one can stay busy and not just look busy; however, the importance of the latter must be discussed.

PRESENTATION

Follow the *Don't Get Fired!* lesson, assigning parts to interns.

GUIDED PRACTICE

Lead a discussion based on the questions at the end of the *Don't Get Fired!* lesson.

REAL-WORLD APPLICATION

Have the on-site instructors give nonjudgmental feedback to interns based on this lesson during the coming week.

Personal Growth: Crocodile Creek

Use Appendix 3.8, Crocodile Creek, for this value-oriented exercise.

Timely Topics: Beginning the Job Search

Talk about the determination necessary to conduct a successful job search. Set up expectations that an intern will not "hit" on a good job opportunity until his or her 20th lead, and that is the number to beat. Review the best sources and techniques of job search, and discuss an important feature of the Career Ladders program: Interns will

be released from the program, but still receive their credits, if they find a suitable and approved job by the end of the semester and agree to intermittent monitoring by Career Ladders staff. Finally, discuss the similarities between a job search and dating: doing things to impress the other person, letting him or her know that you are sincerely interested, psyching yourself up for some rejections before the right person comes along.

Job Search Skills: Complete a Personal Resume

Introduce job-seeking vocabulary, such as *resume*, *objective*, *references*, and a list of action verbs, such as *file*, *type*, *clean*, *organize*, *supervise*, *sweep*, *prepare*, *cut*, *chop*, *cook*, *deliver*, *distribute*, *coordinate*.

WARM-UP/REVIEW

Use the intern-generated list of job search skills necessary to find a job from previous weeks. Put these responses on the board again. The list might include interview skills, resumes, job applications, and job leads.

PRESENTATION

Show the interns two resumes that contrast markedly in quality (see Appendix 3.9). Ask the interns to identify which resume is neater, easier to read, and contains the most important information.

GUIDED PRACTICE

Discuss good general work objectives, references, other job-related interests or responsibilities, and work experience. Take a few examples of interns' work experience and "punch them up" with assistance from the class using the list of action verbs and information from their personal data sheets.

REAL-WORLD APPLICATION

Have the interns write their own resume using a model supplied by the instructor (see the first resume in Appendix 3.9) and the various sheets from previous weeks on which they have brainstormed their contacts (for references), interests and hobbies, skills (job duties), their personal data sheet, and so on. Pair up the most competent interns and provide individualized instruction for those who need help.

Final resumes are to be prepared by on-site instructors, kept on disk and in a student's electronic portfolio,[2] and forwarded to the transition specialist.

Send two new previously chosen interns out on a supported job search.

Interpersonal Growth: Asking for Help or Instructions

WARM-UP/REVIEW

The purpose of this lesson is to show interns the importance of asking for help and instructions on the job. Ask the interns who taught them their job and who is their supervisor; interns must name at least two people. Present the rationale for learning the skill of asking for help. Ask interns for any stories from the job site where this skill might have been useful, and invite discussion of problems the interns have had using the skill. Briefly review the problem-solving process (see Personal Growth, Week 4) to get some ideas and a sense of what the skill is.

PRESENTATION

Read this case study aloud to the group:

> Reggie's boss rushed in and gave him a job to do. His boss explained the job very quickly and there were many things to be done. Reggie didn't have any paper to take notes so he tried to listen very carefully as his boss talked, but she was in a hurry and talked very fast. Before his boss ran off, she asked Reggie, "Do you understand?" Reggie said he thought he did. Reggie started to do the job but he couldn't remember which letter went in the envelope and which was to be put into the folder. He thought about it for some time, but still wasn't quite sure. His boss was very busy and not always friendly. Should he disturb her or should he just do what he thinks is best?
>
> Choose *bother her* or *not bother her*.

Once the interns have chosen, explain the consequences of each choice. After *bothering her*, Reggie's boss thanks him for stopping to ask more questions. She apologizes for not taking more time to explain the job and says she's never too busy to answer questions.

After *not bothering her*, Reggie's boss comes back to pick up the work and realizes that it's been done wrong. She needs the work in 5 minutes for an important meeting. She has to correct the work herself and will be late for the meeting. She looks at Reggie and says, "I wish you had asked me if you had a question. It would have taken me much less time to answer your question than to fix your mistake."

GUIDED PRACTICE AND REAL-WORLD APPLICATION

Have interns role-play asking for instructions and giving instructions. Introduce the rating sheet (Appendix 3.10) on a transparency. Group interns into threes. One person can observe and give feedback to the other two, and the two who are role playing can also give each other feedback. Rotate so that each person has an opportunity to play each role. Interns should use coworkers' names and real job situations. The role-playing interns should rate themselves in their role of instruction giver or taker.

Week 10

Lessons In

- ☒ Job Skills
- ☒ Job-Keeping Skills
- ☒ Job Search Skills
- ☒ Personal Growth
- ☒ Interpersonal Growth
- ☒ Timely Topics

Job Skills: Tasks Imported from the Community Classroom II

Repeat Week 7 activity.

---

[2]Many high schools are developing portfolios and electronic (Web-based) portfolios in which students collect summaries of their academic work and career preparation materials. Career Ladders student products are appropriate for electronic portfolios.

Job-Keeping Skills: Following Directions and Making an Extra Effort

Ask interns for actual incidents from the job sites when knowing how to follow instructions has been important. The on-site instructors may have more information than the interns. Take care to present incidents accurately, neither humiliating the interns nor glossing over any examples where they needed to perform this skill better. Give an assessment that measures instruction-following ability. Watch interns carefully for signs of test anxiety; reassure them that the test is not being graded and will only be used to help them improve performance on the job and to help find them appropriate job placement.

Read aloud the following case study, then discuss it using the questions at the end:

> The setting is a very busy department store 2 days before Christmas. Debbie, a popular salesperson who is friendly with the boss and everyone else, was scheduled to work. She called in about an hour before she was due for work to say she was sick and couldn't come in. The manager called other salespeople, but everyone was busy with last-minute Christmas shopping and it looked as if nobody would be able to cover. Then the boss called Joan. Joan was a nice, quiet worker who did her job well. She was reluctant to go to work that day because she too had planned to do her last-minute Christmas shopping, but the boss really needed her and she was always willing to help. Joan went to work that day and about 4 hours later Debbie walked in with her arms full of shopping bags. Debbie greeted the boss and all the other workers. She was friendly and very happy that she was able to get so much shopping done. She admitted she wasn't really sick and joked with the boss while Joan continued working quietly. After the Christmas season the boss called a staff meeting to thank everyone for working so hard and for making the Christmas sales go so well. The boss said she wanted to mention one person in particular who had worked very hard. Joan sat up, straightened her dress, and got ready to accept the recognition that she was due, although she was a little embarrassed because she was a shy person. Joan was speechless when the boss called out Debbie's name. Everyone was happy for Debbie; she was very popular. Of course, Joan never said anything to the boss about it because she was a quiet person.

Discussion Questions: Why did the boss recognize Debbie for outstanding performance, while Joan was overlooked? Why did the boss like Debbie? Did the boss dislike Joan? Was Joan a good worker? Did Joan deserve the recognition? Was Debbie a good worker? Have you seen something like this happen?

Personal Growth: Decision Agent

Use the "Decision Agent" exercise from *Peer-to-Peer Asset Building* (Varenhorst, in press). This unique exercise simulates the feeling of gaining or losing control over decisions in life, and is thus extremely practical and useful for youth in transition. You may also want to use other exercises (see also Clark, 1979; Gibbs, 2001; Simon, Howe, & Kirschenbaum, 1995) that compel interns to rank values. Provide opportunities for the interns to debrief the experience, learning to value and to understand that each individual's value system is unique.

Timely Topics: Reevaluating Career Objectives

Have interns reevaluate their career objectives from Timely Topics in Week 5 or from the resume-writing exercises based on what they have learned from the "Decision Agent" exercise. Discuss what might look best on their resume as a career objective and encourage them to develop some longer term goals.

Job Search Skills: Baseline Job Interviews

Conduct baseline job interviews; provide no in-depth feedback, no instruction. This is a "test-flight" just to record the basic performance levels. Videotape if possible. Give all interns similar questions to answer and provide light praise rather than criticism or instruction. Take a lot of notes, however, on their performance. Instruction will begin at the next session. Because you provide no feedback during these baseline interviews, it is possible to get through the entire group in one day.

WARM-UP/REVIEW

Use the intern-generated list of job search skills necessary to finding a job from previous weeks. Put these responses on the board again. The list might include interview skills, resumes, job applications, and job leads.

PRESENTATION

Ask how many interns have gone on job interviews, how it felt, what helped the most, what areas are in need of improvement, what areas have improved since the first interview, and how much they have improved.

GUIDED PRACTICE

Have the interns (in small groups of six) review the list of intern- and teacher-generated interview questions from Week 6. They can informally role-play, practicing and discussing good answers to the interview questions.

REAL-WORLD APPLICATION

Conduct practice interviews with the interns. Act as the interviewer to get a baseline of the interns' areas of weakness. Videotape the session if possible. (The results, good and bad, can be discussed in a later session.)

Send a new pair of previously chosen interns out on a supported job search.

Interpersonal Growth: Asking for Help or Instructions

Practice "Asking for Help or Instructions" from Week 9. Encourage on-site instructors to find ways to prompt the interns to practice this skill appropriately on the job. Ask for examples from those interns who have used this skill on the job.

Week 11

Lessons In

- ☒ Job Skills
- ☒ Job-Keeping Skills
- ☒ Job Search Skills
- ☒ Personal Growth
- ☒ Interpersonal Growth
- ☒ Timely Topics

Job Skills: Tasks Imported from the Community Classroom II

Repeat Week 7 activity.

Job-Keeping Skills: Give Good Service

Discuss the concept of good service. Listen to stories from the job site and use the problem-solving process when possible. For example, how would one cope with an unpleasant customer using the feelings–issues–alternatives–testing–strategy process (see Personal Growth, Week 4)? This topic will be addressed in great detail in social skills training sessions to come.

WARM-UP/REVIEW

Discuss the advantages of being able to give good service.

PRESENTATION

Use the *Don't Get Fired!* (Anema & Lefkowitz, 1996) lesson on this topic.

GUIDED PRACTICE

Have a discussion based on the questions at the end of the *Don't Get Fired!* lesson.

REAL-WORLD APPLICATION

Have the on-site instructors give nonjudgmental feedback during the week based on the points of this lesson.

Personal Growth: Values Ranking

Do a values-ranking exercise from Week 10 if you did not do one with the "Decision Agent" exercise.

This is the final personal growth activity for the semester. Show the interns how they have made discoveries about themselves, how they have begun to develop more sensitivity to others, and finally, how values are growing out of these activities. Remind interns that these processes are ongoing and that they can continue to use these tools in their personal relationships with family, peers, other interns, on-site instructors, the transition specialist, and even employers. The nuts and bolts of maintaining relationships with others and working on sensitivity will continue in the interpersonal growth segments of the upcoming workshops. However, continue to offer opportunities for interns to speak honestly and make friends through personal growth activities.

Timely Topics: Past Interns' Anecdotes

Give the interns a realistic sense of their future by telling them the outcomes of past interns. Describe success stories, and try to illuminate the key to each person's success: dependability, good social skills, determination, and so on. Give examples of past interns who have not done as well and explain why: friends visiting on the job, poor attendance, poor interview skills, dishonesty, and so on. Ask alumni to visit as guest speakers if possible.

Job Search Skills: Mock Interviews

Begin mock job interviews in earnest, modeling the format after the social skills training sessions and integrating that script into a job interview. Model the particular interview skill that will be emphasized today: the recitation of job duties. Demonstrate how the ordering of job duties can be integrated into the job interview. The interns should be enthusiastic about this task because they are now generalizing the well-practiced skill of ordering job duties to a new context. Give the interns opportunities to practice and to give each other nonjudgmental feedback.

WARM-UP/REVIEW

Use the intern-generated list of the job search skills necessary to find a job from previous weeks. Put these responses on the board again. The list might include interview skills, resumes, job applications, and job leads.

PRESENTATION

Ask how many interns have gone on job interviews, how it felt, what helped them the most, what areas of improvement they noticed, whether they have improved since their first interview, and, if so, how.

GUIDED PRACTICE

Have interns (in small groups of six) review the list of intern- and teacher-generated interview ques-

tions from Week 6. They can informally role-play, practicing and discussing good answers to the interview questions.

REAL-WORLD APPLICATION

Conduct practice interviews with the interns. Act as the interviewer and videotape the session if possible. Following each interview, discuss the positive aspects and areas in need of improvement with the group of interns.

Send a new pair of previously chosen interns out on a supported job search.

Interpersonal Growth: Having a Conversation

The purpose of this exercise is to identify socially appropriate and inappropriate subject matter for conversations at the job site, such as weekend activities versus pay or subjects of a personal nature; inappropriate people with whom to talk casually, such as the boss; and inappropriate times and ways to talk, such as during staff meetings or too softly.

At this point in the semester, the interns should already have a good feel for this topic and be able to experience success in this exercise because they are building on skills learned in exercises early in the semester. The following activity will check the interns' progress using a more structured approach. The process of making nonjudgmental observations in the format of this exercise is the same process that was used in the observation exercises in Week 8.

WARM-UP/REVIEW

Repeat the exercise from Week 6 in which interns deliver positive statements to each other.

PRESENTATION

Use an overhead transparency to guide the interns through the rating form, Starting a Conversation (Appendix 3.10). Discuss the meaning of the different areas, such as complimentary comments. Discuss possible topics of conversation, taboo topics, and when and with whom to talk. Ask a few interns to role-play having a conversation and then ask them to rate themselves. Observing interns may also participate in the rating.

Have interns pair off using a random system. That is, pair them with other interns with whom they do not usually socialize. They should practice having a conversation for approximately 10 minutes, then get back in a whole group and use the rating sheet to discuss how the conversations went.

REAL-WORLD APPLICATION

Have the interns select a person at work whom they would like to know better. Select a topic of conversation and, if necessary, role-play a conversation with the interns. Have the interns report back next week about the topic of the conversation and then rate their performance.

Week 12

Lessons In

- ☒ Job Skills
- ☒ Job-Keeping Skills
- ☒ Job Search Skills
- ☐ Personal Growth
- ☒ Interpersonal Growth
- ☒ Timely Topics

Job Skills: Tasks Imported from the Community Classroom II

Repeat Week 7 activity.

Job-Keeping Skills: Leave Your Personal Problems at Home

Give examples of past interns who have hurt their status on the job by revealing their personal problems at work. Be sensitive to interns' personal problems and use the problem-solving process to generate ideas about how interns can deal with situations in which personal problems seem likely to overwhelm a job situation.

WARM-UP/REVIEW

Ask interns about the consequences of failing to leave personal problems at home.

PRESENTATION

Use the *Don't Get Fired!* (Anema & Lefkowitz, 1996) lesson, "Leave Your Blues at Home."

GUIDED PRACTICE

Lead a discussion based on the questions at the end of the *Don't Get Fired!* lesson.

REAL-WORLD APPLICATION

Have the on-site instructors give nonjudgmental feedback during the week based on the points of the lesson.

Timely Topics: Capitalism 101

Explain that we live in a society with a capitalist economy, and describe the basic forces of supply, demand, and profit that so dramatically affect the lives of the interns. Explain that they will not retain employment unless their employer makes more money than their wages plus benefits when they are at work. Discuss what may or may not be regrettable about this situation and give the interns other employment options, such as starting a business. Use the problem-solving process to help interns generate ideas about other ways to go about making a living, so that they understand the range, possibilities, and limitations of their options. Discuss how the economy determines the types of jobs that are available.

Interpersonal Growth: Giving Negative Feedback

WARM-UP/REVIEW

Ask the interns if they have ever had a fight with the boss or problems on the job and discuss the situation. Introduce the idea of negative feedback, and explain its necessity and how to minimize its antagonistic aspects (nobody *likes* to get negative feedback, even when it is appreciated) without sacrificing the value of being direct. Explain that negative feedback can be very valuable and that it can come from caring about someone and how he or she is performing. Negative feedback does not necessarily result from disliking someone else. Say that if another person on the job really wanted the intern to do poorly, the person probably would not give negative feedback that would ultimately help the intern.

Generate situations that interns can use to role-play the skill by asking them for examples of real situations they have faced during the semester. Take the time to get a deep sense of the situation, and walk the interns who will be role-playing through the script even more carefully than usual. The script should be well rehearsed so that the actors can bring real anger to their roles. Using the rating sheets, have observers watch for the following features of a good performance: *Listen* to the person giving the feedback, *apologize* if you were in the wrong, *understand* what is behind the anger if you feel you are not in the wrong, *ask* for suggestions so that the situation does not recur, *ask* if it is okay to tell your side of the story, and *accept* the power differential if it is your boss who is giving the feedback.

Be sure also to explain the difference between appropriate negative feedback and verbal abuse. The workshop, peer support groups, human resource departments, and union advocates are all good resources for helping interns to understand a situation and decide on the best course of action. This lesson is about learning how to accept and give negative feedback appropriately and within the standards and characteristics of a socially healthy workplace.

PRESENTATION

Role-play two different approaches to giving and accepting negative feedback (i.e., one that goes well and one that goes poorly). Make a video that depicts scenarios of a negative feedback situation with varying levels of competence, or purchase published tapes such as ASSET (Hazel, Schumaker, Sherman, & Sheldon-Wildgen, 1981). Ask the interns how they felt viewing each of the situations, and have them identify the positive steps that helped calm the situation.

GUIDED PRACTICE

Have the interns view a transparency of the steps to giving and accepting negative feedback (Appendix 3.10). Refer back to the video to show how these steps are used.

REAL-WORLD APPLICATION

Break the interns into groups of three and give them a situation or have them give you a real-life situation in which they can practice giving and accepting negative feedback. One intern observes and the other two take roles, rotating three times so each intern has an opportunity in each role. The role-playing interns must rate themselves before the observer gives his or her feedback.

Job Search Skills: Mock Interviews

Continue the mock interviews that began last week. Have the interns report on how their job searches are proceeding. Ensure interns are keeping records and making call backs on their job searches using Appendix 3.6.

Send two new interns who have been previously chosen out on a supported job search.

Make sure that resume writing is included in this lesson if interns have not yet completed theirs (see Week 9).

Week 13

Lessons In

☒	Job Skills
☒	Job-Keeping Skills
☒	Job Search Skills
☐	Personal Growth
☒	Interpersonal Growth
☒	Timely Topics

Job Skills: Tasks Imported from the Community Classroom III

Those interns benefiting most from continued practice on their imported task thus far should continue. Other interns who have had specific tasks from the work site identified and transferred to the workshop setting can work on these tasks. Or, if a change in work station has presented the intern with new job duties, new and relevant tasks should be identified and imported. Examples include learning new software and customer service procedures, taking telephone messages, filing, processing forms, performing data entry, preparing recipes, counting and reporting inventory, and learning the local geography. All tasks undertaken during this period should be specific to the internship job or to a potential placement. Some interns may work on job search skills such as filling out applications or investigating college options. This is a good time for a third visit by the transition specialist, who starts assessing postsecondary needs and begins deeper relationships with those interns who are likely to need the most intensive services beyond graduation.

Job-Keeping Skills: Get Along with Others

WARM-UP/REVIEW

Have the interns talk about why it is important to get along with others.

PRESENTATION

Use the *Don't Get Fired!* (Anema & Lefkowitz, 1996) lesson on this topic, assigning interns to read the parts in the script.

GUIDED PRACTICE

Conduct the "Deep Think," "Decision Time," and "Discussion" activities at the end of the lesson. Allow the interns to take the discussion in whichever direction they choose.

REAL-WORLD APPLICATION

During the coming week, have on-site instructors give interns feedback on how they are getting along with others, referring back to the points of the lesson as agreed-upon standards. Note that this lesson fits well with the interpersonal growth lesson for this week.

Job Search Skills: Mock Interviews

Remind the interns to use the job search contact sheets they created in Week 7 (see example in Appendix 3.6) as they conduct their job search. They can bring the contact sheets in to work and meet with their on-site instructors to plan strategies.

Discuss career objectives today. Interns need a realistic picture of their career options and what they may hope to achieve. They need to hear that many people do not figure out what they want to do until at least the age of 30, but that it is therefore all the more crucial that they set a career goal before that time, so that they do not waste the early postsecondary years. If they invest in a job or education, when a serious career goal emerges, they will have the money or education necessary to pursue it. If, on the other hand, they spend the next 10 years "hanging out" and waiting for their career aspirations to surface, then when they are ready to pursue their goals the odds will be seriously stacked against them. Compare this to the situation of a person who has earned a college degree, or at least saved some money to buy the training time; consider the person who has developed a resume of skills that provides entry into the field he or she has finally decided to pursue.

Talk now about what kind of career goal will look best on the resume of a recent high school graduate who may be looking for an entry-level position, looking to grow with a company, looking for experience, looking to combine a college education with a stable employment situation, and so on.

The group should complete the first round of mock job interviews today and begin the second. Provide serious dialogue and feedback to hone the interns' interviewing skills. This is a core activity, and the one that many graduates have appreciated most from the workshop.

Interpersonal Growth: Giving Negative Feedback

See Week 12, and continue working on the "Giving Negative Feedback" exercise. In taking the time to effectively teach this skill, expect only two to five interns to get through a role play each week.

Timely Topics: Job Search Strategies

This is a good time to discuss job search techniques in a fashion that highlights the "consulting" mode in which the program and workshop now operate. In other words, this lecture covers useful tips to help interns be successful in their job searches, and staff will assist to the extent that interns ask for assistance, but the burden has shifted to them (we are moving from "testing" to "consulting") and *they* need to make the decision to use these tips. Give the interns the following speech:

> A good resume can put you on the offensive in a job interview, even (and especially) a walk-in interview, because you control the flow of information, unlike a review of your job application. Make your resume a powerful and persuasive presentation of your strengths, keep it up to date and sharp looking, and always have several copies handy.
>
> Do not forget that Career Ladders is a high-class job. When you are asked about your most recent job or work experience, Career Ladders is it, and it is with a reputable company, that is, the sponsor of your community classroom internship. Refer to Career Ladders as a training experience, an education, *and* a job.
>
> Mock interviews are not a joke, nor are they busywork. As soon as you have your first real job interview, you will be glad you had a chance to practice here. Many of our past interns have told us this. If you go to a real interview and have a problem, bring it back to the workshop and share it with us; we can work on it.
>
> Most people get jobs through a self–family–friend network. You too will probably have to start your search with the people you know who are in a field that interests you. And just because you know them does not mean that you should stop trying to impress them and sell them on your reliability as a good employee.
>
> If you are making a cold call to a business, have a strategy: be well groomed, go at a slow business hour, avoid Mondays and Fridays, get the names of the people who hire and of receptionists, get business cards, get two copies of the application, have your resume and personal data sheet (see Appendix 3.7) ready, find out when to call back, and so on. Of course, do not forget to call back.
>
> Though some people enjoy them, fast-food jobs are typically not desirable starting points for most. Nevertheless, they do provide employment, and they can serve as a decent "bottom rung" on a ladder to better and better paying jobs. Some of you may have management potential.
>
> Keep a job search contact sheet (see Appendix 3.6) up to date with employers' names, times to call back, phone numbers, addresses, and so on. Do not count on your memory.
>
> Consider the advantages of "crab-walking" your way up the career ladder with two part-time jobs,

or of balancing a job with part-time school. If your first job is not the job you want, you will need other irons in the fire.

> Do not give up, and do not be afraid to let us help you.

Week 14

Lessons In

- ☒ Job Skills
- ☒ Job-Keeping Skills
- ☒ Job Search Skills
- ☐ Personal Growth
- ☒ Interpersonal Growth
- ☒ Timely Topics

Job Skills: Tasks Imported from the Community Classroom III

Repeat Week 13 activity.

Job-Keeping Skills: Take Pride in Your Work

WARM-UP/REVIEW

Have the interns talk about why it is important for them to take pride in their work, both for the sake of the employer and for self-esteem and self-respect.

PRESENTATION

Use the *Don't Get Fired!* (Anema & Lefkowitz, 1996) lesson on this topic, assigning interns to read the parts in the script.

GUIDED PRACTICE

Conduct the "Deep Think," "Decision Time," and "Discussion" activities at the end of the *Don't Get Fired!* lesson. Allow the interns to take the discussion in the direction they choose.

REAL-WORLD APPLICATION

During the coming week, the interns should give feedback to the on-site instructors about whether the interns are taking pride in their work, referring back to the points of the lesson. Do the on-site instructors sense that this pride is sincere? If so, they should help the interns rehearse articulating this pride and receiving the good feelings of being praised for accomplishing it.

Job Search Skills: Mock Interviews

To help develop the interns' resumes and job interview skills, discuss the importance of interests and hobbies. They can be mentioned by the interviewee (though not emphasized) in interviews, and can sometimes provide the edge in getting a job (e.g., when an interest or hobby coincides with that of the interviewer, or simply by demonstrating breadth, and therefore the balance and potential of a candidate). Interests and hobbies also can help a person become more socially integrated on the job.

Continue the second round of mock job interviews.

Interpersonal Growth: Giving Negative Feedback

Continue the role-playing activity that began in Week 12.

Timely Topics: Waiting for the Job You Want

As a continuation of last week's discussion, repeat the main points of the lecture, this time using the hypothetical example of a youth who is not going to take a "lousy fast-food job" at minimum wage, but is going to wait for the higher paying and challenging job that suits him. Then present role plays of this person competing for the ideal job, when it does come around, with a peer who *was* working in a fast-food job while the other was waiting. Who is going to get the job? Praise the youth who sets high goals, but develop the concept of having a strategy and reaching goals in steps. It is critical that interns find some productive activity in work or school, and preferably both, that will in time empower them to get the job they want.

Week 15

Lessons In

- ☒ Job Skills
- ☒ Job-Keeping Skills
- ☒ Job Search Skills
- ☐ Personal Growth

- ☒ Interpersonal Growth
- ☒ Timely Topics

Job Skills: Tasks Imported from the Community Classroom III

Repeat Week 13 activity.

Job-Keeping Skills: Don't Talk Back to Your Boss

WARM-UP/REVIEW

Have the interns talk about why it is important not to argue with the boss.

PRESENTATION

Use the *Don't Get Fired!* (Anema & Lefkowitz, 1996) lesson on this topic, assigning interns to read the parts in the script.

GUIDED PRACTICE

Conduct the "Deep Think," "Decision Time," and "Discussion" activities at the end of the lesson. Allow the interns to take the discussion in any direction they choose.

REAL-WORLD APPLICATION

See if the interns can recall instances when they could have argued or did argue with their supervisors. Have them discuss the various consequences of different routes they could have taken. Present situations in which they might want to argue with the boss, and let them articulate what would most likely happen if they did. During the coming week, see if on-site instructors can identify scenarios of potential conflict on the job, and point them out to the interns to heighten their awareness of these incidents and of opportunities to avoid trouble.

Job Search Skills: Mock Interviews

Complete the second round of mock interviews today, and begin the third round. Let interns know that actual employers will come to the workshop and be used as the final exam on interview skills. Have interns who have been going out on job searches report to the group on their successes and frustrations. Reinforce the importance of persistence and the certainty of employment if the interns do persist. Praise highly, and allow the group to praise, any intern who has already achieved an interview or job.

Interpersonal Growth: Accepting Negative Feedback

Present this lesson in learning to *accept* negative feedback as the converse to the one interns have been learning over the last 3 weeks. Now that they have learned to be cool in a situation where they are angry, they can take on the reciprocal skill of being cool when someone else is angry.

As a model, use the same videotapes and the rating sheets found in Appendix 3.10.

Review the principles of social skills training. Ask why it is important to learn this. Demonstrate the skill. Let someone try it. Discuss it with non-judgmental feedback. Provide opportunities to practice it.

Timely Topics: Realities of the Work World

Present the interns with the following eight realities of the work world (Clark, 1979; Clark & Kolstoe, 1990) paraphrased here:

1. Work is still the unstated but real card of citizenship and self-respect in our society (regardless of constitutional rights); the unemployed feel guilt, anxiety, and worthlessness.

2. Work often requires mobility and adaptation to another place.
   a. Travel
   b. Social standards of a workplace: dress, behavior, and so on

3. Paid work is largely impersonal.
   a. Qualities associated with play, recreation, and love are not to be expected on the job.
   b. This may turn off an intern initially, but will avert a later failure.

4. Work has rewards.
   a. Money
   b. Learning skills
   c. Being of service through volunteer work
   d. Opportunity to pursue interests and abilities
   e. Ability to meet and interact with people

f. Avoidance of boredom
g. Increase in self-respect and self-esteem

5. Work is bound by time.
   a. On-task behavior required
   b. Prescribed times for breaks, eating, cleaning up, and so on

6. Work is seldom performed in complete isolation or independence; therefore, one must be able to sustain critical relationships.
   a. Worker to supervisor
   b. Worker to worker
   c. Worker to customer
   d. Worker to subordinate

7. Settings rarely exist in isolation.
   a. They are interdependent (e.g., manufacturer, wholesaler, distributor, retailer).
   b. Interns can learn the importance of all work groups.

8. Not everyone who wants to work can obtain work nor can everyone who obtains work be employed in the work of their choice (and jobs will change over one's life span).
   a. This is presented as a general fact (not just for youth or youth in special circumstances).
   b. Job dissatisfaction is the rule, not the exception.
   c. Career education is a way to confront and cope with job dissatisfaction.

Week 16

Lessons In

☒ Job Skills
☐ Job-Keeping Skills
☒ Job Search Skills
☐ Personal Growth
☒ Interpersonal Growth
☒ Timely Topics

Job Skills: Tasks Imported from the Community Classroom III

Repeat Week 13 activity.

Job Search Skills: Mock Interviews

Interns should be well into the third round of mock interviews. For next week, all interns will have an appointment with a cooperating employer who has agreed to come in and conduct mock interviews. Try to use more than one employer to give the interns a choice of field and to avoid taking undue advantage of the employer's goodwill. Interns should interview with a stranger. Give the cooperating employer copies of Appendix 3.5, Interview Rating Sheet, or another way to provide written feedback to the interviewees.

Review and discuss various intern job searches, giving support and praise to those who have been putting time into it, and providing assistance to those who are working on applications or who request more mock interview practice.

Interpersonal Growth: Accepting Negative Feedback

Repeat Week 15 exercise on this topic.

Timely Topics: What Is Postsecondary Life Like?

Ask all instructional staff to relate stories of their first jobs after high school, of the progression of their careers, and of the progression of the careers of friends and family members whose paths have been particularly interesting. Interns should hear stories of both success and failure. Hopefully, they will be able to apply this information to themselves as their lives continue beyond high school. Other appropriate topics for discussion include moving out of the family home and setting up independent living, going to college, self-monitoring recreation and leisure pursuits, and parenting and raising a family.

If possible, this is a good time to bring in program alumni who have done particularly well and who can discuss their career paths since high school.

Week 17

Lessons In

- ☒ Job Skills
- ☐ Job-Keeping Skills
- ☒ Job Search Skills
- ☐ Personal Growth
- ☒ Interpersonal Growth
- ☒ Timely Topics

Job Skills: Continuing Development

At this point, the interns have derived the maximum benefit possible from the time offered during the workshop to learn new job skills. Today, devote this period to helping interns devise a strategy for continuing the development of the job skills they have been practicing and determining the resources they will use, such as community college, tutorials, self-teaching, or other adult service providers that can offer opportunities to make the interns' skills more marketable. Interns should make relevant inquiries (letters, phone calls, etc.) during class if possible. Every intern should write out a strategy.

Job Search Skills: "Real" Mock Interviews

As mentioned last week, this week each intern interviews with an actual guest employer representing a career of interest to the intern. The interviews are videotaped, and the employer, fellow group members, and you rate the intern's final performance.

Simultaneously to these in-class interviews, other interns are out on prearranged mock or informational interviews with real employers at their place of business. Sometimes these interviews can turn into real jobs. This is the preferred method because having interns go to employers is both more convenient for the employer and more like an actual job interview.

Interpersonal Growth: Accepting Negative Feedback

Continue exercises from Week 15.

Timely Topics: Open Forum

Review the purpose of Career Ladders (i.e., improved postsecondary opportunities, not pleasing the teacher or getting a good grade) and offer to review anything that is requested. If possible, let interns lead their own group discussion on their topic of choice. Encourage them to function as a support group, exchange phone numbers, pass on job tips, and stay in touch with instructors and each other beyond the semester. The workshop has created relationships based on the value of postsecondary success, and thus continuing those relationships should extend that value beyond the life of the workshop.

Week 18

Lessons In

- ☐ Job Skills
- ☒ Job-Keeping Skills
- ☐ Job Search Skills
- ☐ Personal Growth
- ☐ Interpersonal Growth
- ☒ Timely Topics

Job-Keeping Skills: Using an Appointment Calendar

WARM-UP/REVIEW

Ask the interns why a person might want to keep an appointment calendar. What is it used for? After they have given their rationale, add the following information if necessary.

Explain that an appointment calendar is a powerful tool for maintaining a job and developing a career. For maintaining a job, a calendar is a way to help a person remember appointments (e.g., appointments with doctors, Social Security representatives, lawyers), and when work must be missed for such an appointment, the calendar can help the person remember to notify the employer ahead of time. For career development, the calendar is a place to track appointments with career counselors, adult-agency caseworkers, college counselors, and so on. Explain that the interns have already learned that being on time and making appointments are crucial. Calendars can help them do that, and in a world that is so complex, being able to keep a calendar is essential. Instructors can obtain free calendars from companies that use them for promotional purposes.

PRESENTATION/GUIDED PRACTICE

Have the interns do the following:

- Write their name and phone numbers in the appointment calendars

- Find their birthday and mark it

- Find the birthdays of two other interns and mark them

- Mark the day they graduate from high school

- Write in any appointments coming in the near future

- Call or meet with the transition specialist and make an appointment to see him or her before graduation; mark times in the calendar to call and check in with the transition specialist, starting 2 weeks after graduation and continuing every 6 weeks thereafter, until the end of the year

- Set aside and mark three times in the next 2 weeks when they will either explore college (call and make an appointment with a counselor) or engage in a job search (try to make a job interview appointment over the phone or set aside the time to do walking or phone searches)

- Arrange right now a day and time during which they will meet with their on-site instructor the next week for coffee and to review the use of the calendar (this can be during break time on the job)

- Pick a date by which they will reach a goal (e.g., get into college, get a job paying a certain amount) and mark that date in the calendar

REAL-WORLD APPLICATION

During the coming week, interns who did not complete the above practice in class should make the necessary appointments and show the completed work (the calendar itself) to the on-site instructor, who can then help those who are having any problems with it. If today is the last day of the program, the appointment calendars can be checked during the date made with the on-site instructors, or by the transition specialist.

Timely Topics: Making Choices

1. Discuss the basic tenets of evolution, that creatures came out of the ocean and that, in vari-

ous ways, choices were made for them by their ability to cope with the environment. Their adaptability enabled them to survive and turned them into different creatures, from reptiles to rodents to mammals to birds. Distinguish between the external nature of choices that are made for us and the fact that human beings make choices on a more sophisticated level than other beings. Although a person may be born into difficult situations or have to live around risks (like drugs or violence), he or she can still make choices. That is how humans differ from other beings. But like other animals, once a person makes a choice, it becomes a part of him or her.

2. Emphasize that the interns are in the best program of its kind. There are two reasons that it is the best. The first and most important is that the staff and interns are all sitting down together and saying that, yes, it is the best one. The reason so many Career Ladders interns succeed is that they make the choice to do so. They simply affirm that they are going to hold a job, go to college, and so on. The other reason Career Ladders is successful is the staff. Draw an analogy to the wealthy person who has a staff that lines up to serve his or her needs in sequence, such as a maid and butler who dress, groom, and prepare him or her for the day. The Career Ladders concept is similar in that first the referring counselor, then the on-site instructor, help the intern along, each of them under the direction of the program manager. Finally, the transition specialist does the final brushing off of the intern who is dressed in the coat and tails of ennoblement and empowerment. When the interns really make the choice, staff are there to back them up.

3. Though the staff is in fact there to serve the interns, it is not by way of giving out jobs, money, or even skills. Career Ladders staff give them the arsenal—social skills, assistance in navigating adult services, knowledge of what they will need to succeed on a job, on-the-job support—for the struggle to come. When the choice is made and the journey begun, there are still no guarantees. Each intern must face the struggle alone, and each will need to be a pioneer, a warrior, and a hero.

Closing Rituals

The transition specialists should attend today's workshop. They can bring guest speakers, particularly admissions counselors from the community colleges.

Lecture the interns about the emphasis of the program, and leave them with a message—not on jobs, but on literacy. Explain that it is through literacy, once they have established themselves economically, that true growth and empowerment will come. To demonstrate the power of being able to write, have them all write comments giving feedback on the program thus far. Make it clear that these comments will be used to revise the workshop and community classroom for the next cohort of interns. Thus, their ability to write and express themselves is, in this case, powerful.

Explain that the program is not over, that it never ends. They have merely completed the first phase. Explain also that Career Ladders staff are available but will leave them alone if that is their desire; you do want to know how they are doing at least twice a year (see Appendix 4.7, Follow-up Protocol/Questionnaire) but use of services is optional.

Have certificates of completion made out for each intern, and hold a graduation ceremony where you and Career Ladders instructors, along with the sponsoring employers, can show appreciation. This ceremony can have significant value as a rite of passage for many students in which the usual rewards of scholarships, sports, and academic achievements are not at the forefront of the class activities. Interns are officially "passed forward" from the community classroom staff to the transition specialist staff. As the interns receive their certificates, they should recite their name, job title, and job duties. The last person to congratulate them should be the transition specialist, who can set up their first appointments.

APPENDIX 3.1

List of Feelings

HAPPY
gay
convivial
festive
contented
satisfied
serene
comfortable
peaceful
tranquil
joyous
ecstatic
rapturous
transported
enthusiastic
inspired
glad
beatific
pleased
blissful
cheerful
genial
sunny
blithe
lighthearted
buoyant
debonair
bright
free and easy
airy
saucy
jaunty
sprightly
lively
spirited
animated
vivacious
brisk
sparkling
merry
mirthful
hilarious
exhilarated
jovial
jolly
jocular
playful
gleeful
frisky
elated
exultant
jubilant

SAD
sorrowful
downcast
dejected
unhappy
woeful
woebegone
depressed
disconsolate
melancholy
gloomy
cheerless
somber
dismal
heavyhearted
joyless
spiritless
dark
clouded
frowning
lugubrious
funereal
mournful
dreadful
dreary
flat
dull
oppressed
downhearted
in the dumps
sullen
mopey
moody
glum
sulky
discontented
out of sorts
ill at ease
low-spirited
low
discouraged
disheartened
despondent
crestfallen

ANGRY
resentful
irritated
enraged
furious
annoyed
inflamed

provoked
piqued
incensed
infuriated
offended
appalled
wrought up
worked up
indignant
irate
wrathful
cross
bitter
virulent
acrimonious
boiling
fuming
in a stew
up in arms
in a huff

HURT
injured
offended
grieved
distressed
in pain
suffering
afflicted
worried
aching
crushed
victimized
heartbroken
hapless
in despair
agonized
tortured
dolorous
piteous
woeful
rueful
mournful
sad
pathetic
tragic

AFRAID
fearful
frightened
in fear
timid

timorous
chicken
nervous
diffident
fainthearted
tremulous
shaky
apprehensive
fidgety
aghast
terrified
panicked
hysterical
yellow
alarmed
shocked
horrified
insecure
anxious
worried
misgiving
doubtful
suspicious
hesitant
irresolute
awed
dismayed
scared
trembling
quaking
cowardly
threatened
menaced
petrified

INTERESTED
concerned
affected
fascinated
engrossed
intrigued
absorbed
excited
curious
inquisitive
inquiring
nosy
snoopy

FEARLESS
encouraged
courageous

confident
secure
reassured
bold
brave
daring
gallant
heroic
self-reliant
spirited
resolute
stouthearted
enterprising
hardy
determined
audacious
dauntless
certain

DOUBTFUL
unbelieving
skeptical
distrustful
suspicious
dubious
uncertain
questioning
wavering
hesitant
perplexed
indecisive
misgiving

EAGER
keen
earnest
intent
zealous
ardent
agog
avid
anxious
enthusiastic
desirous
fervent
fervid

APPENDIX 3.2

The Paper Chase: One Big Step on the Career Ladder

NA	= You don't need this.
✓	= It's done!
	= You still need to get this in to get paid.

Intern

Intern	Copy of Valid ID	School Application	Applicant Survey	Copy of Social Security Card	Work Permit (If Under 18)	Proof of Negative TB Test	W-4 Form	I-9 Form (Employment Eligibility Verification)			

APPENDIX 3.3
Counselor–Job Seeker Agreement

This agreement is not a legally binding document. Its purpose is to provide a complete understanding by the counselor and the job seeker as to what they can expect of each other and to assure each other that each person has a sincere commitment and intention to carry out his or her responsibilities. The agreement will be read aloud and questions about any part of it should be discussed.

Duties of the Counselor. The principal duty of the counselor (Career Ladders instructor, transition specialist, or anyone else in this role) is to help you obtain a job. All of these services are free. You pay nothing.

The following are specific services of the counselor:

1. To provide you with job interview practice and information on how to answer common questions
2. To provide necessary photocopying service of letters of recommendation, applications, resumes, and other job-seeking material
3. To provide a telephone for your use
4. To provide typing service if necessary for your resume and job-seeking letters
5. To provide you with the specific statements you should make on the telephone when asking about a job and to arrange practice and discussion of these calls
6. To help you write a resume of your job qualifications and make copies of it
7. To store your resume electronically and add it to your electronic portfolio
8. To answer all questions you have on how to improve your job-finding chances
9. To write to other agencies, if you desire, to inform them of your job-seeking efforts

Duties of the Job Seeker. The principal duty of the job seeker is to carry out the counselor's instructions quickly and completely and to consider the job search as a [full-time (for graduates)] job.

The following are specific duties of the job seeker:

1. To attend all scheduled meetings and to be on time
2. To call beforehand if you absolutely cannot attend a meeting so the leader can give you any new job leads that have come up
3. To attend all scheduled interviews on time, and to fill out a job search contact sheet immediately after the interview
4. To be honest with the counselor so she or he can know how to help you solve any special problems
5. To keep a lookout for job leads that may be useful to other clients just as they are for you
6. To continue attending sessions until a job offer is definite

As a counselor, I hereby agree to do everything possible to provide the services listed above.

_____   _____
On-site Instructor   Career Ladders Supervisor

As a job seeker, I hereby agree to do everything possible to perform the activities listed above.

_____
Career Ladders Intern/Job Seeker

APPENDIX 3.4
Typical Job Interview Questions

Tell me about yourself.

What kinds of experience do you have?

Why do you want to work here?

Why should we hire you?

Tell me some of your strengths.

Tell me some of your weaknesses.

What makes a good boss?

What would you like to be doing 1 year from now?

What about 5 years from now?

What hobbies and interests do you have?

What was the worst and best part of your last job?

Why did you quit your last job?

Do you have any questions for us?

APPENDIX 3.5

Interview Rating Sheet

Date _____

Scoring Key:

3 = Excellent

2 = Good

1 = Okay

0 = Needs Improvement

The interviewee:

Was convincing . . . . _____

Was polite and friendly . . . . _____

Looked sharp . . . . _____

Used good English . . . . _____

Had the right kind of experience . . . . _____

Asked good questions . . . . _____

Showed genuine interest in the company . . . . _____

Made a good overall impression . . . . _____

Total Score _____

Scoring Results:

18–24 = Excellent

10–17 = Good

7–9 = Okay

0–6 = Needs Improvement

Person Interviewed _____

Rated By _____

APPENDIX 3.6

Job Search Contact Sheet

Company	Address	Phone Number	Date	Contact Person	Callback Date

APPENDIX 3.7

Personal Data Sheet

First	Middle	Last	
Street	City	State	ZIP Code
Phone Number	Date of Birth	Social Security Number	

Can you type? _____ wpm Can you take dictation? _____ wpm	Software you know:

Have you ever been convicted of a crime? If yes, give date, offense, and penalty of conviction   Yes ☐   No ☐

Driver's License Number:	Circle highest grade completed: 9 10 11 12

Name of High School: _____

City and State: _____ Receive Diploma? _____

List college, business, trade, or other courses below.

Name and location of school	Courses taken	From	To
1.			
2.			

Employment Record: Begin with most recent employment.

Job 1

Employment Dates From: Mo: Yr: To: Mo: Yr:	Employer's Name, Address, and Phone Number
Total Time Employed	Supervisor

Occupation and Description of Job Duties	Salary	Reason for Leaving

Job 2

Employment Dates From: Mo: Yr: To: Mo: Yr:	Employer's Name, Address, and Phone Number
Total Time Employed	Supervisor

Occupation and Description of Job Duties	Salary	Reason for Leaving

Job 3	Employment Dates From: Mo: Yr: To: Mo: Yr:	Employer's Name, Address, and Phone Number	

Total Time Employed	Supervisor

Occupation and Description of Job Duties	Salary	Reason for Leaving

Special Job Skills, Activities, Special Training, Experiences, etc.		
Personal References Name	Address and Phone Number	Position and Years Known

Additional Information

APPENDIX 3.8

Crocodile Creek

Rationale   This activity is designed to develop awareness of personal values and show that values differ from person to person. Further, it is designed to promote acceptance of difference as being neither right nor wrong in itself, just different.

Materials   The Crocodile Creek artwork at the end of this appendix or similar artwork is vital for keeping track of the characters and for voting. The story is too complex to be effectively remembered by most people (adults included). The leader will probably need a chalkboard or some other large surface to keep a tally of opinions. Group members have always been very interested in seeing how the group as a whole voted.

Activity   Pass out artwork page, then read the story to the group. Then follow procedures in "Discussion" section.

Crocodile Creek

Once upon a moment there was a girl by the name of Abigail who was very much in love with a boy named Abner. Now, Abigail lived on the other side of the river from Abner and in order for her to meet with him she would have to cross the bridge.

One morning on her way to see Abner to give him a present that she had spent all of her hard-earned money on and carefully wrapped, she found that the bridge had fallen down during a storm and she could not get across. She was desperate.

While Abigail sat by the water's edge and sobbed pitifully, Sinbad came rowing down the river in his rowboat. "What's the matter, Abigail?" called out Sinbad, and she proceeded to tell him of her problem. She then asked him if he would row her across the river in his boat. "Why, of course," said Sinbad, "but you will have to give me something to make it worth my while. You will have to make love (give that beautiful present) to me." "Why, I can't do that!" said Abigail. "Then I won't take you across!" said Sinbad.

Abigail was so distraught, but just then she saw Ivan, the lumberjack, and told him of her problem and of the proposition made by Sinbad. "I'm sorry, I can't help you. I don't want to get involved," said Ivan and he walked away.

Abigail walked back to the river thinking that she might never see her boyfriend, Abner, again. She then decided that she loved Abner so much that she would have to sacrifice in order to see him and said yes to Sinbad. After Sinbad got what he wanted, he rowed her across the river and said goodbye. Abigail ran to Abner, fell into his arms, gave him a hug and tearfully told her story. When she was done, Abner screamed at her, "How could you do such a thing?" and angrily pushed her away from him while saying that he didn't ever want to see her again. "But I did it for you, because I love you!" cried Abigail. "Get out!" screamed Abner.

As Abigail tearfully walked along the river, feeling lonely and rejected, she ran into her old friend Slug. She told him the whole story and that Abner threw her out. Slug said, "Why, he can't do that to you! We'll see about this!" and angrily stormed down the path toward Abner's house. He knocked down the door and grabbed Abner, yelling at him, "You ungrateful slob. You have broken poor Abigail's heart." And he proceeded to punch and kick Abner senseless. All the while Abigail was standing in the doorway and was just smiling.

Discussion Give the following directions: Using the page in front of you, put the number under each name that describes what you think about each person in the story (the teacher may have to summarize names and roles) using the following scale:

1	2	3	4	5
Worst Person	Bad	Not So Bad	Kind of All Right	Best Person

After the students have finished writing their answers, ask for a show of hands when you ask, "Who picked Abigail for the worst?" Then go down the scale for each character, tallying the scores for each one. Ask each student to say why he or she made certain choices. Point out the similarities of choice (value/morals) as well as the differences. Point out that differences make us unique and that they can also bring about problems with respect to understanding between two people. Because each person's values are unique and different, there is no way of telling who is right or who is wrong. In respecting our differences, everyone becomes right and no one becomes wrong. Point out, also, how we as human beings tend to choose friends according to how similar our values are and this makes us comfortable. Note that those who do not share our same values also choose friends whose values match their own. Neither is right, and neither is wrong.

Note. From *Values Clarification*, by S. B. Simon, L. W. Howe, and H. Kirschenbaum, 1995, New York: Warner. Copyright 1995 by Warner. Reprinted with permission.

ABIGAIL

ABNER

SLUG

Crocodile Creek

IVAN

SINBAD

APPENDIX 3.9
Sample Resumes

May Lincoln
1138-F Gateview Ave., T.I.
San Francisco, CA 94130
(415) 555-5055

OBJECTIVE: To secure a full-time entry-level clerical position

EDUCATION:

2001–2005   Galileo High School, date of graduation: January 2005

2005   Career Ladders Employment Skills Workshop

EXPERIENCE:

2005   Career Ladders: File, type, enter data, collate, deliver documents, and receive customers for the Personnel Department at California State Auto Association, San Francisco.

2004   Tutor and assist students with disabilities at Galileo High School in reading and functional skills (calculator, shopping).

2004   Skateland: give out skates, patrol and monitor skating floor, sweep floors, clean snack bars, train new employees in above skills.

2002–2003   Direct traffic, give information at Pacific Bell Park.

Provide child care, care for family members with illness and back injury, clean house, cook.

RELATED ACTIVITIES/HOBBIES:

Music, dancing, bicycling, singing, baseball, football, and basketball

REFERENCES:

John Hodges
Sr. Personnel Specialist/Recruitment
California State Automobile Association
150 Van deKamp Avenue
San Francisco, CA 94102-5279
(415) 555-2190

Shepherd Siegel
Career Ladders Coordinator
San Francisco State University
San Francisco, CA 94132
(415) 555-1161

James Portman
Guidance Counselor
Galileo High School
1150 Francisco Street
San Francisco, CA 94104
(415) 555-3150

Bill Dogget
2835 Merced Ave.
San Francisco, CA 94133
(415) 555-8674

Age: 18 Yrs.
Birth date: 11-17-87
Birth place: S.F. CA
Social Security #: 677-98-4575

PRESENT SCHOOL:

Francis Scott Key Learning Center
1350 43rd Avenue
San Francisco, Ca 94122

Grade: 12

WORK EXPERIENCE:

DECEMBER 11–21, 2005

Serra Shops
Colman State Book Store
1876 Lincoln Ave.
S.F., CA 94132
(415) 555-4678 Marcia

Summer '05
Mayor's Summer Employment Program
Audobon School - Child Care
350 Clay
S.F., CA 94115 Evelyn

Summer 04 Bill's For Sales
3450 Evans Avenue
S.F., CA
431-6843
Jack and Jonny Ross

Summer 03 S.F. YMCA %
Ingleside Branch
4576 Bookman St.
S.F. CA
555-7890

Michael

Summer 02: Polenti Bates Youth Center
1235 Walker St.
S.F., CA 94133
555-1436   David Washington

REFERENCES:

Lana Hessman - Teacher
F.S.K.L.C.
1350 43rd Avenue San Francisco, Ca 94122

Bonnie Porter
Career Training Center
1325 13th Avenue
S.F. CA 94133
555-7989

APPENDIX 3.10

Social Skills Training Rating Forms

Social Skills Rating Form
Ordering Job Duties

	Trials							
	1		2		3		4	
	yes	no	yes	no	yes	no	yes	no
FACE the person								
WAIT for the question								
BEGIN job duties with the word "I"								
TELL them your job title								
LIST a few of the things you do								
ASK if your answer is complete								

Use professional terminology   1 - - - 2 - - - 3 - - - 4
    poor   good

Eye contact   1 - - - 2 - - - 3 - - - 4
    poor   good

Speech loudness   1 - - - 2 - - - 3 - - - 4
    poor   good

Hands away from face   1 - - - 2 - - - 3 - - - 4
    poor   good

Confident voice tone   1 - - - 2 - - - 3 - - - 4
    poor   good

Straight body posture   1 - - - 2 - - - 3 - - - 4
    poor   good

Full sentences   1 - - - 2 - - - 3 - - - 4
    poor   good

Social Skills Rating Form
Starting a Conversation, Giving Positive Feedback

	Trials							
	1		2		3		4	
	yes	no	yes	no	yes	no	yes	no
FACE the person								
INITIATE the conversation								
RETURN the greeting								
GIVE the feedback								
WAIT for the person to respond								
Make SMALL TALK								
DECIDE if the other person is listening								
Bring up the MAIN TOPIC								

Number of conversational questions

1 - - - 2 - - - 3 - - - 4
poor   good

Number of complimentary comments

1 - - - 2 - - - 3 - - - 4
poor   good

Eye contact

1 - - - 2 - - - 3 - - - 4
poor   good

Personal presence (smiling, enthusiastic, sincere)

1 - - - 2 - - - 3 - - - 4
poor   good

Speech loudness

1 - - - 2 - - - 3 - - - 4
poor   good

Relaxed posture and hands away from face

1 - - - 2 - - - 3 - - - 4
poor   good

Social Skills Rating Form
Giving Negative Feedback

<table>
<tr><th colspan="9" align="center">Trials</th></tr>
<tr><th></th><th colspan="2" align="center">1</th><th colspan="2" align="center">2</th><th colspan="2" align="center">3</th><th colspan="2" align="center">4</th></tr>
<tr><th></th><th>yes</th><th>no</th><th>yes</th><th>no</th><th>yes</th><th>no</th><th>yes</th><th>no</th></tr>
<tr><td>ASK if you can talk for a minute</td><td></td><td></td><td></td><td></td><td></td><td></td><td></td><td></td></tr>
<tr><td>First SAY SOMETHING POSITIVE</td><td></td><td></td><td></td><td></td><td></td><td></td><td></td><td></td></tr>
<tr><td>TELL the person you are concerned</td><td></td><td></td><td></td><td></td><td></td><td></td><td></td><td></td></tr>
<tr><td>TELL how you feel or what was done wrong</td><td></td><td></td><td></td><td></td><td></td><td></td><td></td><td></td></tr>
<tr><td>GIVE the person A REASON for changing</td><td></td><td></td><td></td><td></td><td></td><td></td><td></td><td></td></tr>
<tr><td>ASK if the person UNDERSTOOD</td><td></td><td></td><td></td><td></td><td></td><td></td><td></td><td></td></tr>
<tr><td>(If not, EXPLAIN AGAIN)</td><td></td><td></td><td></td><td></td><td></td><td></td><td></td><td></td></tr>
<tr><td>ASK how the person FEELS</td><td></td><td></td><td></td><td></td><td></td><td></td><td></td><td></td></tr>
<tr><td>GIVE the person SUGGESTIONS for changing</td><td></td><td></td><td></td><td></td><td></td><td></td><td></td><td></td></tr>
<tr><td>THANK the person for listening</td><td></td><td></td><td></td><td></td><td></td><td></td><td></td><td></td></tr>
<tr><td>CHANGE the topic</td><td></td><td></td><td></td><td></td><td></td><td></td><td></td><td></td></tr>
</table>

Do not put down the other person   1 - - - 2 - - - 3 - - - 4
poor   good

Face the person   1 - - - 2 - - - 3 - - - 4
poor   good

Keep a serious facial expression   1 - - - 2 - - - 3 - - - 4
poor   good

Use a serious tone of voice   1 - - - 2 - - - 3 - - - 4
poor   good

Keep posture straight and hands away
from face   1 - - - 2 - - - 3 - - - 4
poor   good

Social Skills Rating Form
Accepting Negative Feedback

	Trials							
	1		**2**		**3**		**4**	
	yes	no	yes	no	yes	no	yes	no
STAY NEAR the person								
LISTEN to the person								
(ASK for clarification)								
If you agree, APOLOGIZE								
SAY you understand								
ASK for suggestions								
If you don't agree, SAY you understand								
ASK permission to tell your side								
TELL your side with facts								
If it is an authority figure, ACCEPT THE FEEDBACK								

Face the person   1 - - - 2 - - - 3 - - - 4
                                             poor   good

Eye contact   1 - - - 2 - - - 3 - - - 4
                                             poor   good

Neutral expression   1 - - - 2 - - - 3 - - - 4
                                             poor   good

Normal voice tone   1 - - - 2 - - - 3 - - - 4
                                             poor   good

Straight posture and hands away from face   1 - - - 2 - - - 3 - - - 4
                                             poor   good

Do not interrupt   1 - - - 2 - - - 3 - - - 4
                                             poor   good

Social Skills Rating Form
Asking for Help or Instructions

Trials

	1		2		3		4	
	yes	no	yes	no	yes	no	yes	no
DECIDE what the problem is								
DECIDE if you want help								
THINK about who to ask								
TELL the person about the problem								
ASK the person to help you								

Eye contact — 1 - - - 2 - - - 3 - - - 4 poor / good

Hands away from face — 1 - - - 2 - - - 3 - - - 4 poor / good

Enthusiastic tone of voice — 1 - - - 2 - - - 3 - - - 4 poor / good

Do not sound frustrated — 1 - - - 2 - - - 3 - - - 4 poor / good

Neutral expression — 1 - - - 2 - - - 3 - - - 4 poor / good

Social Skills Rating Form
Following Instructions

Trials

	1		2		3		4	
	yes	no	yes	no	yes	no	yes	no
LISTEN carefully								
ASK questions if you do not understand								
DECIDE if you want to follow the instructions								
REPEAT the instructions to yourself								
DO what you have been asked to do								

Neutral expression

1 - - - 2 - - - 3 - - - 4
poor   good

Eyes on person or work

1 - - - 2 - - - 3 - - - 4
poor   good

Nod your head when listening

1 - - - 2 - - - 3 - - - 4
poor   good

Say "mm-hmm"

1 - - - 2 - - - 3 - - - 4
poor   good

Hands away from face

1 - - - 2 - - - 3 - - - 4
poor   good

Straight body posture

1 - - - 2 - - - 3 - - - 4
poor   good

Social Skills Rating Form
Giving Instructions

	Trials							
	1		2		3		4	
	yes	no	yes	no	yes	no	yes	no
DECIDE what needs to be done								
LABEL the job or task								
THINK about who could do it								
CHOOSE a person								
ASK what you want done								
EXPLAIN the purpose of the job								
SHOW all the materials								
GIVE INSTRUCTIONS step by step								
(CHANGE or REPEAT instructions if you need to)								
ASK if there are any questions								

Eye contact
1 - - - 2 - - - 3 - - - 4
poor   good

Hands away from face
1 - - - 2 - - - 3 - - - 4
poor   good

Patient tone of voice
1 - - - 2 - - - 3 - - - 4
poor   good

Be willing to repeat
1 - - - 2 - - - 3 - - - 4
poor   good

Speak slowly enough
1 - - - 2 - - - 3 - - - 4
poor   good

Postsecondary Services for Youths in Transition

CHAPTER

Matt Robert and Shepherd Siegel ■

WHAT ARE TRANSITION SERVICES?

A simple and reasonable definition of transition services might be "facilitation of the adjustment from high school to adult life," adult life meaning employment, independent living, college and postsecondary education, leisure pursuits, social life, and exercise of citizenship. While the Career Ladders pilot program at one time or another became involved in all of these aspects, the work focused on employment, independent living, college and postsecondary education, and training. Simple definitions fall short of describing the range and intensity of experiences young people encounter, but there are definable approaches to dealing with the day-to-day problems of managing youth transitions, from the tangible to the intangible, from the bureaucratic to the interpersonal. And these approaches can be adapted to most school programs, often using existing resources.

This chapter will outline some practices that have been developed in Career Ladders programs, starting from a general structural–philosophical outline of what an effective transition program should look like, and proceeding to ways of work-ing with individual students with specific problems. Once the initial structure and its philosophical underpinnings are in place, the methods described can be better implemented. We will illustrate the dynamic between these youths' lives and a flexible and responsive service approach.

The transition specialist is a crucial player in the empowerment of youths and the facilitation of their transitions. In Career Ladders pilot programs, transition specialists were funded by a model demonstration grant from the U.S. Office of Special Education and Rehabilitative Services (OSERS). Though the transition specialist's mission clearly aligns with that of vocational rehabilitation, the role goes beyond that which a typical rehabilitation counselor usually plays, and the transition specialist works with a smaller caseload. Communities can find ways to fund transition specialists through grants, partnerships, and special dispensations.

The key premise that underlies this process is that services are shaped to the lives of the youths served. Effective services and self-directed change in the lives of youths can occur within the context of a trusting relationship between the transition specialist and a youth. Planned, systematic, and data-based behavioral and counseling approaches (e.g., follow-along, self-monitoring, charting, and role playing) can enhance the effectiveness of the

The authors gratefully acknowledge the contributions of Kathy Ackerman, Bob Huven, David Kanetomi, Michele Waxman, Mark Johnson, Suzanne Shaw, Desiree French, Igen Chan, Mary Magee, Joe Barrientos, P. J. Connell, and S. Kofi Avoke, who played a major role in the development of transition specialist services.

115

change, but no change will occur if the transition specialist and youth are not given the opportunity to develop trust and a sincere relationship. This relationship, in essence, helps to create and meliorate the community in which they both interact.

FEATURES OF AN EFFECTIVE TRANSITION PROGRAM

The outline of an effective transition program begins with a description of some of the aspects of a transition-oriented service system that is poised to respond to a broader-than-usual set of behaviors from the youths served. This description traces a tenable path from an emotional and philosophical commitment to youths to a more measurable and systematic description of the services that evolve from that commitment. A team of professionals that was developed by the founders of the Career Ladders program included first one, then another new professional—the transition specialist—was assigned to a group of about 100 youths who had graduated from the Career Ladders community classroom program component (see Chapter 2). The team was not required to work within the constraints of any particular system or framework (e.g., special education, rehabilitation). They were simply instructed to do whatever was necessary to assist the graduates in developing their careers. This section describes the first principles that emerged from early Career Ladders programs.

Team Building

It became obvious early on that effective services required interconnectedness among the staff and clear definitions of roles and responsibilities in the transition process. Regular contact between community classroom staff and transition specialist staff was essential because both staffs were involved in planning transitions, and communication between the staffs before the intern graduated helped form a cohesive team and avoid duplication of efforts or working at cross-purposes. Transition specialist staff were briefed by community classroom staff, who were the most current experts on the interns' situations. Community classroom staff were

also able to assist greatly in getting interns to their first appointments with adult service agencies, and so on. This team-building approach is consistent with models of curriculum-based assessment articulated by Stodden and Ianacone (1981), Stodden and Boone (1987), and Irvin (1988), and facilitates a smooth handoff.

Smooth Handoff

Though this chapter emphasizes an approach that reduces and avoids "handoffs" from one system to another, the Career Ladders model does require this one handoff from the school-based staff to the postsecondary staff (i.e., from the community classroom setting to the world at large with a transition specialist). To counteract the risks of losing an intern during the transition, Career Ladders staff make extra efforts to personalize this process and neutralize intern or graduate inhibitions about working with a new professional. When this process is done correctly, the intern already views the transition specialist as part of the team, and by the time the intern leaves high school (and becomes a Career Ladders graduate), the transition specialist has built a rapport, has a personal history with the graduate, and has some knowledge of the graduate's situation. This initial service delivery overlap encourages further coordination between the schools and community agencies because the transition specialist can serve as liaison.

Coordination of Postsecondary Service Delivery

Once the intern has graduated and developed a pattern of contact with the transition specialist (though continuing relationships with the school-based staff are encouraged), the transition specialist acts as the graduate's personal manager. The transition specialist is a generalist who is an expert at understanding and assessing the availability and quality of other community services, agencies, and employers that might be able to serve the graduate's postsecondary needs. By acting as a case manager or liaison between various agencies, the transition specialist can help prevent mix-ups and misuses of services. This is a broader and more longitudinal replication of the team-building approach initiated in the school-based and handoff phases and is one form of ongoing support.

Ongoing Support

Though all staff work to make their services unnecessary, it is only through consistent follow-up and continuous availability of services (i.e., a case is never closed) that efficient prevention of vocational failure or degeneration can be achieved. The majority of youths served in the community classroom are empowered to develop their careers, but Career Ladders' ability to predict who will need services is not perfect. There are many individuals who would subsist without Career Ladders services but who, as a result of the program, have been able to earn more money, get more postsecondary education and training, and work at more challenging jobs because the ongoing support offered by the transition specialist team helps the graduate develop plans and goals.

Long-Range Planning and Goal Setting

Many youths experience a period of floundering (Wilson, 1987) after high school graduation that can last anywhere from 1 month to 12 years. Often this is a phase of unproductive, illegitimate, or ungrounded activity. The most important aspect of this period is that it does taper off. The transition specialist can make the best of this time period by maintaining a relationship with the graduate so that Career Ladders is poised to be the graduate's first point of contact when he or she does feel ready to go to work or back to school. Also, patterns that emerge during the floundering period can be reworked or redirected into the educational or career potential of the graduate, such as creating artwork, working on cars in an informal setting, programming computers, and so on. By at least meeting with the transition specialist on a regular basis, the graduate can develop the ability to plan and set goals. When the graduate is ready to act, the transition specialist may be critical in "greasing the wheels" to help the youth build and maintain

momentum, empowering the graduate to avert or remove obstacles and consequently move more smoothly in the direction of independence and self-determination.

The next section further elaborates and details the services defined above. They are described in this book by way of introduction, and to demonstrate the possible dynamic capacity when a flexible approach is taken. In our past Career Ladders work, we found that the most important feature of the initial staff behaviors was that instead of committing to a particular theory or methodology, Career Ladders staff tried to listen carefully to what was going on in the lives of Career Ladders graduates. This listening was coupled with a dedication to finding out what would help the graduates succeed; the staff were not limited to prescribed tools and services in their efforts to provide assistance. For example, ongoing support is concept grown from an organic manifestation of this commitment in social services. But rather than simply expecting ongoing availability of services to occur naturally, we now believe that it is a valid programmatic component that can be analyzed, systematized, and learned by newcomers to the position, avoiding our trials and errors and taking advantage of the participant observations of our graduates.

The first principles outlined in the sections above are responses to some of the lessons Career Ladders graduates have taught us; these graduates experience floundering periods. A lack of career development can be only partially explained by a clinically assessable disability or special need. Likewise, socioeconomic status, culture, family problems, and so forth are relevant and sometimes critical factors that can impede graduates' careers. By all means these factors must be considered, respected, and addressed. But there are even more contributing pressures that may appear to be only obliquely related or totally independent. Being young is almost always a primary factor, and it conspires with the other factors to create formidable barriers to success.

For example, graduates often manifest the following characteristics: They want to be on their own and do it themselves; they don't want to be associated with anything that might connect them to a special education or other K–12 background; they often lack motivation, and there is no single explanation for this; they are unrealistic in their immediate aspirations; they really do not know what they want, so they bounce around from job to job or program to program; they have serious and inhibiting fears of failure or success, so they bounce around from job to job or program to program; and they exhibit the behaviors characteristic of "learned helplessness," acquired in school or from family, and function consistently in a helpless fashion.

Continuous exposure to these qualities is what inspired Career Ladders staff to develop a service delivery approach based on team building, smooth handoff, coordination of postsecondary service delivery, ongoing support, and long-range planning and goal setting. The next section describes these services in more detail.

ARTICULATION OF TRANSITION SERVICES

Initial Team Building and the Handoff Phase

We envision a society where community is effectively created through a deinstitutionalization process. Such a society is not going to be built all at once, and best efforts to integrate marginalized youth into the workplace both prevent their further institutionalization by the justice, welfare, or mental health systems and create a momentum within the mainstream to accommodate their differences. In other words, we see the successful transition from school to work as one part of a larger movement to create more enduringly committed and caring relationships among all people who attend school and who go to work.

This chapter proposes a step in that direction. Our proposal is practical and feasible within the current service delivery model, and it necessarily retains some of the current model's protocols. For example, though we have worked to personalize transition services and create ongoing relationships with youths in transition, there is currently no way to avoid having some handoff from one part of the program to another. Fortunately, the program includes just one handoff, from the school-based to the postsecondary staff. Although other programs may participate in the youths'

plans, the transition staff can facilitate any additional interventions.

This section will describe how the handoff phase—where the majority of at-risk youths typically fall through the cracks—can be more effectively and humanely implemented. The first step for the transition specialist is to make contact and begin to form relationships *before* the exiting youths graduate from high school. There are a number of times and places in which the transition specialist can do this. As described in Chapter 2, the family meeting provides an excellent opportunity for the participating families to meet the entire team, including the transition specialist. For those interns who are expected to graduate early or who are planning to enter the workforce or college immediately, the transition specialist will contact their family during the semester, assisting with the necessary paperwork, counseling, problem solving, and so forth. In cases where program funding is driven by a case services agreement (i.e., where there is statistical monitoring of the number of successful case closures), this early contact is critical for getting the youth into the plan, so that work performed by the transition specialist is properly credited. A reformed system might reimburse professionals for other types of services to youths who would not otherwise avail themselves of adult services.

The transition specialist can begin contact and acquaintance with interns at the family meeting and develop it during the community classroom semester by visiting the sites where the interns are working. This develops familiarity; the intern views the transition specialist as part of the team and becomes more comfortable with him or her. This later proves to be crucial, because many exiting youths are averse to going into clinical settings such as a vocational rehabilitation office and exposing themselves to procedures reminiscent of more objectionable special education experiences such as standardized and IQ testing. A relationship with the transition specialist desensitizes interns to adult service providers and gives them the critical knowledge that they have an ally in that system (the transition specialist). Also, by seeing an intern in a work setting, the transition specialist can begin informal assessment of the social and work skills of the intern, can suggest what might be viable career fields for the intern to pursue that are consistent with the intern's career interest and ability, and can anticipate some of the barriers to a satisfactory employment experience.

The goals of desensitization and team identification are further achieved when transition specialists attend some of the employment skills workshop sessions (see Chapter 3). The transition specialists can introduce in a workshop format what adult services are, what transition specialist services are, and how the transition specialist can help, emphasizing the unique approach of Career Ladders. When interns are promised ongoing service beyond graduation, they do not really believe it, probably because 13 years of public education with at least 33 different teachers has taught them differently. Thus this message is crucial, and the ongoing commitment must be verbally reinforced throughout the semester and demonstrated immediately afterward. It can often take more than 2 years of contact before the youth realistically appreciates and understands this long-term commitment.

Early contact with interns also serves a procedural function—and can greatly upgrade the efficiency of the shift from school to postsecondary services. That function is that the paperwork initiating the opening of a case with an adult agency can be completed. The first appointments with that agency's counselor can be made and coordinated with the school-based program (community classroom teacher, school counselor, family, etc.). And contact with other agencies relevant to the adult life of the individual (community colleges, child care services, job training programs) can be initiated with the knowledge and aid of the transition specialist, and thus be better coordinated.

Finally, the first contacts with the interns serve to introduce the concept of transition planning and begin to give substance to that concept. For example, the transition specialist may attend an Individualized Education Plan or Individualized Transition Plan meeting, where expectations of the parents, interns, and various professionals can be explored and compared. Possible postsecondary activities, either work or training or education, should be explored at this meeting. And the assessment process, begun in the first contacts, can be developed by exploring the ecosystem of the youth (Hobbs, 1982). Because the services and the service delivery posture are geared toward success with an emphasis on all the factors that will engender success, this is also a critical opportunity for the transition specialist to clear the intern's way. That is, the transition specialist can identify the stressors in the intern's life and plan to make adjustments and preparations for events that may impede or hinder success. When the intern faces such obstacles, the transition specialist's role expands from one that merely facilitates paperwork processing and access to postsecondary opportunities to one that calls for closer involvement in the life situation of the graduating intern. The transition specialist must draw from a wide-ranging palette of transition services designed to empower the youth to overcome whatever obstacles have emerged. These services are described in the next section.

Transition Services

The transition specialist must be an eclectic provider, one who can generalize from a broad base of experience and expertise and be able to respond appropriately to all the different players involved in the graduate's life as well as to the various situational exigencies that may arise. At any time, a transition specialist could wear any of the following hats:

Job coach	Advocate
Job developer	Ombudsman
Academic tutor	Peer counselor
Career manager	Substance abuse counselor
College counselor	
Rehabilitation counselor	Support group facilitator
Social worker	Social skills trainer
Financial consultant	Sounding board
Crisis intervention counselor	Researcher
Personnel consultant	Systems analyst/consultant
Interagency liaison	Philosopher

The purpose of the preceding list is not to denigrate these occupations by grandiosely claiming that a transition specialist can assume any of these individual perspectives at will, nor is it to minimize the profound impact these occupational roles might have on a young person's life. Any one of these roles could represent a career that is much more than a full-time job on its own, requiring years of professional training and developed expertise. The point is that the transition specialist must wear many different hats at any given moment, and must be flexible and able to respond effectively to a range of situations at any given time.

For example, one morning may find the transition specialist facilitating a confident, high-functioning graduate's job search. The biggest help the transition specialist can be to this young woman is to somewhat passively observe her, coach her, positively reinforce her good instincts, and bolster her confidence. During the afternoon, in contrast, the transition specialist may be working with a young man with multiple disabilities, and struggling to help him procure a computerized communication board that he needs for his new job as a mail messenger in a downtown office.

To successfully respond to the varying agendas of all the different players, including parents, teachers, counselors, administrators, rehabilitation counselors, employers, and so on, a transition specialist must change hats easily and make compromises when it is in the best interest of the intern or graduate. The situations in which a transition specialist brings these talents to bear could range from just helping the graduate get through a hard day at work to addressing a drug problem, from coaching on family issues to developing a long-term career plan.

The following is a sample of the transition services Career Ladders transition specialists employ. A summary of these transition services is provided in Appendix 4.1, and Appendix 4.2 shows a self-tracking chart that allows transition specialists to record the frequency with which they deliver each service. When the transition specialist is using the self-tracking chart in Appendix 4.2, entering information in a database for follow-up, or in other situations where the graduates' confidentiality should be protected, we recommend a coding system. Graduates should be identified by a two- or three-digit number instead of by name. The first digit represents the semester when the intern entered Career Ladders, and the second and third digits represent the specific graduate. So for the third semester offering of the community classroom, the 8th, 9th, 10th, and 11th students would

be coded 38, 39, 310, 311, respectively. Later sections will further discuss the organization of the transition specialist's time.

Follow-Up Contact

The transition specialist conducts routine quarterly follow-up to see how graduates are doing, what their employment status is, if they are in school or are planning to be, and if they feel they could benefit from Career Ladders transition services. This contact may be more or less frequent depending on individual circumstances. Follow-up contact also involves obtaining the graduate's permission to visit his or her job site and to contact his or her present employer (when appropriate), coworkers, or other significant support people in the graduate's social network for more sensitive monitoring and as an intervention-oriented assessment.

Regular follow-up is probably the most effective tool the transition specialist can use to make his or her job more manageable. We found that following up with graduates every 3 to 4 months is most effective because people in urban areas and in this population move frequently and their phone numbers change often. If the transition specialist does not maintain contact regularly, graduates tend to get lost. Maintaining regular contact also results in the following benefits:

1. Graduates will eventually learn the transition specialist's phone number so that even if they lose touch for a while they are more likely to recontact the transition specialist in the future.

2. Graduates who are out of touch but who are friends of other graduates who are in contact are more likely to reconnect with the transition specialist.

3. Activities that accompany follow-up contact can initiate and build a group consciousness among the graduates. For example, newsletters that report on successful graduates or peer support groups can make graduating students see the value of staying in touch.

4. Graduates will perceive the persistence of the transition specialist not as a nuisance but as a commitment that can help build trust.

5. By regularly checking in with graduates, the transition specialist can better monitor

progress and ferret out problems the graduates may be having, make suggestions, or intervene before a problem is beyond remediation.

6. Regular contact allows Career Ladders staff to collect invaluable qualitative and quantitative research data as well as documentation for the program's accountability.

7. Access to more information and convergent patterns of ability and interest can help graduates develop a long-range career plan.

8. Graduates learn to use the transition specialist, an expert they can call upon to develop their network of resources, thus facilitating their progress to independence and richer, more productive lives.

Adult Agency Casework

The transition specialist facilitates referrals; case openings and closures; rehabilitation services; post-employment services; case management and program planning with adult service agencies; and consultation, coordination, and communication with counselors about all Career Ladders clients with active or inactive cases.

Facilitating referrals and case openings to adult service providers may sound simple but dealing with adult agencies can be one of the most difficult experiences a graduate (and a graduate's transition specialist) undergoes. Some graduates have a hard time making appointments and getting to them promptly, and some have a hard time with a particular type of appointment. One can hardly blame them. To get their case opened for most vocational rehabilitation programs, they have to undergo evaluation of their disability, intelligence testing, *and* a medical exam—three of the most uncomfortable experiences for anyone. These are especially stressful for youths who have been special education students; many have already had to endure much more of this type of intrusion than the typical person, child or adult, ever does. So these youths' resistance is entirely understandable and often indomitable. Many youths believe that adult agencies are for drug addicts and ex-convicts.

In trying to facilitate the referral process, transition specialists have found the following things helpful: (a) desensitizing interns to an agency by discussing what it is and listening to what the in-

terns' perceptions of it are; (b) telling interns about the agency's history and who the agency helps (e.g., anyone who might experience significant obstacles to successful employment); and (c) explaining why the interns are different from other adult clientele (e.g., the interns are as yet unfledged in their participation in the adult world and in their emergent career development). Also, staff "sell" the rationale and potential benefits of getting a case opened, particularly the financial aspects. It is much easier to get cases opened while interns are still in school because appointments can more easily be coordinated with parents and counselors. Furthermore, when feasible, students can be sent en masse for any testing and medical exams. Groups of three are usually the most manageable, although some clinics will actually go out and examine students at their school site and can see as many as 20 in a day.

Regular contact between graduates and the transition specialist also facilitates case reopening when former clients again need services, because the transition specialist can provide the agency counselor with the evidence he or she needs to justify the reopening. Because counselors are held strictly accountable and must provide rationale and justification for any plans they make or costs they incur, coordination and consultation in assessment, program planning, and management are crucial. The transition specialist negotiates a middle ground where agency protocol is met and pertinent information is brought together so that more effective action can be taken and appropriate services provided to the graduate. In this way the work of transition specialists and agency counselors are complementary and do not serve cross-purposes. Transition specialists should work as a counselor's right arm, providing the more comprehensive case-management service that the counselors would like to provide but cannot due to time and caseload constraints. Many graduates need that extra time and flexibility to succeed.

Postsecondary Education or Training

Transition specialists provide counseling, referral, liaison, and tutoring services for Career Ladders graduates who would like to go to college or to participate in an occupational training program, youth employment program, or similar activity.

This is another area that needs to be closely monitored by the transition specialist. Many Career Ladders graduates plan to go to school, usually to the local community college, which is open to everyone with or without a high school diploma. Graduates often do not realize, however, that college is not like high school in that they are expected to manage the bureaucracy and organizational pitfalls of these institutions essentially on their own. Many graduates are unaware of special services offered such as career counseling, tutoring, and classroom or curriculum accommodations. Often, graduates take inappropriate classes and flunk out after a few semesters. The transition specialist can help to better coordinate the transition to postsecondary education, setting up and going to appointments with graduates when necessary, and sometimes even tutoring them if they need more than what their school provides. Transition specialists help graduates switch from one institution to another if they are in over their heads and would do better in another setting. They also can help set up a limited-enrollment situation in more than one institution if appropriate (e.g., between different community college campuses) or, if desired, they can help graduates manage their schedule to work part-time and go to school.

The transition specialist also coordinates with the community college district, apprenticeship programs, and other agencies that provide training in specific occupations or skills. Different programs come and go, their scheduling and other requirements may change, and some programs may be more appropriate than others for certain graduates. For these reasons, it is crucial for the transition specialist to make contacts, visit sites, follow up with teachers and counselors, and sometimes even attend classes to see what the programs are like and what they demand of graduates, and to help the graduates understand what to expect. Through the best efforts of Career Ladders transition specialists, Career Ladders graduates enrolled in postsecondary training and college twice as often as a representative national sample, but more than half of the graduates failed to pass their classes (Siegel, Robert, Waxman, & Gaylord-Ross, 1992). Clearly, there is a need for increased services to youths with special needs if they are to benefit from access to higher education.

On-the-Job Training

Transition specialists provide job training and coaching, task analysis, accommodations, and mediations for Career Ladders graduates to aid in the development of specific job skills; they also provide coaching in job retention skills such as attendance and appearance.

As in the community classroom component of Career Ladders, transition specialists learn the graduate's job and go to the work site to help train the graduate or reinforce training. Also, transition specialists may use this time to briefly observe the graduate at different periods during the workday to make an on-the-job assessment, to troubleshoot extant or potential problems, or to see if additional training or reinforcement is necessary. They then can provide accommodations, suggestions for adaptations, checklists for self-monitoring, and so on. In a general sense, transition specialists attempt to further reinforce the skills taught in the employment skills workshop and help the graduates apply them to their own work situation.

Counseling

Transition specialists provide counseling and problem solving with graduates about personal, employment, and education or training issues as they directly affect and pertain to their career concerns.

Transition specialists probably do more of this than any other task; their services extend from crisis intervention to periodic pep talks. Therefore it is crucial for them to have some demonstrated background or ability in counseling. For some graduates, this compassionate listening may be the only service the transition specialist provides. Many graduates are either doing adequately on the job or may be in a situation where it might not be advantageous for a transition specialist to spend time with them on the job (e.g., if the presence of the transition specialist might draw unnecessary negative attention to the graduate). Graduates are also adults and have rights, especially the right to privacy (more than they do in the school-based part of the program), and should be encouraged to have their rights respected.

Often, other issues in the graduates' lives that may have been only briefly addressed in the workshop, if at all, will present themselves significantly, prominently, and progressively as adult life takes hold. The crucial role of transition specialists as counselors develops in discovering these issues. Issues that seemed peripheral before may now directly affect a graduate's job performance or job readiness. For example, a student exhibiting chronic avoidance behaviors may be doing so not because of a learning disability, but because of more pervasive issues caused by being the adult child of an alcoholic. Until the primary issues affecting the graduate are addressed, she or he will continue to fail on the job regardless of the transition specialist's efforts. Once a trusting relationship is built with the graduate, the transition specialist can help the graduate address these personal issues and make referrals to other service providers when appropriate. Ironically, it is often the case that transition specialists do more good for graduates by letting them lose a job and then profit from it by helping the graduates address their root problems and see that they need help. In some cases, this might be the most significant thing a transition specialist will do for a graduate's career development.

Independent Living Skills

Transition specialists provide counseling in basic skills that are not necessarily directly related to job retention, but to enhancing the quality of life, such as completing income tax paperwork, finding an apartment, or getting a driver's license.

The level at which a transition specialist works on independent living skills varies dramatically. For example, transition specialist activities in Career Ladders have ranged from working with one graduate on doing household chores and using the public transit system, to consulting with another on how to start his own business, to helping another arrange for child care.

Resource Referral

When appropriate, transition specialists refer graduates to other service providers and community agencies that could potentially enhance graduates' individual transition capabilities.

Such referral is a direct consequence of counseling. There may be a great number of community-based resources, particularly in urban areas, but they are typically very diffuse and decentral-

ized, which limits their accessibility to graduates. It is therefore essential for the transition specialist to know what resources in the community work well with young people, and to develop trusting and cooperative-minded contacts to whom he or she is comfortable making referrals. The transition specialist can get to know referral sources by visiting them. If it is necessary for the transition specialist to make a referral with minimal background knowledge, he or she should make sure the graduate understands this beforehand and returns with feedback about the person or organization. In this context, the graduate not only is being served, but has joined the service delivery team and has taken on more responsibility, expanding the Career Ladders team's knowledge of other agencies. But be warned: A bad referral can and will damage the delicate trust-building process between transition specialist and graduate.

Social Skills Training

Transition specialists provide problem-solving, role-playing, behavioral modeling, self-monitoring, and other techniques to help graduates work through on-the-job and interpersonal problems and to help them better acclimate to their particular social environment at work or in other situations.

Social skills training may be used as an effective adjunct to counseling for working through on-the-job problems. The skills taught can range from something as basic as learning how to say hello to coworkers in the morning to more complex training such as learning the best way to advocate for oneself in asking for a raise. Young people who need social skills training should be provided with and should themselves provide the rationale for why social skills are important. In many workplaces, graduates are thrust into social environments that are entirely new and foreign to them, are extremely diverse (and rife with intercultural clashes), or contain other employees who are much more deficient in their social and interactional abilities than the graduates. The graduates may perceive work situations differently than their coworkers or boss, and although it may seem awkward or distasteful to graduates, social skills are part of a game they must play if they want to reap the benefits of keeping their particular job. In this way, social skills training can be used as a tool to help graduates learn to set and rank priorities and to put them into perspective.

In some situations the transition specialist works with a graduate on *metasocial skills*, such as the graduate's perception, evaluative capacity, and strategy development in more complex social environments with multiple players or problematic personalities. The need for this training will usually be triggered by some on-the-job interpersonal problem the transition specialist observes or the graduate shares. Based on the transition specialist's and the graduate's knowledge of different personalities at the job, past experiences, and the general tenor of the workplace, they troubleshoot potential problem situations and work on ways to negotiate them. For a good example, see the case study about Gloria later in this chapter.

This training is similar to the social skills training interns receive in the employment skills workshop, but usually it has a narrower focus, either more specific to the graduate's situation at the workplace or tailored to a specific social skill area where the graduate is in need.

Some of the techniques commonly used for social skills training, such as role playing, are easy for the transition specialist to implement because the graduates have already been inured to them in the employment skills workshop and now view them as valuable and viable learning tools.

Ecosystematic Intervention

Ecosystematic intervention is a global intervention technique in which key players in a graduate's social network (e.g., coworkers, supervisors, relatives, counselors, teachers, and friends) are enlisted to assist in the manipulation of parameters that have been collectively identified as areas in need of remediation, and to provide support and bolster the graduate's capability to maneuver in a difficult situation toward an ultimately positive result.

In this technique the transition specialist is trying to mediate the general discord between a graduate and his or her environment. The focus is not on the graduate as the locus of the discord but on the interaction of all the people involved, without whom no problem would exist. The transition specialist uncovers the factors in the relationships between the graduate and these other people that are keyed to the problem behaviors. The tran-

sition specialist then serves as the conduit for communication, brainstorming possible solutions among the parties to mitigate the existing dissonance or resorting to more covert methods of manipulating the environment. For example, a young man may have the basic skills to perform the simple filing job for which he has been hired, but he cannot manage it without constant supervision. An arrangement with the employer and coworkers that accommodates his needs and reduces discord may enable him to keep his job. Another worker may have her career development impeded by overprotective parents; counseling them to let go of their child and to develop other interests may make it more possible for the young person to work. Other examples of ecosystematic intervention are cited elsewhere (Hobbs, 1982; Siegel, 1988; Siegel, Avoke, Paul, Robert, & Gaylord-Ross, 1991).

Job Search

Transition specialists provide job search skills such as counseling, support, supported job searches, help with applications or exams, maintaining resumes, interview skills, job leads, job development, and job placement.

The transition specialist's primary function in this area is to assess each graduate's capability of securing a job. What is the graduate looking for? Does he or she need more experience to get the job applied for? Is there another job that would be easier for the graduate to get that would be a step up the ladder to where he or she wants to be headed? Or does the graduate need more training? The transition specialist should never lose sight of the main objective of the program, which is for graduates to be independent. So if graduates are capable of managing their own job search, the transition specialist should do no more than necessary to get them headed in the right direction, then monitor their progress and reevaluate. Other graduates might need the transition specialist to accompany them for moral support when they are applying for jobs (supported job search).

The transition specialist may need to develop some leads and let the graduate pursue them alone. The job search services provided depend on the individual needs of each graduate. The overriding guideline for the transition specialist is to never do things for graduates that they can do for themselves. Determining how much help a particular graduate needs will often be a judgment call and may involve a certain degree of counseling and trial and error. But the transition specialist should remember that he or she is supposed to be sanding the rungs of the ladder so that graduates can get a better grip, not boosting them up every step of the way.

As an ongoing service, the transition specialist always keeps graduates' resumes on disk and helps them update them as needed; helps them fill out applications when necessary; prepares graduates for interviews (often with role playing and mock interviews); and assists in the pursuit of specialized positions or positions with certain companies or governmental agencies. Such training always focuses on helping graduates know ahead of time what to expect.

Pregraduation Contact

Transition specialists provide any needed transition services to interns before they have graduated from Career Ladders.

There are a few instances in which beginning transition specialist services before graduation is necessary, such as when mild retardation requires extra training time for a youth to prepare for postsecondary life; when a youth who leaves the community classroom early by finding a better job still needs some support; or when a teen parent or other youth more urgently needs adult services to develop employability or a college or postsecondary training plan.

Transition Planning

Transition specialists work with school-based teachers, counselors, adult agency personnel, parents, interns, and others to start developing or implementing Individualized Transition Plans (ITPs) for pregraduates and recent graduates.

This is an important way to get more specificity, realistic goals, and a sense of accountability for what will happen when the student leaves high school. A full discussion of this matter is not within the scope of this book, but suffice it to say that present methods of determining what will happen to graduates upon exiting high school and how they can be prepared are vague and woefully inadequate by almost everyone's standards. The agencies that may play a key role in graduates' postsecondary experience should be represented at these meetings, and students should be able to designate someone to represent their interests and advocate for them if they wish. Transition specialists can informally coordinate with the student, parents, counselors, and other agency professionals who may be involved in transition planning. Appendix 4.3 offers samples of the types of activities a transition specialist might engage in over the course of a week.

INTERAGENCY ARTICULATION

In recent years, whenever people from human service agencies got together to talk about their problems or how they could do things better, the term *interagency coordination* inevitably came up, usually with respect to the relationship between agencies with similar or complementary concerns. The phrase had a ring of hope, of a group identity, of collaboration, collective consciousness, and strength. After a few attempts at coordination, however, the subject would begin to cause furrowed brows and an "I've heard it before" look. One would have thought it was a dirty word. Why does this happen, especially in an era of human services budget cutting, where coordination is practically a fiscal necessity?

There are a number of reasons. An underlying conflict, which is smoothed over and only partially reconciled in this chapter, is the difference between the value systems that drive education and adult agencies (DeStefano & Snauwaert, 1989). Furthermore, most hardened veterans of public service are inured to a life of transient funding, understaffing, high turnover, daily emergencies, statistical requirements, and even competition with other agencies that address the same issues. They know that anyone proposing to undertake an endeavor such as coordination is either just naive or paying lip service in a moment of sublime inspiration and courage that will soon fade. The main reason interagency coordination never seems to work is that it simply takes too much time and energy—time and energy that most people with full-time jobs do not have. To really make a breakthrough takes a persistent effort, not just calling someone on the phone once. It means going out to an agency, meeting the staff, seeing the program, sharing information, and then maintaining ongoing contact. It means *articulation*, not just coordination. One has to be able to see and touch something before one can organize or coordinate it.

The reason Career Ladders has had success in the interagency relationships between the school district and various adult agencies is that even from the program's informal beginnings, it was based on articulation. Transition specialists were housed at an adult agency with a desk and phone near the office of the counselor who was assigned to Career Ladders graduates. The transition specialists were able to sit down and discuss cases with the counselor as needed because they were right there in the office, instead of having to try to reach counselors by phone, which can sometimes take days. The transition specialists learned from employees in the office and had access to materials, so they could learn, understand, and respect the agency's procedural and administrative requirements. They could thus make appropriate referrals and recommendations for their clients without stepping on anybody's toes. And they were able to educate the agency about the graduates, the school district, and other community agencies, and provide an enriched form of assessment and a less diffuse form of direct service delivery. Because of the clarity of the Career Ladders mission, the transition specialists could put the youths first and enable the cooperating agencies to serve them better as well. *Coordination* ceased to be a vacuous term because it was tangibly working to everyone's benefit.

But this took a lot of time, energy, mistakes, and troubleshooting, and it continues to require a special effort. Involved parties must make a commitment to do it, set up a manageable itinerary that meets with everyone's satisfaction, and stick to it. Then when problems, inconsistencies, or incompatibilities arise, the agencies can collaborate to overcome them, rather than use them as fodder to denounce the relationship as unmanageable.

Some of the issues that can impede a successful interagency relationship, and that must be confronted, circumvented, reformed, or otherwise dealt with, are described below. Each community and each interagency relationship must try to re-

solve these issues in their own fashion. Advocates of legislative reform and systems change can take note and plan for procedural changes that will nourish collaborative relationships. But success in these relationships is usually derived from an intense personal commitment at the local level that cannot be legislated.

Conflicting Value Systems and Procedures

An employer's concerns are many, but the most decisive one is profit. On the other hand, school districts and adult service agencies share some concerns, but also have many that conflict. For example, schools operate as an entitlement program (and special education on a zero-reject principle) and are mandated to enroll and educate all citizens of school age. Many adult agencies, however, like vocational rehabilitation or agencies funded by the Workforce Investment Act of 1998, are not entitlement programs and can only serve those who are determined to be eligible. One of these eligibility criteria is the likelihood that clients will benefit from services and retain employment. People are often refused services because their problems have not become serious enough. By staying informed and sensitive, transition specialists can ease, if not resolve, inherent conflicts such as these. These system differences are the most burdensome obstacles for exiting youths.

Partial Solutions

Career Ladders staff have been advocating that assessments be streamlined, so that the final educational assessment of a special education student can be equivalent to the assessments that will open a case at an agency or that will obtain admission and services at a community college. Unfortunately, the systems differ in their qualifying criteria and use different tests to determine eligibility. But why not allow success on a state-mandated 10th-grade exam to function also as an entrance exam to a college? The path of contact between the schools and the adult agency should be well known. School-based staff and community-based staff should know who to contact in the schools as well. School counselors and teachers need to know exactly who qualifies for which services and be able to describe those services accurately to their students.

Interagency agreements are one way to formalize a working relationship and to give the counselors on the front line a green light to devise solutions and fashion the system more sensitively to the needs of the youths. Ideally, such an agreement softens the bureaucratic mold and makes it more responsive to graduates' needs; the responsibility shifts more heavily from the system to the people involved in service delivery. In this instance, the system's demands for successful case closures become a subset of superior and more comprehensive service delivery. If effective services are being provided, then successful case closures will follow naturally.

Strategic Advocacy

The beneficiaries of any advocacy by the transition specialist are always the youths being served. This context requires transition specialists to carefully scrutinize assessments or procedures that may be preventing the youths from receiving services. For example, some agencies that would serve a particular youth might reject him or her because of an unwritten "creaming" policy in which only the most ready clients are served. The transition specialist may be able to effectively intercede. An employer or rehabilitation professional may not consider a particular youth for a job because of assessment data that may not be accurate or that do not reflect the possible enhancement of the youth's ability through a job accommodation or other transition specialist services. The transition specialist, through participant-observer[1] relationships with youths, may be able to present evidence that is contrary to test results and get a youth into a program.

Other situations that have called for strategic thinking and advocacy by the transition specialist include those that require protection of confidentiality, regulation of information to employers or other programs, and openness to the likelihood that a particular youth is disabled only in a school setting. Two examples that called for strategic advocacy follow.

A young man working in a fast-food franchise performed so well that his employer wanted to promote him to a managerial position. However, he had to take a reading test soon after the promotion, and when he failed it, he was terminated. When the skills tested do not pertain to the job requirements, such testing can be considered an act of discrimination.

Another young man held an entry-level job as a mover, lifting and loading furniture. He held the job for over a year, but then sought a job with the post office. However, he could qualify for the post office job only through a Schedule A placement that permitted him to bypass the civil service exam. He could not qualify for Schedule A placement unless his rehabilitation case was reopened. Because he was working full-time and demonstrated no apparent vocational handicap, there was no way his case could be legitimately reopened. If he wanted to try for the post office job, he might have to consider quitting his present job just to qualify. These examples represent systematic constraints that limit youths served by vocational rehabilitation agencies (as one example) to entry-level positions and prevent them from developing a career ladder.

In these cases, the advocacy is called *strategic* because it has to be a well-planned, diplomatic process of bringing information together to arrive at solutions that are in the graduate's best interest. For the sake of current and future clients, it is important for transition specialists to avoid adversarial postures that burn bridges. Unfortunately, strategic advocacy does not always work. For example, no vocational rehabilitation services were easily available to the two graduates described above.

Clearly, this discussion only scratches the surface in describing the conflicts in the service delivery system. Rather than providing a lengthy handbook on how to manipulate the system to provide optimum service, we described only a few of the major conflicts and solutions in the previous

---

[1]*Participant observation* is defined by Edgerton (1967) as "learning about the problems of [individuals] by observing and participating in the lives of such persons and by permitting them to present their own lives in their own words . . . participant-observation [includes] trips to recreational areas, grocery shopping, shopping excursions in department stores, sight-seeing drives, social visits in their homes, invitations to restaurants, participation in housework, financial planning, parties, and visits to the homes of friends and relatives" (pp. 16–17).

section in order to set the stage for what we believe to be a sensible reform of that system. In the next section, we propose a new model, inspired by the work of transition specialists. It calls for changes that would free a well-trained and dedicated corps of transition specialists to develop a new state of the art in social service delivery.

COHORT SERVICE DELIVERY MODEL

In a market economy, the provider offers a product or service and must spend less than the customer to remain in business and make a profit. Through advertising, the provider tries to heighten the temptation to buy the product or use the service by promising virtually anything. In most cases, the provider will cut off service as soon as possible after the money has changed hands. The only reason to provide service beyond the sale is to keep the customer coming back, to develop a regular business relationship for repeat business or to provide guarantees that encourage sales.

This model does not isomorphically transfer to social services, but unfortunately, that has been the conventional approach. The goal of current social services is to serve inexpensively, but ideally to avoid repeat business, which is costly to the government. In rehabilitation services, the typical 60-day case closure is the most salient example of this: There is no incentive for the provider to offer service beyond the documentation of a successful case closure. But the high school diploma or handoff to other adult agencies provides similar examples of the disorganized, decentralized, inappropriate, and irresponsible ways our systems ignore youths with special needs. Furthermore, well-meaning professionals are prevented and even discouraged from delivering quality service because of the market-based quota systems imposed on their roles. In the long run, such market-oriented policies are more costly because they do not last long enough to truly empower people to take care of themselves. Good social service professionals are on the run because the constraints of their quotas prevent them from developing quality relationships with the people they serve, and they quickly burn out because they are prevented from sharing in whatever successes occur; they are com-

pelled by their job descriptions to continually deal with the situations in which services are not working. In other words, the social service deliverer in the current system can be characterized as someone who is putting out fires rather than tending blossoms.

Good social service professionals operating in an improved systems environment will be less likely to leave their jobs for the private sector when the naturally occurring rewards of empowering disenfranchised individuals are allowed to be felt. A new model is needed that can deliver on its promises accountably and inexpensively, but that is based on authentic and ongoing human relationships, not a commodity exchange, and is not driven by a quota-oriented fiscal policy. One solution that will ultimately bring value and reward to social service occupations is what we are calling the *cohort service delivery model*.

The concept of cohort service delivery is simple, and it is one we believe has potential for improving social services, ultimately reducing the costs of and need for safety-net programs like Aid to Families with Dependent Children and shelters for the homeless. In a best-case scenario, this model improves the quality of life for clients and all the people involved with them.

First, we describe the current mode of service delivery (and the typical consumer–merchant relationship) as one based on an "in–out box" paradigm. Concern for the condition and outcomes of a consumer is time limited. This means that services are delivered as long as the case is open, that is, the criteria for closing the case have not yet been met, and the likelihood of meeting those criteria is high (in the same way that the merchant delivers services or goods as long as the likelihood of payment is high). The criteria for closing a case are based on some approximation that is thought to indicate an improved quality of life (e.g., high school proficiency exam, 60 or more consecutive days of stable employment, earnings beyond a certain level). In some contexts, such as specific skills training, medical treatment, or certain specific accommodations, this arrangement is efficient and allows a professional to serve a large number of people with some effectiveness. However, in the instances of at-risk youths leaving the public school system, or certain other at-risk populations seeking to enter or reenter mainstream society, such an approach simply will not work.

As is often the case, individuals with the most severe disabilities have led the way by inspiring professionals to develop state-of-the-art services that would later have implications for other special groups. Developers of supported employment for people with profound and multiple disabilities were the first to realize that some of their clients could need lifelong support to retain jobs. Philosophies emanating from the University of Wisconsin, the University of Kansas, Virginia Commonwealth University, San Francisco State University, and the University of California–San Diego in the 1980s were notable in their powerful commitment to this population. If part of one provider's job was to continue to facilitate accommodations for an individual, then so be it. Economic arguments (which can be made) aside, it was believed to be the right thing to do. In fact, this way of thinking can be viewed as only a slightly unconventional extension of the existing interdependence of jobs in the work world.

Career Ladders took its cue from this model. Although the students with so-called mild disabilities we served appeared "normal," they presented a complex and infinitely varying array of problems and explanations for career failure. In short, they demonstrated a need, if not for continuous services, then for continuously *available* services. Measures of success for this group were not easily quantified, and the problems inhibiting career adjustment fell beyond the domains of a conventional in–out box service deliverer's job description.

We have discovered, through our ongoing contact with and availability to Career Ladders graduates, a new way of conceptualizing social service delivery. In place of the in–out box service delivery system, we propose the cohort approach.

In a cohort service delivery system, a transition specialist or other social service professional serves a semifinite number of youths who come under a particular descriptor, for example, every student to leave school A's resource specialist programs over a 6-year period, or every youth released from institution B over a 1-year period, or every teen parent who is served by community agency C over a 2-year period, depending on what the optimal maximum load is.

It is the transition specialist's job to maintain a minimum of three contacts per year with all members of the assigned cohort, and to make services available as needs arise. As far as we know now, the commitment should be ongoing, but it is possible that the need for services will taper off for many over a period of time, say 5 years. Without risking a return to an in–out box approach, a transition specialist could gradually take on new graduates over time.

What, then, is the function of the transition specialist beyond contact? The array of possible services was described previously in the "Articulation of Transition Services" section, but we wish to emphasize here that the function is often that of a generalist, and it is certainly appropriate for a transition specialist to make referrals to other organizations or agencies. However, as the graduates' personal manager, the transition specialist is still obligated to see that the referred services are appropriate, of high quality, delivered, and consumed, and that they realistically fit into the career plans of the graduates. So no matter how many agencies or programs a youth interacts with, the transition specialist who first was designated to serve that youth remains the primary responsible party. Ethically, we believe that this is the most responsible way to deliver services. Practically, we believe it to be more efficient, cost-effective, and compassionate to offer an at-risk youth the expertise and guidance of someone whose job it is to know what services, jobs, educational opportunities, and other activities are available in the community and who can provide appropriate counseling. We call the practical operations of delivering this style of service *continuous cyclical triage*; it develops logically from an initial commitment to ongoing support, which is described in the next section.

Ongoing Support

As mentioned before, in ongoing support a case is never closed; the window of service delivery for a particular graduate through Career Ladders is always open. More and more adult service agencies are waking up to the value of this approach in that they either adopt the method or identify and fill these gaps in service delivery through partnerships. Most agencies cannot currently provide this kind of service because their funding is driven by the number of people served successfully and those numbers are generated by opening and subsequently closing cases. A person's career plans may take many months, sometimes years, of development, but once that person is successfully on the job, his or her case is usually closed after 60 days. One may argue that it is always possible to get a case reopened if necessary, but in some cases the client may no longer be eligible. Clients also cannot go back to get help with a career change just because they are unhappy with their job. Such a request must be justified by their having problems or barriers on the job as a result of a disability. We have found that an overriding problem with this population (i.e., young people) is that, for various reasons, they do not go back and have their cases reopened. It has been our experience in Career Ladders, however, that if the transition specialist is in touch with graduates, he or she can prompt them to have their cases reopened when appropriate. This is part of ongoing support: not just being available, but prompting graduates to avail themselves of services.

Given a cohort service delivery model, how can an agency with only one or two transition specialists possibly provide continuous availability of service at any given time to a group that increases every semester? The answer is that it cannot, at least not in the sense that a staff can work with everyone continuously from the moment they graduate. Some graduates will be more self-sufficient, some will have nothing to do with the agency, some will move, some will become parents, some will continue to pursue a higher education, some will be satisfied with the jobs they secured right out of high school, and the rest should need only periodic support if the community classroom training and employment skills workshop have been implemented effectively. The problems of ongoing support are those of resource management, the primary resource being the transition specialist's time, and of developing reasonable methods of managing the allocation of this time among all the graduates. It is also important to remember that follow-up contact actually makes the transition specialist's job easier in this respect. When follow-up is maintained throughout the floundering period, it has the short-term effect of keeping the graduate on track because problems are avoided or remediated as they arise. This can actually free the transition specialist's time (e.g., helping a graduate stay on a job through ongoing support is more time- and cost-effective than helping the graduate develop a new job every time he or she loses one).

In the long term, such contact helps graduates develop and maintain some direction in their life that will carry them beyond the floundering period. Through success that diminishes or eliminates the need to use other social service agencies later in life, they will be less of a burden on public resources. Most graduates who have less-than-severe impairments should be skilled and independent enough to negotiate their own career development by age 23 or 24.

Continuous Cyclical Triage

The following is a method developed in the Career Ladders program for effectively managing the cohort of graduates and the allocation of the transition specialist's time. First, we borrowed some terminology, the notion of *triage*, which is generally associated with emergency medicine. The word *triage* means, very simply, to sort or cull. For example, in the medical model, the doctor or nurse performing triage in a busy emergency room has to determine who is in the greatest medical need and, consequently, in what order the patients should be seen by the physician on duty. One person may have a minor problem and could go home and see his or her personal doctor the following day. Another might have a potentially life-threatening head injury, while yet another is experiencing a heart attack and requires immediate attention. In a military emergency medical team used in combat situations, the person in charge of triage might have a much graver responsibility over patients' lives. If a particularly large group of wounded came in and taxed the unit to its capacity, triage personnel might need to determine not only who is in the greatest medical need, but who of the most critically wounded has the most reasonable expectation of surviving surgery. In using the above examples as analogy, it is crucial for transition specialists to make such determinations intelligently in their own version of triage, that is, (a) who is in the greatest need of services, and (b) of those in need, who seems to command the greatest expectation of success if the transition specialists intervene. If the transition specialists are overwhelmed by the service need at any particular time, they might have to add the additional criterion of temporarily limiting their service only to those who are actually availing themselves of it. A transition specialist cannot try to drum up business if she or he is already overextended, especially if graduates are not following through on their appointments. Other reasons for prioritizing graduates might be to deal with people who have outstanding cases with an agency or those who have most recently graduated.

Typically, human services agencies in this domain do not have a version of triage that corresponds to the model described above. Once eligibility has been determined, services are rendered. Once the agency has reached the maximum number of open cases, the remaining people go on a waiting list, regardless of their relative need.

Another characteristic that differentiates both this and the medical triage model from the one used in Career Ladders is that if providers and their administrators (who are actually policymakers) are not committed to follow-up, monitoring, or ongoing support, triage is only an expediency of the in–out service model. Eligibility or need is determined (triage); treatment, training, or other services are delivered; and the person goes back out on the street. In many job training programs, a clock starts ticking the moment clients enter, and if they have not been placed in a job by the end of the program's time period, they are out of luck. For those with learning and other mild disabilities, for example, this is particularly problematic because they typically need extra time or repetitions before they understand a procedure or concept.

Because Career Ladders employs a model that incorporates ongoing support, triage is handled quite differently. It becomes more dynamic in relation to time and the changing status of graduates. It also becomes an indispensable tool to help transition specialists allocate resources. There is never any maximum number of active cases allowed at a given time as in time-limited programs.

In Career Ladders, the first step in the triage process is to establish three somewhat gross categories to assign to graduates. We use numerical designations of 1, 2, and 3 to represent each graduate's status in terms of potential need and consequently the level of labor-intensiveness this would indicate to the transition specialist. This taxonomy is done with the realizations that it is imperfect and not a substitute for more comprehensive assessment measures, that many graduates might

fall into gray areas, and that virtually all graduates would change status over time. Thus it is not a means of labeling individuals, but a method for managing time and service deployment for best results.

Those designated as 1s were considered relatively competent, highly motivated graduates, who continually exhibited good job responsibility behaviors. Services they might require were predicted to be minimal (this was not always the case) and would include things such as maintaining resumes, providing job leads, assisting and advising in career changes and postsecondary education, certifying for special programs, and counseling. The 1s were graduates who would probably do fine on their own and could conduct their own job search. We could assist them in enhancing their career potential, upgrading their abilities, and so forth. Though their needs for survival were not dire, we believe that in many of these cases we played a significant role in their climb up the career ladder into better paying and more challenging jobs.

Those designated as 2s usually had problems that held them back a little more. Whether their problem was social–behavioral competence on the job or task-related competence, they needed more guidance and support. These youths were also motivated, but might need remediation in certain areas.

Those designated as 3s usually had some fairly intractable problems. They were severely limited in either their job skills, social skills, or job responsibility skills; they lacked motivation; or they demonstrated various combinations of these characteristics. The individuals in this group could range from highly functioning young people with underlying emotional and behavioral problems to youths with mild retardation who perhaps should have been eligible for supported employment services through regional centers, but who were denied. Individuals in this group often represented a significant time investment on the part of the transition specialist.

A further distinction useful for triage was determining the level of short-term need and long-term need. The above-mentioned categories would typically be used to characterize the level of long-term need, taking into account such issues as degree of self-sufficiency, patterns of behavior, and severity of disability. On the other hand, the short-term level of need might address the temporal exigency of a particular service (e.g., referral to mental health services, application assistance, or certification of other paperwork needed for a special program). Short-term level of need could be illustrated by analogy to the coding system used in the dispatch of emergency vehicles. Code 1 usually means to stack the call, indicating that it is not an emergency; Code 2 means that the call is an emergency and should be attended to as quickly as possible; Code 3 indicates that it is a life-threatening emergency requiring immediate response and all due haste; and Code 4 means that the situation is under control and no further assistance is necessary. For perspicuity and simplicity's sake, we reduced these categories to three, indicating an increasing level of need from lowest to highest.

As a result, a graduate would receive a two-digit designation, the first digit, or *urgency index*, denoted short-term level of need (i.e., what level of service would be immediately delivered). The second digit, or *severity index*, denoted long-term level of need (i.e., the assessment of the overall situation). A young man who is a long-term 3 (severity index) but who is currently refusing service (Code 2 urgency index) might receive a 23 designation; a long-term (severity) 1 who has a great job lead but needs her resume updated immediately and is unable to do it alone (3 urgency) might receive a 31 designation; a graduate who is in jail (3 for severity) but about whom the staff can do nothing until his release date is closer (urgency index of 1) might receive a 13 designation.

After training many teams of transition staff, we realized that the two-digit numeral system can be confusing. We have found color coding to be useful in clarification. Many people find color coding with highlighter pens a more compelling method for conveying the urgency index (red = Code 3; yellow = Code 2; green = Code 1). One quick look at a planning sheet using this method can be very informative, especially if a supervisor suspects one transition specialist may be overwhelmed with high-urgency index cases. Some transition staff have found alphanumeric designations to work better for them: numbers for the urgency index and letters for severity (e.g., A, B, C like the grades or X, Y, Z to avoid the similarity to grades). One rule that helps users generally avoid confusion is making sure the directionality (e.g.,

left to right with letters and numbers) corresponds isomorphically to the change in intensity (e.g., higher or lower).

See Appendix 4.4 for a simple Triage Chart into which a transition specialist can place the names of the Career Ladders graduates being served. Of course, as graduates' lives develop and their circumstances change, so will their designation.

Regular staff meetings were held biweekly where these designations would be debated and assigned. The cohort was divided for even distribution considering the time constraints of the different categories and to make sure that graduates were matched with the transition specialist who was qualitatively most appropriate for their situation. For example, the transition specialist might be of the same sex, linguistic background, or ethnicity as the graduate, or might have a background in dealing effectively with a particular graduate in the past. These concerns were incorporated into the triage process.

At each staff meeting, the transition specialists bring a Career Ladders Job Placement Record for each graduate who has less than a year of stability (see Appendix 4.5) to expedite the meeting and to effectively brief the other members of the team on the current status of different graduates. Using the staff meeting to briefly acquaint all team members with the current history of each graduate serves several purposes: It encourages joint brainstorming and problem solving; it alerts team members and managers if a particular transition specialist is becoming overwhelmed; and it allows the transition specialists to coordinate efforts. If one transition specialist is having a particularly difficult time working with a graduate or having interpersonal differences, or if it is just mutually determined that another transition specialist might be a better match, the meeting facilitates the exchange of responsibility. A form referred to as the Quick Progress Planning and Assessment Sheet (see Appendix 4.6) consists of a list of all the graduates in the cohort and has columns for follow-up (if it is needed and by when), transition specialist (who is the responsible party), and priority (Is this person a priority for follow-up or some other need?), with an additional column for comments about what the graduate is doing or may require in the way of transition services.

Unfortunately, until ongoing follow-up is more widely practiced, transition specialists will have caseloads that are too large to continually manage. They must invoke the concept of triage and sort their group according to the criteria described above, and they must learn to cluster groups of graduates according to their individual circumstances. Transition specialists want to make sure that the graduates most in need are served in addition to the largest number of graduates possible. Therefore the needs of the graduates in different areas should be evaluated, including their triage designation and the amount of time they will require; a schedule should be organized (usually week by week) that is synchronized to graduates' activities. Geographic proximity of different job placements can play into this determination and should also be considered (as it is for community classroom site selection for interns). To keep the whole project manageable, it is crucial to have regular meetings to facilitate the triage process at periodic intervals and on a continuous basis, so the team is always apprised of the status of the cohort and able to respond. Hence the term *continuous cyclical triage*, that is, triage performed at regular, periodic intervals on an ongoing or continuous basis, is appropriate. It may seem to be a redundant process, but we have found this intensified attention paid to the semifinite cohort to be effective.

The whole idea of providing ongoing support and continuous availability of service for an indeterminate number of graduates can be conceptually overwhelming. In this next section we will try to explicate that complexity because it is a main feature of the transition specialist job.

The obvious but unavoidable fact is that the transition specialist only has a finite amount of time available in a given week. The entire cohort is thus not really being served all at once, but rather in manageable clusters of graduates. A cluster might significantly change in a period of a month, or even a week, but there will always be the same number of hours to allocate per week to the transition specialist's cohort. Each transition specialist has a finite number of hours to expend to youths categorized as 1, 2, or 3, as discussed previously. These designations represent the amount of time a transition specialist will be able to devote to graduates at a particular moment. So each transition specialist will have perhaps three to six 3s, twice as many 2s, and a substantial number of 1s.

This triage process marries time management to compassionate and effective case management.

It is a tool that the transition specialist can use to decide how to allocate his or her hours.

However cold it may sound, the reality is that it will frequently be necessary for the transition specialist to determine which graduates are going to be put on hold for the time being. These will generally be the graduates at either end of the triage spectrum. They may be the high-functioning 1s, who are capable of conducting their own job search with minimal suggestions and direction on the part of the transition specialist. They may be high-functioning 1s who want to make a change toward job advancement even though they already have a job that is stable. These students may actually benefit from a transition specialist who will watch from a distance, providing access to support on an as-needed basis, but applauding the graduate's independent efforts. On the other end of the spectrum, the transition specialist may decide to put on hold the intractable 3s who are not ready for a job, refuse to make appointments, and generally are at a point where they just drain the program and the transition specialist's time.

There has to be some reasonable expectation of success to make the time commitment a 3 usually demands. Again, this is not to say that these youths whose situations warrant the designation of 3, who are probably the most at risk, should be abandoned. One of the luxuries of having ongoing support and follow-up is that the transition specialist can stay in contact with them and come back to them when they are in a position to be more receptive to the transition specialist's efforts. This also gives the youths time to see that the program's commitment is real and that someone really has been calling to check on them and see how they are doing, as was promised when they were in high school. If the program is working well, there will be many periods where the transition specialist's time will free up enough to work with this group, or to spend more time with the more self-sufficient graduates. The other graduates who typically will be put on hold include those who, at least for the time being, do not want to associate with the program, such as single parents with infant children who go on a self-imposed hiatus from the program. Finally, the transition specialist cannot work with people who are unreachable (which means that reasonable efforts to contact them have been unsuccessful). But the crucial qualitative difference between the cohort model and conventional social service delivery is that no one is ever forgotten or completely neglected by the system; no case is ever closed.

When a new group of interns graduates, this enlarges the cohort for which the transition specialist is responsible. While the transition specialist's focus will switch to the new graduates, there will still be members of older groups who return to the program with a renewed interest or need for services. Once the size of the cohort reaches the point where it is not feasible or physically possible for the transition specialist team to provide necessary services for the high-urgency 3s and the potentially successful students with severity ratings of 2 or 3, that particular transition specialist team has reached the capacity of graduates who can be served. Either the existing team must be expanded or new teams must be generated to be able to continue serving all the existing groups effectively.

Figure 4.1 illustrates the typical fragmented and depersonalized approach to social services whereby a youth moves from agency to agency. When a needed social service can be handled within discrete boundaries, like a visit to a medical specialist or getting a driver's license, this approach is both efficient and cost-effective. But when the social services are intended to coach and shepherd a young person through a perilous adolescence, through high school exit and on to college, work, family and adult life, then the cohort approach, where the transition specialist moves with the individual through time, is clearly superior.

MANAGEMENT ISSUES
Staff Self-Management

The question of how many transition specialists are necessary to make a cohort service delivery system like Career Ladders run effectively is difficult to answer. It depends on a number of variables, including the characteristics of the cohort, the apparent permanence of its success, idiosyncrasies of the geographic area (e.g., major industries, services available, public transit), and other intangibles such as the capability and commitment of a particular transition specialist to manage a particular caseload. However, there are certain aspects of the po-

sition that should remain relevant across situations, cities, and school districts.

In our experience, as the cohort approach developed, we hired one transition specialist. After a full year in which only one transition specialist served the cohort, it became obvious that two transition specialists could serve 100 graduates better than one could serve 50. One important reason is that this arrangement allows the two sexes to be represented, which can make it much easier for the transition specialists to deal with certain subjects that might be harder to broach for someone of the opposite sex, such as birth control, parenthood, or hygiene and grooming. Another advantage is that graduates are exposed to a positive role model of the same sex. Many graduates come from backgrounds where they may never have had a positive role model of the same sex as they were developing, growing up, becoming socialized, and being educated. A similar argument can be made for having a transition team that does not just respect the varied cultural backgrounds of the graduates being served, but adequately reflects them.

Two well-matched transition specialists bring different strengths and weaknesses to the work and can thus develop complementary styles that enable them to respond more effectively to a broader range of circumstances. Everyone has stylistic differences, individual biases, talents, preferred counseling strategies, and so on. If one transition specialist's style is more suited to a certain graduate for some reason, it might be the crucial factor that engenders the graduate's acceptance of the transition specialist and consequently the graduate's ultimate success. For example, one transition specialist may be good at getting to know the student, building rapport, and identifying personal stressors that may be affecting the student's success, but may have a hard time developing a plan based on this information and getting the graduate to stick to it. Conversely, the other transition specialist may be highly skilled at the needed intervention skill and can work with the first transition specialist to provide more sensitive and comprehensive service.

This diversity in personality combined with frequent meetings easily allows the transition specialists to cover for each other in the event of scheduling conflicts, to switch assignment of a graduate from one transition specialist to the other if it seems that it may be a better match, or to

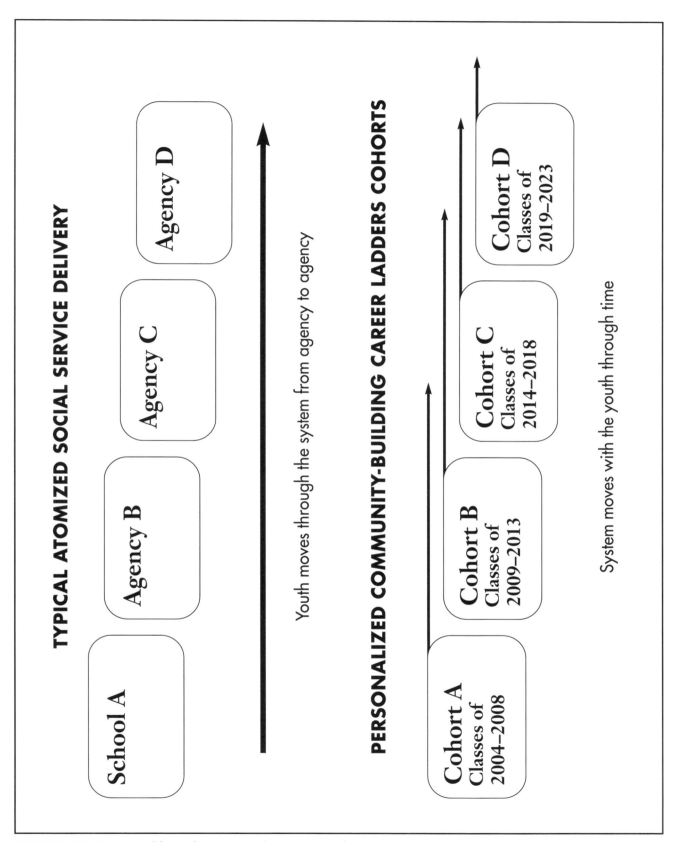

FIGURE 4.1. Career Ladders cohort approach to postsecondary services.

effectively combine efforts to cocounsel one graduate. This last approach can foster the feeling of a team effort, especially for the graduate. It also serves to minimize the typical institutional, client–service provider dichotomy that presents its own problems in this population.

It is also advantageous for transition specialists to have a peer involved in similar activities with similar concerns. We think that this is especially important considering the implicit demands of the job and the fact that the job takes the transition specialist into the field much of the time. This job is almost entirely performed in isolation; the transition specialists are facing a challenging and exclusionary mainstream by themselves. It is important for them to have someone with whom they can share experiences, brainstorm, and develop support systems. Otherwise, they will be much more prone to burnout.

Time Management

Another crucial area that must be addressed in the role of transition specialist is that of time management. Considering the demands placed on transition specialists by the various as-needed services they provide, combined with the programmatic component of ongoing commitment, their hands are more than full. They must get time management down to an art or the demands of the job will take on a life of their own, gain control, and dictate the allocation of time. This can be the genesis of transition specialist burnout.

One method that helps is the clustering approach, working with groups of graduates as described above. This idea can be generalized to help organize time by clustering not only the graduates, but the requisite, ancillary activities their success may hinge upon, such as follow-up, job development, outreach, and interagency articulation. But even with the most masterful organizational skills, the crucial factor in the transition specialist's scheduling technique is flexibility. A person who needs the structure of a 9-to-5 workday will have a hard time as a transition specialist. A number of activities have to be accomplished that make working at odd hours necessary. Many graduates are unreachable during the day because they are working or out of the house; many have

jobs on the weekend or strange shifts. It is also important for the program itself to have a mechanism for dealing with the fluctuating hours of a transition specialist, including issues such as the mode of pay (e.g., salaried, hourly) and compensation for overtime, and scheduling alternatives such as flextime or compensatory time. The necessary flexibility of transition specialists in accommodating other people's schedules should be reflected in the program's personnel and payroll management to protect the interests of the transition specialists as well as their accountability.

Another issue that must be considered in managing time for the transition specialist is travel time. Transition specialists are always on the move and may spend up to 2 hours a day getting from place to place, not including their travel time to and from the office. This can be very costly, especially in a city. Some cities have efficient mass transit systems available, as in the San Francisco area. There, Career Ladders transition specialists rely almost exclusively on public transportation. Using this mode of transportation has advantages. For example, the whole problem of parking, traffic, car maintenance, and keeping track of these costs is obviated by simply buying monthly transportation passes. It also forces transition specialists to become familiar with public transportation so they can give directions to graduates or instruct them in its use. Another potentially catastrophic problem public transportation circumvents is the issue of liability if a transition specialist were to drive a graduate in his or her personal vehicle and an accident occurred. Another potential benefit that may not seem as compelling is that it forces the transition specialist to be more organized in arranging visits for the day; it also allows travel time to be used for reading, paperwork, or other incidentals relevant to the job, instead of attending to driving.

Finally, the chart in Appendix 4.7 illustrates graphically how transition specialists distribute their time during a typical week. The hours shown are longer than a normal 40-hour work week because it is a composite week, intended to describe a range of activities and variation of hours. However, it should be noted that sometimes a transition specialist may have to put in a 10- or 12-hour day if the need arises, and, as mentioned before, arrangements need to be made to adequately compensate him or her in this situation.

JOB DEVELOPMENT

A number of excellent materials on job development already exist, and so the process will not be explicated beyond what is offered in Chapter 5. We particularly like Denise Bissonnette's *Beyond Traditional Job Development: The Art of Creating Opportunity* (1994). The process of teaching interns to conduct their own job search was explained in Chapter 2 and relevant lesson plans were described in Chapter 3. Youths must be taught to conduct their own job searches in every possible instance. However, there is still a place and a need for the transition specialist to develop jobs.

In the process of following up on a graduate, the transition specialist can be a catalyst for re-creating the community that takes care of its own (more common in rural than urban areas) and can parlay one successful placement into others. There have been several instances where a second or third graduate was added to a particular employer's workforce, or where a graduate who left a job for school or a better job was replaced by another, more recent graduate.

Clearly, rushing or pressuring a graduate into a job without considering the quality of the match is a poor way to develop jobs, and research (Siegel & Gaylord-Ross, 1991) and experience have taught us this lesson. Quota systems encourage this kind of expediency, and in many cases, a 60-day placement can be obtained, but a poor job match is ultimately destructive to the youth, the credibility of the job developer, the employer, and the authentic servicing of career growth.

A transition specialist must also develop the fine art of knowing how to disclose information about a candidate that honestly informs the employer about the youth's strengths and limitations, but does not compromise that youth or predispose the employer against her or him. We recommend the transition specialist develop nonjudgmental behavioral descriptions and relevant data that can help an employer anticipate the special needs of a new employee, and that can enable the transition specialist to negotiate the support services that will help engineer success.

Sometimes a person may be an excellent transition specialist in every area except job development, or may be new to an area and lacking in contacts, or may be severely time constrained due to the intensity of other duties, especially that of enabling job retention for those already hired. In such cases, it may be necessary to bring in as a new team member a job developer who can create training and job placements for the transition specialist team to fill (see Chapter 5). This situation creates a new interdependency and need for articulation among the team because the transition specialist must deliver on promises made by the job developer. In this revision of the model, the job developer makes the cold calls, knocks on doors, and performs other activities that might eat up the transition specialist's primary direct service time with graduates. A well-connected job developer can save program staff many hours in trying to break into a big company by his or her ability to contact an executive at a high enough level to open that company's doors.

Finally, an essential aspect of job development and initial placement is the ability of the job developer or transition specialist to sell and deliver to the employer tax credits or training stipends. To effectively build a network, the work site must be assessed and a good match made. The intensity of initial service must be likewise assessed, and the commitment made. Finally, the promise of ongoing support and regular contact with the employer must be delivered as well.

DOCUMENTATION

Another important task for the transition specialist is that of record keeping and documentation. There are a number of reasons for this requirement and several ways it can be accomplished. Because the concept of the transition specialist is fairly new and innovative, documentation can provide invaluable information to others who want to replicate this role, or for troubleshooting within the program to increase the efficacy of the transition specialist and revise the job description. Documentation also can help an overwhelmed transition specialist see ways to improve efficiency. It is an important advocacy tool that can justify the position, provide accountability, and aid in research.

Probably the easiest and most effective way to document efforts is by keeping a daily journal.

Although the journal does not need to be extremely detailed, it should contain a list of the day's activities with brief descriptions of all interaction with contacts and of services provided to graduates or interns.

The journal can be useful in a number of ways, one of the more important being to help the transition specialist with accountability. Because transition specialists are out on their own most of the time, a journal that documents dates and services can protect them. The journal can also be used to justify certain activities or the amount of time spent on them if the need arises.

The journal can also serve as a valuable tool for following individual graduates, charting their progress and problems, and discerning patterns in their emergent career development, and it can provide evidence the transition specialist may need to advocate for a graduate. For example, a rehabilitation counselor may believe that a certain type of job is not indicated for a graduate because of his or her test scores, but the transition specialist may be able to provide compelling observational evidence to the contrary (using information recorded in the journal), and thus help justify the graduate's plan. In addition, the journal can be used as a general way of keeping track of graduates; it is possible to go back and glean the journal, discovering information that was not previously recognized as being important, and supplying this information at a later time (e.g., for particular research concerns or for graduates who need their resumes updated).

The journal can serve as a valuable adjunct to more formal data collection or research projects, especially because its information can be used right away. It also can provide useful information in the development of other instruments as the Career Ladders program progresses. The importance of the research component of a program cannot be overemphasized because it is often what drives the funding of special programs.

Research makes a program more objectively valuable and determines its potential for replicability. The journal, other instruments, and accompanying research can help answer questions and clarify issues about the program. Clearly, this book is only a first step, and those who attempt to replicate Career Ladders will improve upon the suggestions made here.

FOLLOW-UP

A rich, multifaceted information base is a by-product of the ongoing support component of the program. Regular follow-up can easily yield rich data that can in turn be stored and analyzed in a database. It is important not just to offer service, chart success, and prove results, but also to maintain contact and to avoid losing people. We have reevaluated and modified the content and methods of follow-up in the Career Ladders program a number of times. The most recent procedures for follow-up in Career Ladders were developed according to the following criteria:

1. The follow-up procedures are convenient and minimally time-intensive for the program staff.

2. The follow-up procedures are convenient and minimally disruptive to the graduate.

3. The database compares to the databases of others conducting similar studies.

4. The database has simple data coding and storage for maximum flexibility and manipulability.

5. Most important, follow-up procedures confirm the verisimilitude of the main treatise of the program: Career Ladders services are shaped to the lives of its participants.

Are we really helping these students to climb a career ladder? Career Ladders' published follow-up data showed favorable program results as compared to the national survey of youth with disabilities being conducted by the Stanford Research Institute. Graduates of Career Ladders experienced a 92% success rate (employed, going to college, or some combination of the two) compared to a national average of 60% with a comparable group (Siegel, Avoke, Paul, Robert, & Gaylord-Ross, 1991; Siegel, Robert, Waxman, & Gaylord-Ross, 1992; Wagner & Shaver, 1989). Appendix 4.8 shows the simple protocol that yielded the data used in these studies. The protocol is also an excellent tool for evaluating program effectiveness. The protocol requires only about 15 minutes per interview with a minimum of two contacts per year. We were able to track 117 of the original

127 Career Ladders interns over a 5-year period. The protocol measures postsecondary progress as well as the level of services delivered.

Such rich follow-up data fulfill both the quantitative and qualitative needs of a program like Career Ladders. Combined with a journal, follow-up data are very useful for developing ethnographic or anecdotal case histories, and for demonstrating the program's process. When interaction with graduates is established, ethnographic, interpretive information can continually corroborate the quantitative data collection and sustain a reasonably high level of social validity.

CASE STUDY

The following case study illustrates some of the principles of case management described in the previous sections. Rather than describe techniques in isolation, our intention is to demonstrate theory in practice and to show how the transition specialist takes an ecosystematic approach to a given case. It is impossible to reduce the role of the transition specialist to a simple formula or procedure. By telling this story we hope to capture the complexity of the different technical, bureaucratic, and human issues that the transition specialist must confront, and show how they all interact in the case of a particular young person.

The responses and reactions of the transition specialist in this case study demonstrate how professionals can and must respond creatively and flexibly to the problems that arise as an at-risk youth attempts to enter the workforce. Finally, we hope to illustrate the importance of the transition specialist keeping informed regularly and frequently during the first 2 years of employment. The transition specialist in Gloria's story is the first author.

 GLORIA

Gloria participated in Career Ladders as an intern in the spring, a year before the advent of my position, a full-time transition specialist. Her community classroom experience was in a large insurance office where she performed basic office duties including photocopying, filing, and minimal typing. The general consensus among program staff and employee evaluators was that Gloria was a good worker, was responsible, and had good grooming habits and job-keeping skills, but the staff was concerned about one area: her shyness. They thought that her shyness might hold her back in the future. After graduation, Career Ladders placed Gloria in a retail store in the financial district of San Francisco that seemed like a good match for her demonstrated skills and abilities. After an initial training period of about 2 months, the employer seemed to be happy with Gloria, so the Career Ladders instructor's monitoring of the situation faded.

Gloria did well on the job, but she did have some problems involving her level of social sophistication as it pertained to this particular environment. Her perceptions of certain on-the-job situations and her consequent behavior were often incompatible with the expectations of her supervisor. For example, Gloria's job occasionally required her to lift and move boxes around. This was not beyond her physical capability, yet Gloria routinely enlisted the help of male coworkers in these tasks. She was oblivious to the fact that this behavior greatly annoyed her female manager, to whom it appeared that Gloria was being manipulative and shirking responsibility. Though this was a factor to be considered, it did not directly affect her employment status. She ultimately did lose the job, however, because no one contacted her employer when Gloria was forced to go on medical leave after being hospitalized for a nervous breakdown.

About 6 months after her hospitalization, Gloria first met with me to discuss her plans and have her case reopened with the Department of Rehabilitation. She was attractive, well groomed, and cooperative, but a little shy, nervous, and somewhat withdrawn. She had been in therapy since her hospitalization, and her psychiatrist was now recommending that she go back to work on a limited basis. Her doctor was very cooperative and gave me as much information as possible, listened to my concerns about Gloria, and addressed them as best he could. Gloria had had adverse reactions to the medication she took, which necessitated further medication to counteract the serious side effects of the primary medication. These medicines in turn had their own unpleasant, although more tolerable, side effects. The doctor had tried to reduce Gloria's dosage in the past but she had experienced a major decompensation. Because of her situation at home and her need to bolster her self-concept in recovery from her mental illness, the doctor felt it was important for her to be out of the house as much as possible doing something constructive like work or school.

Gloria concurred with the doctor's recommendations. Her situation at home was not entirely unsupportive, but she had several brothers who were troublemakers and she worried about them, sometimes obsessively. She and her doctor agreed that she needed to take some initiative with her own life. Because her mother and brothers essentially supported her in this plan and because her mother could not speak English, I did not involve the family directly other than introducing myself and letting them know what my role was. In other situations, I might have consulted with family members more intensively to encourage them as natural support systems for the young person in transition. This is especially true in situations where youths may be exceptionally at risk, or where demands may be made on them by their family, either knowingly or unknowingly, that could potentially sabotage their success on the job. But because the family was supportive of her efforts and Gloria, though withdrawn, was honest and forthright, I felt confident that she could report to the family any relevant information. I might have investigated the family dynamics further to see if I could make any suggestions to enhance Gloria's chances for success, but after assessing the situation between the relevant players (i.e., Gloria, her doctor, her brothers, and her mother), I determined that to do anything further might be too ambitious or invasive and therefore possibly counterproductive. At this point, the overriding priority was to get Gloria out of the house as much as possible by finding her a job and some kind of remedial education program. The doctor was helping Gloria deal with her family problems and seemed to be doing a good job, so there was no reason to supplant, duplicate, or do anything else that would create interference between services. I had gleaned enough information to make this determination through coordination with Gloria's existing support network.

Gloria's immediate vocational goals were to get a clerical job and enroll in remedial education to upgrade her basic skills, particularly reading and writing. She liked the idea of working in an office atmosphere but had little clerical experience other than the routine stock work she had done at her previous job. She had no real typing or phone skills, and I wanted to avoid putting her into too challenging a setting right away because too much pressure was the last thing she needed in her state of recovery. Gloria could file fairly well and perform most other basic office tasks. Her reading level was low but workable, and she also had a problem with vocabulary and lexical access to some common English words. It was not clear whether this was due to her learning disability, her level of English proficiency, potential side effects of the medication, or a combination of all three.

I set up an interview for Gloria at a large law firm that needed an interoffice messenger. Gloria made a good impression in the interview and they decided to try her out. The personnel manager was a little concerned about her shyness, but he figured that it would subside once she became comfortable with the job. Because I was confident that Gloria could perform all the tasks the job required, I did little more than offer my services if Gloria needed any help learning the job. The personnel manager himself was new, inexperienced, and a little nervous about just how he was going to perform at his new job. So I felt that the best approach at this point was one of reassurance, rather than drawing unnecessary, potentially negative attention to her. I said that I thought Gloria would do well and I would be available to handle any problems if they came up. Sometimes, giving too much background information to an employer can actually do more harm than good.

I discussed setting up a remedial education program with Gloria and we agreed to hold off until we established how she was tolerating the job.

Gloria started working part-time, 4 hours a day, from 9:00 A.M. to 1:00 P.M. I checked in the first day and made sure everything was going smoothly. The mailroom was cramped and because I already knew the job through a previous placement, I could tell that Gloria was in good hands (she was getting one-on-one training from a person who had exactly the same job) and she seemed comfortable, so I just observed for awhile, making sure she was understanding her instruction, and then left. I called Gloria that night and fairly regularly for the next 2 weeks, and also called her supervisor the first, third, and seventh days, then once a week for the first month. There were no complaints, and everything seemed to be going well. The only ancillary service I provided for Gloria at this time was to get a voucher from the Department of Rehabilitation for shoes and pants because she did not have enough clothes for appropriate outfits for an average work week.

Then one day, after about 8 weeks, I was in the office with a graduate who was interviewing for another position in the firm, when Gloria's supervisor pulled me aside. He asked if there was anything particularly wrong with Gloria and I asked what he meant. He said there had been a few complaints that she had been making mistakes, delivering documents to the wrong offices. He said it was not serious, but because of the time constraints on attorneys it was important that documents went where they were supposed to in a timely manner. He also said that something else was wrong that he could not quite put his finger on. He said he liked Gloria, that she was nice, always appropriately dressed, on time, and so forth, but that there was something different about her. For some reason, she did not quite fit in. I asked a few questions to see if I could elicit more helpful information to further pinpoint the problem, but that was as far as I could get. She just did not quite fit in and the supervisor was at a loss. He said that he did not want to let her go but might have to if things did not improve or if they got any worse. I thanked him for his honest feedback and reaffirmed that I was there to help in just this sort of situation. I asked the supervisor if I could work with Gloria for 1 to 2 weeks and see if I could somehow remediate the situation. The supervisor happily agreed and gave me permission to come in and work with her whenever I liked.

My next hurdle was approaching Gloria because she was in a fairly fragile emotional state. I did not want to unnecessarily frighten her or initiate any undue stress that might cause her to become ill, regress, or behave on the job in a way that might make the situation even worse. But I needed to make her aware that she needed to make some changes to keep the job. I first interviewed her to see if she liked the job. It would be pointless to try to keep her on the job if she were unhappy with it. But she really did like the job. She had met one or two people she liked and had conversations with, and she thought that she was doing all right. She mentioned having a task-related problem that involved memorizing the names of the attorneys, so I offered to come in and work with her a little each day of the following week to see if I could come up with some strategies to help her with this task.

It took fewer than two visits to assess and establish what the problems were and to see that they were in no way insuperable, except for the additional element of the time. If I had not taken the supervisor's word that Gloria was doing so well and had done an on-the-job assessment sooner, she could have been working on these things for a few weeks at this point.

I started out by showing up when Gloria started work in the morning and essentially just shadowed her for a few hours, asking her questions about what she was doing to make sure she understood everything. If she did not, I encouraged her to ask questions of the appropriate employee. In shadowing her I was able to get a reading on the general tenor of the office, to see which people might be enlisted as potential allies for Gloria and which might be potential detractors to be avoided. I was able to accomplish all of this in less than a week so that it appeared that I was just another employee who was being trained by Gloria. By the time any of the office workers had a chance to figure out my role, I was gone.

There were three basic areas I identified as needing attention if Gloria was to keep the job: (1) basic job skills and the accommodations and adaptations needed to enhance them, (2) things she could do to fit in better socially at the workplace, and (3) the opportunity for her to have more time to learn the job, to allow the effects of the remediation plan to take hold, and to let the social ecology of the workplace begin responding positively to her and accepting her. I set separate appointments away from the job to work with her on these things, then arranged to shadow her on the job a few more times to evaluate the effects of my training and also to cue her and reinforce certain areas if needed.

During my first day of shadowing, I got an excellent clue as to what was going on the moment I arrived. Gilda, the head receptionist who had been with the company for 15 years, had her own commentary about what she thought the problem was. Gilda was one of the only people in the office who knew that Gloria came from a special program because she had made a point of asking me a lot of questions on the occasions when I had visited the personnel manager. At that time, she had gone on and on about what a wonderful program she thought it was; she said she wished her neighbor had known about it for her son. But it was clear on this visit that she did not really have Gloria's best interests at heart. She made a point of filling me in on all the mistakes Gloria had made and said that it appeared she could not read at all because she would often stare in a confused way at the list of attorneys she used to make deliveries and at other documents. All of this was offered up in a rather petulant tone, as if I might be at fault for putting Gloria in a job she was not capable of doing. Consequently, one of my first instructions to Gloria was to give Gilda a wide berth.

The next thing I did was to inspect the system Gloria used to make deliveries. Generally, a Post-it note with the attorney's initials was stuck on the document. Until a person was familiar with all the initials, he or she had to use a list that gave the attorney's full name next to the initials in alphabetical order, along with the name of each attorney's secretary. Some interoffice mail was to always go to the secretary and some to the attorney. So Gloria had to match the initials on the Post-it note to the initials on the list, figure out the attorney's name (and there were some unusual ones), match the name to the sign on each attorney's door (which could be on any one of three floors), and learn who all the secretaries were. There were over 100 attorneys and secretaries in the firm.

The first problem was with the list. It had been reduced so many times to fit onto a tiny 6-by-9-inch piece of paper that it was almost unreadable to me. So I had a more perspicuous version of the list enlarged and color-coded according to floor. I had several sessions with Gloria on pronouncing the difficult names and developed mnemonics to help her remember the exceptional ones. She started showing improvement after two sessions, which her supervisor and I noticed. I also contacted her doctor and asked if the medication she was taking could be making the task harder for her and might account for some of her apparent confusion and spaciness. He said that it easily could and that he would try to start reducing her dosage as much as he could. Gloria also responded positively to this. At this time I also accompanied her to speak with a counselor at the community college and she enrolled in some remedial classes in basic skills: reading, vocabulary, spelling, and math. She again responded positively. She improved measurably in a short time, especially in vocabulary, the area where she was most noticeably deficient.

The next area I addressed was improving the way Gloria was assimilating into the social environment at work. I felt that in her case it was an especially delicate subject to broach. I wanted to present it in such a way that it did not affect the progress her success at this job was having on her self-esteem. At the same time, I needed to alert her that some changes had to be made or she would be in danger of losing the job. And the truth is, it was not Gloria's fault that she was shy; it had to do with the insensitivity built into the office environment, which can be especially unforgiving in this regard. So that is approximately how I broached the subject with Gloria—by emphasizing the fact that there was nothing wrong with her, but that this was an unusual situation that had different rules. I told her that just as you might not talk and behave the same way around your mother as you do around your friends, there are certain modes of behavior that are more acceptable in the office environment outside of just showing up to work on time and doing your job.

I came up with three simple, manageable ways for Gloria to change her behavior, which could be viewed as tools to *empower* her and allow her to *play the game* of the workplace, not to change her personality because she was a bad person or did not fit in. I included her in this experiment, telling her that if she tried a few techniques, she would be surprised by the way that people would treat her differently. What I had her do was (a) smile and address people a little more often when she passed them in the halls or when she entered a room to make deliveries, (b) speak up a little when talking, and (c) move a little faster from place to place while she was working. This again was put in the context that these changes were not necessary to execute her duties because she was doing fine in that regard; they would just help her to make a positive impression on the attorneys, her supervisors, and her coworkers, using techniques that might not have been readily apparent to her.

I shadowed her a few more times to make sure that she was exhibiting the behaviors I had coached her in, and she was doing so quite competently. I next approached her supervisor to see how he felt about her quick progress. Unfortunately, what I feared most was about to happen. Things had gone on too long without any intervention, and he was still getting complaints about Gloria and pressure to replace her. In an attempt to buy a little more time, I reminded the supervisor that there really had not been enough time for my attempts at remediation to take hold. The supervisor apologized and said that he would have to let her go but would wait a few weeks, until after the holidays, to do so, more out of respect for Gloria than anything else. A week later, I contacted him to ask when Gloria's last day would be so I could place her into another job as soon as possible. The supervisor said that they had put the idea of terminating Gloria on hold temporarily because she seemed to be improving and there had been no complaints about her work since the last time he and I spoke. I kept checking in until it was obvious that Gloria was succeeding. In fact, she was the best messenger in the office, second only to the person who trained her (who was also a graduate of Career Ladders). Gloria is now completely off any medication for her psychiatric condition, has been working successfully for over a year and a half, continues to improve, and is now working with me on plans for further training to be a medical assistant and possibly eventually a licensed vocational nurse.

The preceding case study about Gloria was an example of a difficult transition for a young person, but it was also an example of how the transition specialist formed a relationship of mutual trust and respect with the young person. Gloria was compliant, motivated, realistic, and possessed sufficient social and technical skill to succeed at her job placement. But many students in Gloria's cohort were not like her—often they were closer to her exact opposite: noncompliant, unrealistic, incompatible, and lacking requisite technical and social skills for the workplace. Here is another short sketch outlining a possible approach for working with such a student—this time a young man.

Imagine a high school student with severe dyslexia who reads at the third-grade level at best, yet insists on following his dream of going to medical school and becoming a surgeon. The transition specialist knows that there is little chance he could read and understand a college application, let alone fill it out, complete the required coursework, and so on. A natural reaction might be to advise the student that this is an unrealistic goal. One problem with this response, however, is that the energy the student has put into nurturing this goal, although misguided and unrealistic, has been what has kept this young person going for some time. Such a young person may become intractably resistant to any attempts to see reason and may perceive the bearers of such information as not having his best interests in mind. He may even accuse the transition specialist of trying to crush his dream, and the more the transition specialist attempts to get him to be realistic, the deeper he will dig in his heels. In this particular case, several well-intentioned counselors had suggested to this young man that he should try to secure a position in patient transport at a local hospital where his family had connections. One teacher suggested that he might even move up to a medical interpreter position because he spoke both English and Haitian Creole, a language important to a large portion of the clientele at that hospital. Both of these suggestions angered the young man and prompted him to go to the school administrator and complain about lack of support for his aspirations.

One of the most important messages for a transition specialist to give a graduate is that he or she is being treated as an adult. This can be difficult, however, particularly when the graduates themselves can often maladaptively insist on pursuing rather daunting and unrealistic career goals. In keeping with the transition specialist's position, a more effective way to approach a student like the one described above might be to accept the student's goal for the time being and realistically outline the entire process and time commitment of becoming a physician. Explain everything, from prerequisite coursework to applying to college, getting into medical school, and finishing an internship and residency. The transition specialist may then challenge the student to get started with a plan, because it clearly means so much to him. He should be reminded that this process has to start right away, with a focused look at his transcript, a plan for taking courses the following semester, the possible necessity of attending community college, and so on.

Why should a transition specialist spend precious time working toward an unrealistic goal? There is only one reason to do so: to bring the student to the point where he will recognize the value of a more realistic goal. In the process described here, the transition specialist may make the quite accurate suggestion that many aspiring medical students take hospital jobs as orderlies or patient transport workers to get practical experience in a medical setting. Explaining to him that this is what everyone who wants to go into medicine must ac-

complish may induce him to give it a try. Such plans challenge the student to do what is necessary to move toward his dream and will elicit the student's trust that the transition specialist has the student's best interests at heart. The student will gradually deal with his inability to carry out the many tasks on the path to medical school, but in the meantime he will have secured gainful employment in a prestigious setting that is attractive to him and where he has the potential for advancement.

CONCLUSION: 10 YEARS AFTER

It has been 10 years since the first edition of Career Ladders was published, and much has changed. However, though many things have changed, some radically, in many ways things seem oddly the same. In the early 1990s the biggest happening was the Americans with Disabilities Act of 1990, which took what was then the more rarefied buzzword *access* and injected it into the American mainstream where it has remained since. At first people were worried that the more circumscribed meaning of the word and the law might be overapplied with rather untoward consequences. It was feared that overzealous advocates would jeopardize local businesses in the name of compliance, and that persons with more severe physical disabilities or more obvious visible disabilities would garner fiscal priority over those with more subtle conditions such as learning disabilities and mental illness. What money was left would be scrapped over by litigious lawyers and suit-happy clients.

None of this happened to the degree feared. Eventually, the public began to view the law in a positive light (like getting a tax credit for making a parent's kitchen easier to navigate). The term *access* began to broaden in scope as well. It came to encompass not just physical access, but access to literacy, to education, to employment, to the further exercise of citizenship. It also began to apply to making services more available to groups like out-of-school youth, senior citizens, minority citizens, veterans, and the unemployed.

This focus on access to more and greater services and necessities of life to an ever-broadening array of disparate groups conspired with the needs of a fluctuating economy to generate some of the most significant changes in the last decade. After years of renewed attention to access, research, model programs based on research, evaluation of model programs, replication of model programs, and so on, the federal government eventually created some appropriate legislation: the Workforce Investment Act of 1998 (see http://usworkforce .org). If this law is successful in the scope of the programs it intends to orchestrate and populations it purports to serve, it will be due to the following seven key principles on which it rests (the description of these principles is paraphrased based on text on this Web site):

1. Streamlining services through better integration and articulation at the street level in the one-stop delivery system. Programs, providers, information, and activities are integrated and coordinated in one place to make the system more accessible to consumers and businesses alike. Service delivery in this manner better approaches the ideal of "seamless."

2. Empowering individuals (thus attracting them) in three critical ways: (1) with creative financial assistance (allowing more flexible use of funds for training); (2) through making available greater levels of pertinent information and guidance; and (3) providing direct advice, guidance, and support at the local level via the one-stop system.

3. Universal access. *Any* individual will have access to the one-stop system and its core employment-related services, including information regarding employment vacancies, career options, employment trends, educational financial aid, and training in job search skills.

4. Increased accountability (and more effective accountability measures and incentives) from programs and providers who receive funding under the Workforce Investment Act with provider performance and consumer satisfaction a priority. Minimum core performance standards must be maintained for providers to continue to receive funding; providers that exceed standards may receive incentive funds.

5. A strong role for local workforce and private sector investment boards. Local businesses may act like a board of directors focusing on strategic planning, policy development, and oversight of the local Workforce Investment Act of 1998 system. This is important because it emphasizes local control and *all* players are at the table to make their needs known—business and labor, community service providers, and consumers. Business and labor have a direct stake in the quality of these workforce investment systems. Employers also contribute critical information about the job market, what skills are currently or projected to be in demand, what local programs can do to address local business needs.

6. State and local flexibility. States, regions, and localities have greater flexibility to build on existing reforms and address the needs of regional and local employers. This flexibility again emphasizes local control.

7. Improved youth programs with a stronger association between local labor needs, community youth services, academic and occupational programs, community service and citizenship activities, adult mentoring and follow-up, and more comprehensive targeting of at-risk populations.

These are all significant and progressive changes, if they bear out what they promise. However, as we reflected on what has changed over the past 10 years, we asked ourselves, is there still a role for the transition specialist? With these new "one-stop" career centers, services of all kinds will be provided in a way that may make the transition specialist's brokering and interagency liaison work unnecessary.

But then we realized that not everything has changed: young people have not changed. They are still loud and brash. They are still rebellious. They still demand honesty. They still demand independence. They are still angry. And they are still impressionable, vulnerable, and at risk, still close to their early development and the bumps and bruises that they may have gotten along the way. They are still afraid, and at the same time defiant, in the face of adulthood.

Young people today face an ever-growing and daunting array of circumstances in their transition from school to adult life—a volatile economy and shrinking budgets, volatile unemployment rates, a threatened and deteriorating environment, decreased educational opportunities, drugs, homelessness, and more. With this in mind, it is obvious that our youths with special needs face an even greater, seemingly insurmountable, challenge. Approaches like supported employment that strive to develop natural supports in the workplace can enhance the potential for vocational success. But it seems unlikely that job coaches, employers, coworkers, or even involved family members can by themselves have the resources to adequately make an impact on the myriad issues facing the majority of these youths.

The transition specialist ideally takes into account the complicated, interactive sets of circumstances that affect a young person's acculturation, assimilation, and integration into the workplace and adjustment to adult life. To this purpose, the transition specialist attempts to develop a global, ecosystematic, and more humanistic profile of the youth in transition as a person developing a long-term career. The transition specialist then acts as a counselor, case manager, and resource developer for the youth, making appropriate linkages with family, employers, school staff, and other adult service providers (see Appendix 4.1).

We thought about thrusting these youths on the brink of growing up into one of these exciting new one-stop career centers, with their multitude of providers, programs, services, and options, and we realized that they are still young and they need guidance. They need guidance from someone with whom they can talk, someone who knows the wheels and workings of the adult world, and someone who knows what the young person is trying to do—someone with whom they have had an opportunity to develop a relationship based on trust. They need someone to help them troubleshoot, to help them form a strategy, to help them learn how to make choices and test ideas, and to filter through the white noise that surrounds their life.

When it comes down to it, this is the most valuable role the transition specialist plays and it is what we hoped to convey in this chapter. The most important role of the transition specialist is to provide guidance as a trusted individual and to help the young person more easily negotiate the hazards and pitfalls on the road to adult life. The one-stop centers may have all the services anyone might ever need, but young people will need somebody in a transition specialist–like role—a mentor who can help guide them through life's complications.

It is from this perspective that Career Ladders and its participants have enjoyed significant success. We hope that this role, or one with similar philosophical underpinnings, can be developed further, thus enhancing the quality of postsecondary service delivery, independence, and success of youths in transition, and dispelling the notion that vocational and employment services are pawns in a larger scheme of tracking individuals into entry-level jobs and leaving them there.

APPENDIX 4.1
Summary of Transition Services

Follow-up contact. Routine quarterly follow-up to see how former interns (graduates) are doing (this contact may be more or less frequent depending on individual circumstances), what their employment status is, if they are in school or are planning to be, and whether they feel they could benefit from Career Ladders transition services.

Adult agency casework. Facilitating referrals; case openings and closures; reopenings; rehabilitation services; postemployment services; case management and program planning with adult service agencies; and consultation, coordination, and communication with counselors about all Career Ladders clients with active or inactive cases.

Postsecondary education or training. Counseling, referral, liaison, and tutoring services for Career Ladders graduates who would like to go to college or participate in an occupational training program, youth employment program, or similar activity.

On-the-job training. Job training and coaching, task analysis, accommodations, and mediations for Career Ladders graduates to aid in the development of specific job skills. Also coaching in job retention skills such as attendance and appearance.

Counseling. Counseling and problem solving with graduates on personal, employment, and education or training issues as they directly pertain to their career concerns.

Independent living skills. Counseling in basic skills that are not necessarily directly related to job retention, but to enhancing the quality of life (e.g., filing income tax paperwork, finding an apartment, getting a driver's license).

Resource referral. When appropriate, referring graduates to other service providers and community agencies that could potentially enhance the graduates' individual transition capabilities.

Social skills training. Problem solving, role playing, behavioral modeling, self-monitoring, and other techniques to help graduates work through on-the-job and interpersonal problems and to help them better acclimate to the particular social environment at work or in other situations.

Ecosystematic intervention. A global intervention technique where a number of key players in the graduate's social network (e.g., coworkers, supervisors, relatives, counselors, teachers, friends) are enlisted in some way to assist in the manipulation of parameters that have been collectively identified as areas in need of remediation, and to provide support and bolster the graduate's capability to maneuver in a difficult or crisis situation toward an ultimately positive result.

Job search. Counseling, support, supported job search, help with applications or exams, resume maintainance, interview skills, job leads, job development, and placement.

Pregraduation contact. Providing any needed transition services to interns before they have graduated from Career Ladders.

Transition planning. Working with school-based teachers, counselors, adult agency personnel, parents, interns, and others to start developing or implementing Individualized Transition Plans for pregraduates and recent graduates.

APPENDIX 4.2

Transition Specialist Self-Tracking Chart

Month _____

Intern Code	Follow-Up	Agency Casework	Postsecondary Education/Training	On-the-Job Training	Counseling	Independent Living Skills	Resource Referral	Social Skills Training	Ecosystematic Intervention	Job Search	Pregraduation Contact	Transition Planning

APPENDIX 4.3

Activities in Which a Transition Specialist Might Engage Over the Course of a Hypothetical Week

Make a home visit to a family to collaboratively make, and engender support for, a career plan for Career Ladders graduate.

Make on-site visit to a Career Ladders graduate who is enrolled in a training program (e.g., a program where the graduate is learning how to tune up cars and replace brakes). Check graduate's progress, check quality of the program and adequacy of the placement, and begin to make plans for what will occur after the training program ends.

Spend solid time listening to a Career Ladders graduate discuss family, sexual, drug, social, or other problems. This may lead to a referral or further establish the transition specialist as a trusted confidant and source of support. It may help to solve a job search or job retention problem.

Assist an agency counselor in the paperwork and procedures necessary to open or close the case of a Career Ladders graduate, facilitate the delivery of a service normally funded by the agency, or advocate for the delivery of such services through the presentation of documentation to the agency.

Conduct a supported job search by "pounding the pavement" with one or two Career Ladders graduates who have good but not great job search skills.

Develop jobs for Career Ladders graduates who lack job search skills but who have demonstrated good job retention skills (this is done for less-than-high-functioning youths).

Facilitate a support group of Career Ladders graduates. This could be a heterogeneous group of newcomers to post–high-school life, a mix of newcomers and veterans, or a group that shares a particular circumstance, such as parenting, drug involvement, alcoholic parents, or job dissatisfaction.

Tutor a Career Ladders graduate in courses taken at a community college, such as a course that would go toward a youth earning a credential in early childhood education and thus be able to climb a career ladder in the childcare field.

APPENDIX 4.4
Triage Chart

Urgency

	1	2	3
Severity 1			
2			
3			

APPENDIX 4.5

Career Ladders Job Placement Record

Intern/Graduate _____   Career Ladders Staff _____
Position _____   Agency Counselor _____
Employer _____   Supervisor _____
Address _____   Telephone _____
First Day of Work _____   Perm. ____ Temp. ____ Hours per Week ____
Wage _____   Name of Union _____
Benefits _____
Job Duties _____
_____
_____

Remarks _____
_____
_____

30-Day Follow-Up
Date _____ Remarks _____
_____
_____
_____
_____

60-Day Follow-Up
Date _____ Remarks _____
_____
_____
_____
_____

90-Day Follow-Up
Date _____ Remarks _____
_____
_____
_____
_____

120-Day Follow-Up
Date _____ Remarks _____
_____
_____
_____
_____

APPENDIX 4.6

Quick Progress Planning and Assessment Sheet

Date				
Name	F°up	TS	Pri	Comments

Instructions:

- F°up (follow-up) column—Necessary?, yes or no, date to follow up by, ASAP, or other instructions
- TS (transition specialist) column—Initials of transition specialist or other Career Ladders staff responsible
- Pri (priority) column—Indicate if person is a priority and the degree of priority: (blank) = no pri, (–) = low pri, (•, •+) = high; or use numbers, like 1, 2, 3

APPENDIX 4.7
Transition Specialist's Composite Week

	Monday	Tuesday	Wednesday	Thursday	Friday
7AM / 7:30	Job coach BD at cafe	Job coach BD at cafe	Job coach BD at cafe	Job coach BD at cafe	—OFF—
8:00 / 8:30	Staffing with counselor	Job development: SFO	Supported job search, CC, GH, CT; inverview for CT	Counseling appointments, in office	DR case staffings
9:00 / 9:30	Mock interview, resume for DS				Phone calls, follow-up
10:00 / 10:30	Supported job search for CC and GH	Job development: Serramonte		—OFF—	Job Fair at Hilton
11:00 / 11:30	Check on BD and other grads downtown		—OFF—	Phone calls, follow-up with grads, employers; paperwork	
12PM / 12:30	Check with City Coll on reg. status, progress	CL staff meeting	Peer support group at pizza parlor (recent grads)	Parent meeting at CSAA	Lunch
1:00 / 1:30	Staffing with TS / Check on LL at auto tech program				Check on grads working downtown
2:00 / 2:30	Help BD close cafe	Help BD close cafe	Meet with City Coll Enabler	Visit Employment Skills Workshop at Transition Center	
3:00 / 3:30	Return phone calls	Office intake w/DR cnslr	re: student referrals	—OFF—	Help BD close cafe
4:00 / 4:30	Discuss voc. plan with JB's parents	Return phone calls; paperwork, etc.	Return phone calls	—OFF—	—OFF— (COMP TIME)
5:00 / 5:30	Reports, letters, misc. paperwork		—OFF—	—OFF—	
6:00 / 6:30	Dinner	Dinner	—OFF—	—OFF—	
7:00 / 8:00	Phone calls, data entry	Parent meeting at Transition Center	—OFF—	—OFF—	

APPENDIX 4.8

Follow-Up Protocol/ Questionnaire

Date _____ Interviewer _____ Participant Code _____

Social Security Number _____

Months post–Career Ladders (circle one):

    6   12   18   24   30   36   42   48   54   60   66   72   78

Employment Information: Find out the following information for each 6-month period since leaving Career Ladders (January 1 to June 30/July 1 to December 31). Use one sheet per 6-month period.

1. How many jobs has the person had from ___/___/___ to ___/___/___ ? _____

2. Job titles? (please number jobs) _____

3. Dates of employment for these jobs? (indicate continuous employment from last period)

    _____

4. How many hours per week did person work? _____

5. How much was person paid? (hourly wage) _____

6. Does the person receive benefits?

    ___ Medical ___ Dental ___ Pd. Vacation ___ Sick ___ Pension

    ___ Other _____

7. Any wage changes in this period? (record raises or reductions) _____

Determine (prompt with examples) the number and nature of job changes, from job to job or within a job (including promotions/demotions, benefits activated, job duties changed, moved to another department, etc.). Try to elicit the following information:

8. How many changes were made? (include wage changes) _____

9. What were they? _____

10. Which were perceived as positive changes? _____

11. Which were perceived as negative changes? _____

12. During this 6-month period was this person enrolled in any postsecondary education or

    training? _____

    Where? (Please check appropriate box)
    - ☐ Still in high school
    - ☐ Enrolled in remedial studies, GED
    - ☐ Enrolled in other postsecondary training
    - ☐ Enrolled in apprenticeship
    - ☐ Enrolled in college
    - ☐ Completed a year of college
    - ☐ Completed professional trade training
    - ☐ Matriculated with a BA or BS

13. How many postsecondary course hours has the person completed? _____

    List courses, if possible _____

    _____

14. Amount of intervention:
    - 4 ☐ Intensive, either on the job, or ecosystematic (counseling, other situations)
    - 3 ☐ Intense, but less than constant intervention (<3 actions per week for at least 3 weeks)
    - 2 ☐ Agency casework more than simple processing and placement (e.g., difficult processing)
    - 1 ☐ Minimal, at most the opening or closing of a case and/or referral to job/agency/ services
    - 0 ☐ No intervention beyond follow-up contact

    List type of interventions: _____

    _____

    Name, address, and phone number of person who will always know how to get in touch with graduate:

    _____

Job and Site Development for Community Classrooms

5
CHAPTER

Gary Meyer and Shepherd Siegel ■

The person in the Career Ladders program who initiates the liaison between the school community and the employment community is called the *job* or *site developer*. This individual could be a program manager, teacher, on-site instructor, or transition specialist. Any number of staff persons can play this role, but in some cases, program staff may decide that they want a person to serve exclusively as the caretaker of the program's relationship with the business community. Certainly, all staff will have critical contact with the employment community and can benefit from familiarity with the job developer's skills. On the other hand, when a specialized job developer shares his or her duties with other Career Ladders staff, the program's presence in the community is maximized through the activation of a broad network—everyone on the staff is pursuing his or her own contacts. Also, sharing the task reduces both compartmentalization of roles and the number of people the business contacts have to know, thus making the program's service more personal. For example, if the job developer and transition specialist are the same person, the employer works only with one person. A specialized job developer, however, must turn the site over to a transition specialist once it has been developed. But given that not all staff members can develop all skills, a competent job developer will in many cases free other staff to train and maintain youths in jobs. In most cases,

the business community can tolerate the "pass off" from job developer to transition specialist.

This chapter is about job-site development, but perhaps it would be better to call it Sales 101, because the most important lesson to be learned in job development is that it is really a sales job; the person doing job development is trying to sell a service to an employer. In Career Ladders, that service is a student or young adult facing special circumstances, such as disability, below-average academic achievement, or other risk factors. The only way to break down the possible apprehension the employer might have is by the job developer showing good sales skills. This means that *job developers sell themselves first, the program second, and the student third.*

SELLING

In any business that sells a product or service, the best salespeople are those who have the most sincere belief in the quality of the product. In the business of increasing career opportunities for marginalized youth, the potential for a high order of belief and commitment is enormous. This work can never be approached as just a job. A job developer's enthusiasm can be fueled by a deeper understanding of the forces that make certain youths difficult to employ, and a moral position supporting their right to citizenship and the dignity of a meaningful and legitimate career. Such belief can create an engaging and convincing momentum that will make employers want to participate in the program and join the team in service to these youths. Take, for example, the job developer who truly believes in the integrity, honor, and rightness of integrating marginalized youths into the mainstream. Even if the content of that job developer's sales pitch solely addresses the profit advantages, his or her underlying belief will still be communicated nonverbally and will create the winning atmosphere—it will sell the program.

In one form or another, everyone has had to sell something. Perhaps you convinced your parents to let you stay out late or borrow the family car. At that point in developing a relationship with your parents, you were trying to show your trustworthiness and your responsibility, to meet the needs, desires, and requirements they had of you as their children. If you were successful in selling your talents, you got the family car. The same pertains to job development. If you understand an employer's needs, desires, and requirements, you have a better likelihood of success.

The employer's decisions will be based on his or her perception of the job developers or transition specialists, and how well they think the Career Ladders people understand the employer's problems. The competition is not just another individual who is trying to do job development; it is *all* the salespeople who call on a given employer. Hence, dress, mannerisms, and business knowledge are important. In many cases, job developers in our programs come from an academic background, which gives them book knowledge, skills in working with youths, and a research perspective. On the other hand, they may lack the experience in business that is required for success. A good job developer should have some sales experience.

Selling Yourself

One of the first things a prospective job developer should consider is his or her appearance. Very often, people from the school community dress in a comfortable and relaxed manner. Yet the prospective employer is accustomed to seeing salespeople in business attire: suits and ties for men, tailored clothes for women. If a job developer does not appear to be a businessperson in front of the employer, he or she starts off on the wrong foot.

Many times an employer will decide in the first few seconds of the meeting whether you represent a problem or a solution. There is an old adage that says that you never have a second chance to make a good first impression. Hence, you should eliminate things that can be perceived negatively. In this case, you want to blend in, so dress becomes important. Job developers who are men should wear a suit, tie, and dress shirt, or perhaps a sport jacket with slacks, but always a tie and shirt. Women should wear tailored business clothes. Even salespeople calling on blue-collar organizations generally wear traditional business attire. You should dress in a manner that acknowledges the policies that each corporation requires for its employees. Also, your first contacts are frequently gatekeepers. If they are Human Resources staff, and they take an interest in your program, they will be surmising what kind of impression you will make on the people *they* hope to impress within their company. You must show them that you can make a good impression for them in any setting.

Another fact to recognize is that the corporate person with whom you meet probably spends each day barraged by professional salespeople who are experienced in presenting their product and their company at the highest possible level. A job developer who is hurled from an educational environment into this highly competitive, highly stressful business world is going to be judged overwhelmingly by the prospective employer's opinion of the developer, and not necessarily by the program or the worthiness of the possible employee. So appearance, sales presentation, follow-up, and a thorough presentation are key.

Unfortunately, for the most part job developers do not have the experience necessary to successfully present their product, which in this case is a student or young adult. Job developers need sales and marketing skills for success. These skills begin with physical appearance and include a knowledge of the product and of the customer's needs. They must present solutions to an employer in a manner that will make the employer want to do business with the organization, to employ students, to see it as a way to solve company problems, and to bring profitability and credibility to her or his company.

Although major corporations have made limited attempts to help society, they operate according to one basic premise: If you do not make money, you do not last. From the chief executive officer down to the smallest department head, corporate administrators are ultimately judged by their ability to make money. As a result, when job developers discuss job opportunities for students, they must present profit as the bottom-line reason for employing Career Ladders students. If job developers can show middle managers (who in today's business climate are getting squeezed for more work with fewer people) that Career Ladders can supply them with long-term working people with positive attitudes, Career Ladders can ultimately increase the managers' profits and solve problems.

One of the most common mistakes made by new salespeople is their desire to hit a home run, or make a long touchdown pass. In other words, they want to find an employer in the community who will hire all the students on a regular basis. This is like the case of the new salesperson who hopes to make a giant sale at the major corporation, fulfill the quota, and take Fridays off for the rest of the year. The simple fact is that it just does not happen this way. Successful salespeople build successful careers by creating a solid foundation and rising from that foundation to the level of success that they need to fulfill their goals and desires. Hence, job developers who hope to find the perfect corporation will be very disappointed, and the students for whom they are responsible will not have the opportunities they would have had if the job developers had made a more realistically planned marketing effort.

A successful marketing plan consists of many elements: some cold-calling, some new calls (partially developed customers), and some return visits to present customers. The terminology used here is that of a business atmosphere, rather than the nomenclature used by counselors and teachers because to be successful in the business world, one must operate like a business. One advantage of cold-calling is that presenting your ideas and personnel to a prospective employer with whom you have had no previous contact gives you the opportunity to practice your presentation with nothing to lose. A successful salesperson's presentation answers most of the customer's concerns and questions before they are even asked. When you do this, you come across as a knowledgeable, well-prepared salesperson. The only way to learn what

those questions are is by constantly making cold calls, discovering the most frequently asked questions, and developing your sales presentation based on them. In the cold-call situation, a mistake costs you nothing as compared with a more high-stakes call on a partially developed prospect.

The advantage of making calls on your existing employers, on the other hand, is that it gives you the opportunity to make sure that you are maintaining a high level of expertise and a high level of service, so that the employer will continue to want to work with you. It also gives you the opportunity to develop more jobs within the organization, and more important, it gives you the opportunity to find out if your contact, who meets regularly with peers and competitors, can suggest other places where you can place people.

A salesperson always wants a big order, but the customer often will give only a small one. In Career Ladders, you may want an employer to hire 10 to 12 of your students, but all he or she will consider is the possibility of one. Because this employer is offering only one job, you may be tempted to place just anybody there. But the key actually is to place one of your best students there, the student who is sure to be a success. This is because you now have your foot in the door and it is very important to be successful with the first placement. A satisfied customer is the easiest customer to sell to a second time. A satisfied employer is the easiest one to convince to hire additional personnel from your organization. If you develop enough "singles" and "doubles" in the early stages of your work, you are more likely to eventually score that home run. Social service people are sometimes averse to this strategy and see it as "creaming." But there is a huge difference between having your star performing youths open the door for more difficult-to-employ participants, and losing the employer altogether due to a bad start, or the actual creaming method where the more challenging youths never get an opportunity.

If you can develop a personal relationship, a manager may decide to work with your program simply because he or she likes working with you. The program must still be as excellent as you claim, but the personal relationship may be the factor that causes the employer to work with you. As the Career Ladders interns are told, the decision to hire them is the decision to like them. The function of the transition specialist at one of our sites was to have coffee with the manager and listen to her complain about all her other employees, but not Career Ladders graduates. In this case, when the transition specialist assumed a counseling role, the placement of Career Ladders youth was rarely the topic of discussion. Nonetheless, the Career Ladders youth's position with the company was protected by this additional service provided by the transition specialist.

Selling the Program

There are two ways to present yourself to an employer at the first meeting. One is as a person from the school who is trying to do something in the community and who is looking for work for the school's students. The other is as a person who has a solution to a problem the employer has, which will benefit the corporation and increase its profit margin, while at the same time providing a community service of which the corporation can be proud.

One of the most important things you can do to ensure success is to develop a concise written proposal that can be presented to a prospective employer and that thoroughly explains the program you are offering. This proposal should include a history of the program, some success stories, how the program works, and the program's basic foundation. If the program has any tax advantages, explain how those might work, as well as any other information the employer may need. The reasons for putting this information into a written formal proposal that you give to the prospective employer are twofold. First, your contact will have something to take forward to her or his supervisor for final approval in a way that conveys your most important points to the ultimate decision-maker. Second, a written proposal that you give to the employer during a presentation ensures that you will not forget to make the most important points about the program. Written documentation also provides consistency among all the job developers who work within the same organization; the same story is being told throughout the community.

Appendix 5.1 is a sample brochure that introduces the program to employers, educators, and families. You can reproduce it or create something similar. Photocopy it onto card stock in colors that identify your program, then cut the trapezoidal shapes in the example and put the promotional package together in a pouch folder. This is an inexpensive way that you can have finished looking materials that present Career Ladders to diverse participants. Appendixes 5.2 and 5.3 consist of examples of a letter of introduction and a business proposal that have been used in Career Ladders to develop both community classroom sites and job placements. Here are some additional guidelines on how to sell a work experience/job placement program.

1. *Scan the market.* Conduct research on a few major businesses in the area. For each business find out: How many employees work there? What kinds of skills are they looking for? Is there a union involved? What is the product and its future in the marketplace? The local chamber of commerce bulletin lists names of businesses, number of employees in each, and the types of jobs they offer. Equally valuable are service clubs such as Lions, Kiwanis, and Rotary. They are often more interested in giving money than service, but if you are a guest at one of their meetings, collect business cards and follow up. If you are invited to speak at one of their meetings, remember that they want to be entertained as well as informed. You can entertain, inform, then challenge them at the end to contribute to the effort.

2. *Pick your times wisely.* Never contact employers on Monday morning, the day after a holiday, or right before the weekend. Avoid pre- and during-meal rush hours in eating establishments.

3. *Consider the walk-in approach.* Sometimes an unannounced visit can catch the right person at the right time. "Can I see Mr. Padilla for 5 minutes, please? I represent the [Your Local] School District. Mr. Padilla, my name is Louise Mann. I was just in the neighborhood following up on one of the youths in our program, and I saw your sign . . . ."

4. *Do not hide limitations, but point to successes if you can.*

5. *Give business cards with your name, school district, and phone number.*

6. *Respect the receptionist.* Receptionists are often powerful people in organizations, and their favor can help you develop contacts. If receptionists

do not feel respected, they can damage potential or current relationships.

7. *Ask for just 5 or 10 minutes.* If that is what you are granted, do not take more uninvited. At the end of your time, ask employers to talk about their business, and listen attentively when they do.

8. *Provide a flyer or brochure that explains the objectives of the program.* If the flyer is successful in gaining interest, prepare a proposal such as the one in Appendix 5.3 to follow up and demonstrate that the program is serious and accountable.

9. *Send a follow-up letter after every visit.* Customize each letter from a basic format. Send the letter no matter whether you were initially successful. It will play a role in most of your eventual successes. And without it, initial rejections will never turn around.

10. *Continuously develop more leads.* Ask yourself which employers can benefit from the program. Some employers who cannot immediately work with you may have associates in other companies who can.

11. *Be upbeat and positive.* Emphasize the strong points of the students and the supportive services your program offers, which are like a warranty. Be able to describe all the advantages, and be knowledgeable about the program's benefits (e.g., no increase in workers' compensation, possible minimum wage exemptions during training, tax credits, on-the-job training contracts with the local workforce development council). Stress in the presentation that your interns and graduates will adhere to all the corporate rules that apply to employees within the company. If 100% of the men in the company wear suits, white shirts, and ties, your interns and graduates would do the same. Present to your contacts, whose primary responsibility is to ensure the profitability of the corporation, the idea that your interns and graduates will be a solution to their problem, contribute to their success, make them successful within the corporation, and make their department more profitable for the corporation.

12. *Ask for a tour of the business.* It is wiser and you will earn more respect if you take the tour after you have explained your program and before you make any requests.

13. *Negotiate an initial low wage with raises rather than starting at a high wage.* Without losing any self-respect, these youths need, like anyone else, to first get their foot in the door.

14. *Negotiate a scale of commitment.* If in fact employers are receiving incentives like tax breaks or subsidies to hire at-risk youths, then they must be willing to make some accommodations or take some extra training time. The agreement is a two-way street, and at this point, the job developer should articulate, advocate, and negotiate what the employer must provide to help make the placement a success.

15. *Try large companies with affirmative action policies.* You may be able to find a go-getter in the company who is eager to have an exemplary program. Perhaps you have a friend who will act as a contact and introduce you, or you may know of a parent on a board or citizens' advisory council. Companies with more than 25 employees are generally an easier setting for obtaining placements. Though smaller businesses should not be disregarded, these companies usually require more skills per person, and many candidates may lack the necessary versatility. Unionized companies can require more time for developing a placement because union representatives must be involved in the process of bringing on youths from special populations, especially in a work experience program. In such companies seek out both union and management leadership for support.

16. *Work with unions.* Organized labor is typically very supportive of programs like Career Ladders, but need to be included near the beginning of new developments, including the initial establishment of a special program for youths.

17. *Develop a network.* A successful job developer will spend a lot of time at meetings, conferences, social gatherings, fraternal organizations, business clubs, and organizations. Because you have an opportunity to meet people socially, over lunch or dinner, or perhaps at a social function, you have the opportunity to become a friend. As one telephone company says, the most important business calls are personal. If you can develop personal relationships with individuals, more doors will open for you, making sales calls on prospective employers easier. Attend as many meetings

and workshops as you can. Get involved in civic functions; they increase your opportunities to meet people. These are places to make contacts and to develop critical skills. Your sources are going to consist of cold-calling, leads from present employers, social parties, business meetings, and personal friends. Do not forget the possibility that parents of Career Ladders youth might be able to open doors at their place of employment. They may be reluctant to get their own child hired, but they may not mind helping out another youth. A parents committee might in fact help with job development.

18. *Work with the food industry.* Like it or not, this is the first proving ground for many new workers and a major force in the huge American service sector. Fast-food establishments and restaurants provide a beginning work experience that is valuable to many youths.

19. *Develop relationships with employment agencies.* This is an unexplored potential resource. Of course, your state's employment development department, workforce development council, or department of vocational rehabilitation may already play an active role in your program. Implementation of collaborative arrangements with these agencies takes work. The work experience coordinators at your schools are good information resources who generally know the job market.

20. *Develop relationships with other adult service agencies.* Often, a student or graduate can stay in your program and at the same time participate in another one, which might offer further subsidies of wages or other means of support. But you must be alert to situations where employers exploit youths by terminating them when the benefit or subsidy expires. For more information on collaborative relationships, see Chapter 4.

Selling the Applicant

Many youths are hired into entry-level positions. The problems most employers encounter at the entry level is that many of the workers have not been trained in job survival skills, and many do not have the patience to stay with the job for long. As a result, employers are forced to terminate some people because of lack of effort on the employee's part. The employees the manager likes often end up quitting because they become dissatisfied with the position quickly. In developing the relationship, the employer may initially be considering sponsorship of a community classroom or hiring a graduate. If seeking a job placement, the job developer should emphasize the job survival training that the students have already completed—the community classroom experience. The proposal also should contain descriptions of some of these job survival skills so that the employer will understand that in some cases interns and graduates might require additional training. Because many of the youths have received classroom training in preparation for that first job, they have an edge over other entry-level employees. Hence, there is a higher likelihood of Career Ladders students staying on the job for a longer period of time, which extends the period in which the employer receives benefits from employing an entry-level person. This likelihood of more extended employment also reduces the company's training costs and turnover.

It is very important for the job developer to repeatedly emphasize why it is profitable to employ students with learning, intellectual, sensory, emotional, and physical disabilities. Because you cannot rely entirely on the corporations' responsibility to the community, you must rely also on the economic benefits of employing these youths. Emphasize to the prospective employer that the youths placed are not a handicap to the operation of the business, but a solution. This youth has been trained to survive in the workplace, is eager to please, and will benefit the employer. He or she is the best candidate for the job.

Many large corporations believe that people coming from a program such as Career Ladders are not prepared to go directly into full-time employment. But these corporations can be convinced of the need to give students on-the-job experience and are often willing to set up community classrooms within their facilities to give students the opportunity to learn job survival skills, how to dress, and how to behave in a business environment. Ultimately these employers will select people from this classroom to whom they will give an employment opportunity.

MAINTAINING THE RELATIONSHIP

You will not be able to hit home runs. There is no shortcut; there is just hard work. The job developer's goal is just to get a few positive hits each week.

When a youth is placed in a position you have developed with an employer, the work has just begun. If you are a job developer who is now handing the care of a youth over to a transition specialist, it will be up to the transition specialist to help make that placement the greatest possible success. Even in this handoff situation, there are two activities that will turn your good work—developing the job placement—into quality work.

First, meet with the transition specialist who will be placing and supporting the new employee, or who perhaps is sending a few candidates to be interviewed. Share all the information about the job and the job environment. The single most important factor in turning a placement into a success is the job match; you want to make sure that the most appropriate candidates are referred. At this point, it is best to avoid meeting with the employer again and introducing another new face. But if you have doubts about the match or the job, you should go to the site again, perhaps with the transition specialist, and get detailed information about the job and working conditions. An employer who sees the care with which you are approaching the placement will doubtlessly appreciate the service you are providing.

The second important activity to ensure success is to make at least two follow-up visits with the employer. You are calling to make sure that the youth is working out and that the support services are adequate and excellent. If the rest of your team is now doing a good job and the match was good, there is no reason why the employer will not start calling you to ask you to send more candidates. This is where home runs come from: the follow-up support that makes a job developed through your organization a truly satisfying experience.

If you are the transition specialist, your role in enhancing job retention for the new employee is even more involved (see Chapter 4), and your follow-up with the employer should be systematic and extensive. If there is no additional support necessary for the new employee, the job developer's role becomes either part of a burnout cycle because the job developer is just moving from one candidate to the next with no relationship building, or part of a training program so excellent that its graduates do not need additional support. However, such candidates usually do not need job developer services, so this is not a likelihood under the current program.

Long-term, dependable relationships are what people, regardless of their role in life, value most. If what began as a sales call brings about long-term, dependable, and profitable relationships with new employees, with the program's staff, and with you, the job developer, then you have begun to move beyond the dollar value of the service provided, and into the realm where community is built. The employer sees the need to employ and work with the youths you represent and reaps the human as well as monetary value that comes from bringing individuals into the economic mainstream who might otherwise live on the margins. The work you have done is not an intellectual exercise, but the creation of human relationships that nourish everyone.

THE BIG PICTURE

Though this chapter has taken a strong position about accommodating the business perspective, the altruistic element is not lost and has an important value and place in the job developer's work. When you are out developing new jobs, you will find that employers can be approached through the value of profitability and convenience, but that the altruistic value has its place as well. Sometimes, as part of a larger company, employers have been instructed to begin hiring people from disadvantaged groups, either as part of a commitment to diversity or because the management has assessed the profitability of tax credits. In such cases the employer is already convinced or directed and will be looking for the job service that is the most convenient and will supply the best candidates.

But what about the moral appeal? In fact, the business world is full of people who run profitable businesses and retain a sense of conscience and social responsibility. As individuals, everyone shares a common culture based on progressing human rights, regardless of whether they work in the private, public, or nonprofit sector. The job developer can build on this common ground.

Large companies that are not particularly oriented toward social responsibility often have a sizable number of workers who feel alienated from their jobs. These people may be trapped; they make too good a wage and have too many debts to maintain their lifestyle without working. Thus they feel imprisoned in a job they do not really like. They may not be the manager or personnel specialist, but they will be among the coworkers who are going to work alongside your candidates. Many of these people are looking for a way to make their jobs more meaningful, and they will be grateful for a chance to keep their well-paying but otherwise mundane and socially irrelevant job, and still make a contribution to improving social welfare. As they get a chance to contribute to the improvement of society, their own job becomes more interesting. Why? Because they are working directly with students with special needs, and there is little of the risk that would be involved if they quit their jobs in search of more socially relevant ones. You are offering that opportunity and, for many workers, you have the most valuable product on the market: meaningfulness.

Some employers can be approached on the basis of ultimate social cost. A youth who is given an opportunity early on to be integrated into the workforce is much less likely to become an expense to society later: to be disabled or poor and need welfare support or institutionalization, to become a drug abuser and need treatment or institutionalization, or to get into crime and steal goods, driving up the cost of commodities, law enforcement, and institutionalization.

The alternative is to turn this person into a taxpayer and a contributor to society, rather than an expense. This is a strong argument that effectively combines altruistic and economic considerations.

Finally, everyone is part of a family. And among virtually all extended families are people with disabilities. It does not take long before an employer will probably reveal that he or she knows or is related to someone who fits this category, and perhaps even someone who needed a special opportunity at one time.

Coping with a disability, poverty, or low skills is a serious disadvantage. To overcome it requires a struggle. No one really engages in this struggle alone or succeeds without the help of someone else. Employers may be willing to share stories of how they struggled to succeed, and with skill and insight, you can show a relationship between their personal stories and the lives of the youths you are serving.

Finally, the underlying message that should be carried in every interaction with the employment world is that you and they are of one community. Profits cannot be made without a healthy community that buys the goods and services offered. There is really no point to making a profit if it is not part of a community life. Business, government, and education are all there to serve people, and the greater participation of marginalized youth in the world of business and employment can and must appeal to everyone's sense of fairness. Giving an employer the opportunity to actively participate in this movement by hiring a youth who is at risk is truly the greatest investment an individual can make.

APPENDIX 5.1

Sample Career Ladders Brochure

Career Ladders is an innovative and highly successful school-to-career program that serves those students who want or need to make their transition directly from school to a job. Many Career Ladders graduates do go on to attend some form of college or postsecondary training, but the model best serves those young people eager to earn a paycheck and begin climbing their career ladder early. The overarching principle of Career Ladders is that **services are shaped to meet the career needs of the students served.** Career Ladders provides:

- ▲ **A principles-based approach to developing a school-to-career program that fits the unique needs of your community.**

- ▲ **Supervised work-based learning, called a *community classroom.***

- ▲ **Weekly school-based seminars where interns integrate the community classroom experience, called the *employment skills workshop.***

- ▲ **Connecting activities through the ongoing availability of transition services for high school graduates of the program.**

- ▲ **Highly effective training that emphasizes the building of consensus and the practical implementation of a locally driven Career Ladders program.**

How Do We Know this Program Gets Results?

Published follow-up studies of the first group of Career Ladders interns showed that after 5 years, 92% of the graduates ($N = 127$) were employed, enrolled in college, or engaged in some combination of the two. This first group was composed of youths with mild disabilities who were typically employed at a 60% rate. More than 30 other school districts across the nation have adopted the model, serving a wide range of students with great success.

How Does Career Ladders Work?

Career Ladders provides a supervised work internship during one of the last semesters of high school. This experience, called a **community classroom**, provides a structured approach to work-based learning that students who are at risk of being left out of the job market (low income, foster care, disabled, pregnant and parenting, substance abusing, adjudicated, speaking English as a second language) can benefit from most. Many work experience programs "fill slots" and monitor. The Career Ladders community classroom reproduces the competitive marketplace, yet it provides the supervision and support that teaches student interns how to survive and thrive in the real work world.

The **employment skills workshop** is a carefully crafted 18-week seminar that is conducted concurrently with the community classroom. It is designed to offer interns an opportunity to process the often difficult experience of going to work and joining the work culture. Besides teaching the fundamentals of job application and job search skills, interns begin to form the peer networks that will support them through the school-to-career transition, and ultimately provide opportunities for employment and full participation in their communities.

The community classroom and employment skills workshop work together to create a foundation from which students can make the leap to a successful adult life as competent employees and citizens. But it is the final and most innovative component of Career Ladders, the **ongoing availability of transition services** that makes the most of these orientation experiences and truly puts a dent into low employment rates. Without the first two components, the third is impossible to implement properly. Without the third, the first two are to no avail.

Career Ladders' transition services beyond high school finally achieve the program's ultimate mission, which is to **build community** in a way that includes and employs those youths who would otherwise be left out. Career Ladders transition specialists perform three critical functions: they form mentoring relationships with the Career Ladders graduates and their families that serve to empower youths to ultimately not need services; they become expert at understanding the network of existing services, referring and advocating for graduates as their needs arise; and they provide direct services like counseling, on-the-job training, career planning, tutoring in postsecondary programs, and social skills training.

How Can We Get Started with Career Ladders?

The adoption process begins with an entertaining and information-packed 2-day training session, conducted by Dr. Shepherd Siegel, the program's founder and designer. Facilitated planning sessions and follow-up consultations ensure that the training is translated into action and successful implementation. The training is codified into one easy-to-understand manual, *Career Ladders: Transition from High School to Adult Life*, and illustrated through the award-winning video, *Career Ladders*. The impetus to establish **Career Ladders** in your community can come from any of the principal participants needed to make it a reality: families and youths, school districts, community employment agencies, or employers.

Community & Employment Agencies

▲ build partnerships with schools

▲ avoid burnout by allowing your providers to develop long-term relationships with consumers

▲ accept and recruit well-prepared candidates from your local school districts ready and motivated to go to work and postsecondary school

▲ expand your mission to serve more diverse populations

▲ shape the trends of the school-to-work and adult life transition movement through the interagency nature of the program, which keeps your organization current and in the loop

▲ **BUILD COMMUNITY** through a strong linkage to families, schools, and employers, and allow your staff to identify and succeed as the primary community builders

Families and Youth

▲ get involved in the school-to-adult life transition process

▲ receive a supervised work experience in a real work setting—some employers may even hire directly from the program

▲ benefit from the ongoing availability of service after graduation from high school

▲ learn job search skills and develop the community network that is likely to support the climb up the career ladder through an educational weekly workshop

▲ **BUILD COMMUNITY** by making a contribution to society through your vocation: You can fully participate in the world of work and in an economic democracy

Employers

▲ hire the candidates you like from among the students you sponsor because the program is an internship that functions like a semester-long interview

▲ select the students you want to enroll as interns

▲ help your people become more meaningfully engaged in their jobs as they act as mentors

▲ share responsibility for the performance of the interns with your local school districts

▲ **BUILD COMMUNITY** by having an employer-driven approach to working with schools and agencies, and provide successful career opportunities to youths who would otherwise run the risks of un- and underemployment

School Districts

▼ build a credible reputation with the business community

▼ develop a cost-effective way to provide a state-of-the-art transition program to a wide range of students

▼ offer students a real work experience in the business community that is cost-effective and efficient

▼ choose excellence over expedience in a school-to-work program that makes no unnecessary compromises—it reconciles the school culture with the work culture in a way that students can grasp

▼ **BUILD COMMUNITY** by having your staff take education beyond the schoolhouse walls and integrating your schools with the postschool environment in a direct and meaningful way

APPENDIX 5.2
Letter of Introduction

Dear Employer:

Many employers in the area have told me that their business has two important employment aims. First, they want to find competent, reliable employees and match them to the right job within their organization with minimal trial and error and employee turnover. Second, they want to make economically sound personnel decisions to fill entry-level positions and, at the same time, support the development of the community in which their business operates. I am writing to tell you about a youth employment program that will help your business achieve these goals.

Career Ladders is an innovative collaboration between major community agencies and employers in San Francisco. It offers you, the employer, a number of benefits:

- *Screening of Applicants.* Career Ladders screens applicants for potential jobs and refers only qualified individuals, avoiding undue inconvenience for the employer and unnecessarily setting up the potential employee for failure.

- *Preemployment Training.* Career Ladders interns receive extensive on-the-job training in a professional work environment to develop marketable job skills in their particular areas of interest.

- *Job Retention and Social Skills.* In concert with their on-the-job training, interns attend weekly workshops to further develop a general repertoire of desirable work habits and learn techniques that enable them to interact more cooperatively and effectively with their coworkers.

- *Tax Credits and Employer Incentives.* Career Ladders can facilitate certification for tax credits and other incentive programs to eligible employers.

- *Ongoing Commitment.* Career Ladders makes an ongoing commitment to its clients and employers, and at no cost to them provides further on-site training, follow-up, job coaching, accommodations, mediations, and other services as the employer feels they are necessary.

The motivation of Career Ladders is to create an opportunity that is cost-effective and beneficial to both the employer and the community at large, and one that establishes a two-sided commitment—a win–win situation for everyone involved.

I have enclosed some information describing the program in more detail. I will call you in a few days to set up an appointment to discuss this program, which my colleagues believe could be very beneficial to your organization. Thank you so much for your time and consideration.

Sincerely,

Mark Roberts
Transition Specialist
Career Ladders

APPENDIX 5.3
Business Proposal

To complete a business proposal, include just a few samples of materials that explain how your staff operates and delivers quality service. Phase I samples: community classroom instructional materials (Appendix 2.11). Phase II samples: postsecondary service materials (Appendix 4.1, record-keeping materials).

A Proposal

Made by

CAREER LADDERS

to

ABC Corporation

for

Phase _____ Career Ladders Services

_____, representing Career Ladders

_____, representing ABC

January 15, 2005

Career Ladders is an interagency collaboration between [Your School District] and [Your Job Placement Agency]. Its purpose is to enable the successful transition from school to work or college for youths in our area. It grows from an original program begun in 1985, between the San Francisco Unified School District, San Francisco State University, and several local agencies and employers. Our success rate of program graduates who are employed or in school 5 years after the program is approximately 90%, which means we can offer low turnover, intelligent matching of candidates to job descriptions, and an excellent return on investment to participating employers.

The core of the program is a semester-long on-the-job training program. We provide a half-day work experience for interns at a real work setting that is accommodated by the presence of an instructor from the program's staff. We call it a *community classroom*. Four days a week Career Ladders interns go to work for 3 hours at one of our sponsoring sites. Some sponsoring sites have included California State Auto Association Insurance, Westin Hotel, Seattle Symphony, Marriott Food Service, Photo and Sound Company, and the University of California Medical Center. In the beginning of the semester, the interns receive intensive supervision from the on-site instructors. As they demonstrate competence and independence, the instruction is gradually faded until the end of the semester, when our presence is no longer necessary on the job.

Interns are assessed in employment and social skills and must meet objectives if they are to successfully complete the program. One day a week, they attend an employment skills workshop, where they learn entry-level job skills, job-keeping skills, social skills, peer counseling techniques, and job search skills.

If an intern successfully completes the program, we make an ongoing commitment to the career development of that individual. A transition specialist follows each of the interns who have graduated Career Ladders, providing services that range from on-the-job training and supported job searches to counseling in social skills and assistance in college enrollment. We believe in career development—a career ladder—for every Career Ladders graduate. A participating company gains not only the production of the new employee or intern, but the services of an entire team of professionals dedicated to the success of our youths and the satisfaction of the employer.

PHASE I
Sponsoring a Community Classroom

Who are Career Ladders interns?

Career Ladders interns are high school juniors and seniors from the [Your School District]. They have motivation to work, family support, and good attendance records. Though interns face challenges in their lives, they are each matched to a job site where they get support, and their life circumstances will not impede their ability to become competent workers.

What services are provided?

The school district employs an instructor who is on the job site with the interns. The instructor comes to the site several days before the interns to learn the job tasks. The instructor then provides the necessary training to the interns and enables the regular supervisors to eventually take over. The educational supervision is faded over time—our aim is to make the interns employable and competitive with the labor force at large. A program coordinator provides ongoing supervision and monitoring of Career Ladders. The [Your Agency] makes its services available as well, and provides a link to the world beyond high school. Our transition specialists serve as liaisons to postsecondary activities such as college, work, and training.

What does Career Ladders want from the employer?

Most important, we need work for the interns to do. Our interns need a place where they can develop and perfect the skills that will make them good employees. We have found four afternoons a week of 3 hours each to be effective, but other arrangements can be made. We would like to send at least two candidates for each intern position in your company, and have you make the final selection of interns based on a job interview. There should always be enough work for them to do. As they reach competency in the job tasks and work behaviors, supervision should come from the regular job-site supervisors, enabling the interns to work more independently and freeing the instructor to work with those interns in need of more training.

How much extra supervision will these interns require?

Each intern is individually assessed, and direct supervision, provided by the on-site instructor, is adjusted according to the intern's needs. As interns demonstrate competence, the program supervision is faded out incrementally, engineering a successful experience that acclimates the youth to the work environment and demands. Some interns require almost no extra supervision from the very first day. Others are watched and guided more gradually toward independent performance. Eventually, all interns work with about the same level of employer supervision that is provided to any entry-level employee with your organization.

What about liability?

The interns receive school credit for their time on the job. [If applicable] They are employees of the school district and are enrolled as full-time students. Because they are enrolled students in an approved program, they are insured against injury or liability by the school district, at no cost to you.

PHASE II
Postsecondary Services Received When Hiring a Career Ladders Graduate

What happens to the interns after their internship ends?

Interns are all close to their high school graduation, and in Career Ladders, our goal is to have them employed full-time as soon as possible. Interns attend a weekly employment skills workshop where they learn job-keeping, job search, and job interview skills. Their search begins in earnest during the last half of the semester. Although we hope that all our interns will have become highly desirable employees by this time, we only request that they be seriously considered by Career Ladders sponsors for permanent positions. Career Ladders makes an ongoing commitment to the careers of its interns and will provide services not only to help them get their first job, but also to sustain employment.

Who are Career Ladders graduates?

Career Ladders graduates have exited the public schools and met all of the stringent training requirements of a Career Ladders internship (see Phase I). They are trained in job-keeping skills and are motivated and prepared to enter the job market. Some Career Ladders graduates have special needs: perhaps they do not read well or have a specific learning style. Career Ladders staff addresses these needs by matching the graduate to a job where this difference is not relevant, by providing additional support and accommodation, or by assisting in the provision of an accommodation at the workplace.

What are the advantages of hiring Career Ladders graduates?

The advantages are many. As shown on the Return on Investment chart for Phase II, tax credits, training costs, and accommodations can be arranged and financed. When you work directly with our transition specialists, we screen our graduates to make sure that we send you candidates who are qualified and motivated to work in the field. Our graduates all have work experience. They are acclimated to the demands of the workplace. They are eager to develop their careers and grow with a company. Finally, they are not "dropped off at your door" and forgotten. They and you will have the ongoing support of our transition specialists to ensure that the job placement is satisfactory and successful. The enclosed Summary of Transition Services [Appendix 4.1 of this book] outlines the types of services we provide.

How do I know that this program works?

As part of various mandates to enlarge transition opportunities for youths, Career Ladders engages in rigorous studies, evaluations, and revisions of its services. Employers, parents, and the graduates themselves provide us with the feedback we use to upgrade our services. Furthermore, part of our evaluation is to follow up on the outcomes of our graduates. The last formal evaluation showed that more than 92% of Career Ladders graduates were working, in postsecondary school, or in a combination of the two. Their job retention rate is excellent. Endorsements from the people we serve, media coverage, and the continued support of the main social service agencies in the area testify to the profitability and positive contribution of Career Ladders. When you meet with any of our staff, we will be happy to refer you to participating employers who can describe to you themselves the experience of working with us.

Phase I: Return on Investment

	Sponsor	Career Ladders
Costs	No initial costs	On-site instructor Extra supervision Transition specialist Employability instruction Minimum wage stipend
Commitments	3 hours' work per day for each intern Willingness to assume supervision over an 18-week period	Initial supervision Instruction Career counseling Demand of excellence
Returns	Production Positive public service Positive public relations	Employability Integrated workforce Continuation of services

Phase II: Return on Investment

	Employer	Career Ladders
Costs	Entry-level wage and benefits	Transition specialist Rehabilitation case services
Commitments	Whatever is offered to other entry-level employees	Ongoing support for the career development of Career Ladders graduate
Returns	Low turnover Already trained—cuts costs Motivated Acclimated to workplace Meets affirmative action guidelines Possible tax credits or subsidies through placement agencies or federal programs	Employability Integrated workforce Continuation of services

To pursue the development of your affiliation with
Career Ladders, contact:

Phase I. Mary Jones 555-4999

Phase II: Mark Roberts 555-3330

Career Ladders: 555-7858
H. Caulfield, Coordinator
Gerry Marks, Site Developer
J. Stanford, Project Director

Job Shadowing for Students in Grades 7 to 10

6

CHAPTER

Shepherd Siegel ■

One high school senior's first exposure to the world of work is an on-the-job training program designed to help her make the transition from school to her first job in an area of identified interest and ability. She chooses a clerical setting in a large business. Five weeks into the semester, the young woman realizes that she is not really interested in this kind of work, and she no longer wishes to work there or to participate in the program, but changing her placement is no longer feasible.

A young man with cerebral palsy has severely limited physical movement, and generally does not speak out or use his communication board. However, his family, physical therapist, and educational team all agree that he has at least average intelligence, and in fact he performs above grade level in math. He is offered and accepts a training opportunity entering billing and invoice data on a hospital computer system. Even though he has physical limitations, the main concern of his on-site instructors is not whether he can perform the job tasks, but the fact that he has never before been exposed to a work environment. They fear that he will not be able to establish himself socially or communicate his needs.

One employer's only contacts with students are the perennial offers by subsidized jobs programs to place a youth with her business during the summer months. While the idea appealed to her initially, the programs sent her youths who were unaccustomed to the requirements of the work world, and brought little understanding of what her business was about and how it or any business had to function. Even though she was not paying the wage, she was unable to integrate the youths into her business because they could not be counted on to show up, and they lacked good job-keeping skills or knowledge of workplace decorum. The monitoring of the youths was insufficient, and the employer felt burned by the program. She now gets her extra help through a temporary agency, and has no time to bother with school or youth-oriented social programs. She would rather pay the wage.

Another employer has a business that does not lend itself to young or entry-level employees. He employs a small, well-trained and educated group of employees, and operates with a very small overhead. He and his employees are a dedicated bunch and have no time to learn about teen parents or youths with special needs, including those of low income, from different cultures, or having any physical, sensory, emotional, or cognitive disabilities.

A young man lives in a neighborhood where no person and no thing indicate that he will ever prosper in a legitimate career. He cannot bring himself to the decision to get out of his impoverished environment because there are no models, no access, no options, and no space for him to even imagine himself as part of the mainstream. Alienated and frustrated, he breaks into the store of a local merchant and steals the things he has always wanted but never believed he could earn.

The above anecdotes are all true. And they are all demonstrations of the need for career-oriented services to youths well before they enter high school. By career orientation, we mean simply avenues where the values and realities of the adult work world can travel to youths facing risky circumstances in ways that they can understand. We believe that the above anecdotes need not always be true, that they can be history, not current events. The job shadowing program described in this chapter is one way to send students the message at an earlier age that meaningful and gainful careers are options within their reach. And the shadowing program is a way for them to find out earlier in life which career direction will resonate with their interests, passions, abilities, and values.

WHAT ARE WE HOPING TO ACCOMPLISH?

As children reach the beginning of their adolescence, they enter a phase in which they begin to realize that adulthood is in fact in their future. They will become adults. But what is horribly inadequate are the efforts we make as adults, in our schools and our communities, to introduce students to the adult world and send them the message that there is a place there for them. There are too few legitimate role models, especially for those who may not have working parents or who live in neighborhoods with low employment rates. And even for adolescents in more affluent conditions, the range of possible adult roles is often extremely narrow because of what is expected of them (i.e., the pursuit of a bachelor's degree, even if it conflicts with their interests).

An elementary school in Seattle has a yearly project called Village Day. Each class, from kindergarten to fifth grade, picks a business to operate on Village Day: radio station, bank, pet store, pizzeria, gift shop of recycled materials, and so on. Once or twice a year, the school coins its own money (putting the principal on the dollar bill), sets up booth-like shops in the hallways and classrooms, puts up festive and colorful decorations, and opens the school to the community.

The school is filled with curious and proud families, elected officials, local merchants, and community members, while these very young children, for one afternoon, are noisily and gleefully playing the adult roles of a village. The experience is all the more striking and poignant because this is a school where 16% of the students come from homeless families. There is no underestimating the dramatic and palpable effects of this role playing, where children coming from families where their parents are definitively "nobody" receive a powerful message: You are going to be somebody. This is the essence of why exposure to career possibilities must come early and often in every student's education.

Field trips are a time-honored, or perhaps timeworn, method for exposing groups of students to the adult world and adult career roles. This methodology can be updated and made more academically substantive when students fully study the related fields (e.g., learning about architecture, engineering, and construction before visiting a major construction site). Students can prepare a list of serious and challenging questions to ask while on site, and then continue studies when they have returned to the classroom.

But students need more than field trips as a means of introduction to the world of work; they need effective educational tools, such as career pathways. Career pathways, or clusters, are broad categories of types of careers, such as health science or manufacturing. The purpose of grouping careers together into categorical clusters is to provide a means for students to get a handle on the world of work.

The U.S. Department of Education has identified 16 career clusters:

- Agriculture and Natural Resources
- Architecture and Construction
- Arts, Audio/Visual Technology, and Communications
- Business and Administration
- Education and Training
- Finance
- Government and Public Administration
- Health Science
- Hospitality and Tourism

- Human Services
- Information Technology
- Law and Public Safety
- Manufacturing
- Retail/Wholesale Sales and Services
- Scientific Research and Engineering
- Transportation, Distribution, and Logistics

More information about career clusters, a U.S. Department of Education initiative, can be found on the Internet at www.careerclusters.org. For younger students, career categories can be even further simplified into four basic career pathways. If not profoundly comprehensive, at least these four categories provide an excellent first step to help students get their minds wrapped around the world of career possibilities, and will mesh well with their development of values. These four, easy to learn and memorize, pathways are as follows:

- *Arts, Humanities, Communications, and Media.* This pathway involves working with performance, images, information, and sound. It includes careers such as performing visual, literary, and media arts; architecture; creative writing; film; fine arts; graphic design; media production; journalism; foreign languages; radio and television broadcasting; advertising; and public relations. And it can encompass the classic liberal arts and humanities education.

- *Business and Marketing.* This pathway provides goods and services. It includes careers in entrepreneurship, sales, marketing, hospitality and tourism, computers and information systems, finance, accounting, personnel, economics, and business management.

- *Health and Human Services.* This pathway provides services intended to improve physical, social, and mental well-being. It includes careers such as medicine, dentistry, nursing, therapy and rehabilitation, nutrition, fitness and hygiene, education, legal services, law enforcement, public administration, child and family services, religion, and social services.

- *Science, Engineering, and Industry.* This pathway involves solving technical and science-oriented problems with a hands-on approach. It includes careers such as agriculture, earth science, fisheries science, drafting, horticulture, manufacturing technology, mechanics and repair, electronics, building trades, and engineering.

As young students learn, discover, and articulate their values, they see that people who like to build things and solve technical problems often connect to careers in the Science, Engineering, and Industry pathway. People who like to work with other people and help them usually work in the Health and Human Services pathway, and so on. Information technology has become so large and critical to our economy, it could easily constitute a fifth pathway on its own. However, we prefer to teach it as an academic literacy, like reading or math, which is essential to and spans all career pathways.

Career pathways are not the same as tracking. As a matter of fact, career pathways, and the experimental selection of a pathway some time early in a student's high school career, is the opposite of tracking. Tracking occurs when students, against their will, are grouped together based on normative assessments of their abilities. Career pathways occurs when students make a choice based on their interest, and spend time with other students of all abilities who share that interest. In a world where adults have decided what nonnegotiable academic standards all students must meet, it is so important that students be empowered to determine the direction, character, and flavor of their education. This is especially critical for those students easily disengaged from conventional school experiences.

It is a myth that having students choose career pathways will limit their options and set them on a narrow career track. The United States tends to be the land of "you can always change your mind," and career pathways will do little to change that. Career pathways can transform a general education high school program that is about nothing in particular into a project-based, passion-inducing experience that is very much about something. Students who, for example, devote their high school experience to classes and activities in business and marketing, but decide upon high school graduation that they want to pursue the arts as a career, will in many ways be in a better position to succeed. Students who change their career pathway every year will develop eclectic interests and learn the consequences of making a decision, and the consequences of changing decisions. Students who reject the classification scheme and come up with a high school and beyond plan that combines attributes of all four pathways are likely the creative leaders of tomorrow. At least the presentation of pathways challenged them to think substantively about the value their education has for their future.

WHAT IS A JOB SHADOW?

A job shadow is the substantive experience that makes career pathways and other school-based career curriculum meaningful. It is more intense than a field trip and less intense than an internship. It is an opportunity for up to three students to spend 3 to 6 hours at a workplace on a single day, with one person. Rather than getting the mile-wide and inch-deep overview a field trip provides, students delve into one aspect of an organization's work. They get an opportunity to begin what could be an authentic professional relationship with an engaged adult worker. They get to try some tasks that this adult worker does. Over lunch, they learn more about the kind of person who chooses, pursues, and loves this kind of work. It is one of the best forms of career exploration.

A transitional experience that can be used as early as the sixth grade and is more viable with fewer resources is the group job shadow. This follows the tenets described below, but allows up to 10 students to participate. It is a little more like a field trip, yet still allows for a closer and more academically rigorous experience. The trade-off is that because of the number of students, the connection between the host and the students is diluted, and lasting connections are less likely.

Ideally, students in Grades 7 to 10 would be able to conduct up to three job shadows every semester. Cumulatively, these experiences would create a portfolio of career possibilities that students could explore, reject, or defer. When students have an opportunity to select high school classes, academies, or internships, they will be able to make informed career decisions based on facts they learned from a real doctor, lawyer, or musi-

cian, and not on the images they see on television or in popular culture.

Two very popular career interests among youths in the middle grades, for example, are architect and veterinarian. However, when students have had a chance to observe the daily life of either of these professionals up close, and find out the kind of preparation and requirements of either profession, they sometimes reconsider. They might reject their original choice, having had illusions debunked, and might shift gears and learn about a related profession that still speaks to their passion, or they may pursue the original choice all the more vigorously. These are all good outcomes, and all superior to a student wandering through high school telling all that "I'm going to be a veterinarian" and never having a clue as to what that involves or what preparations are needed.

ELEMENTS OF A QUALITY JOB SHADOWING PROGRAM

An ideal and comprehensive job shadowing program requires resources. This chapter describes the ideal program, but creative educators who cannot obtain these resources often find alternate ways to provide a quality experience. But no matter how a program is formatted, whenever students are going to extend their education into the community, the following three questions must be answered affirmatively: Is the student safe? Is measurable learning occurring? Is the school developing a positive relationship with this partner in the community? If there are not enough resources and energy to ensure a positive answer to all three questions, then the risks outweigh the rewards, and the program should not be pursued.

For the Employer and School

In the ideal job shadowing program, a full-time coordinator develops an array of employer hosts in the communities, in all four of the career pathways described above, and in the public, private, and nonprofit sectors. These employers know what to expect when students arrive, they have designed a unique experience within the parameters of the school program, and they are willing to repeat the experience. A job shadowing program, in fact, is a great opportunity for those employers who cannot commit to hosting internships but who still want to contribute to the career education of students in their community.

Next, in the school environment, the principal and staff have committed to the job shadowing program: transportation and materials are funded, and most important, teachers agree to release students from class up to three times per semester. There are two basic permutations for this arrangement. Either it will be an occurrence whereby different groups of a few students will miss class on a regular basis, or else teachers, aides, parents, and the coordinator will work together so that an entire class or group of classes will disperse into the community on a variety of simultaneous job shadows.

With these elements and commitments in place, the program coordinator generates forms and curriculum. The coordinator provides the employer with a Job Shadow Employer Registration (Appendix 6.1) and Job Shadow Guidelines (Appendix 6.2). A parent consent form should be sent home as arrangements are made. This form can be adapted from the school district's field trip consent form, but the special circumstances of a job shadow—student will not be constantly supervised by school personnel and may be there alone—should be noted. Such forms should be approved by the legal office of the district. A separate form may be necessary for the student to be released from classes for that day.

In a job shadowing program, quality control is extremely important. The continued success of the program hinges almost entirely on the ability of the school's personnel and students to generate positive public relations. As such, students will benefit from rehearsals before going out on job shadows, and teachers should not hesitate to set clear behavioral benchmarks for students to meet (e.g., dress, ability to ask questions, politeness) before they can go out. A Job Shadow Evaluation (Appendix 6.3) provided to participating employers lets them know that the school values quality

and wants to continuously improve. The evaluation gives the employer a chance to provide feedback that will help the coordinator make changes that will help sustain the program and the school's good name. If these arrangements are handled professionally, then the success of the program will rely on the classroom teacher and the students, as it should.

For the Student

Students should be prepared for the job shadow experience by having heard about it from older peers, and by having the teacher refer to it as a future activity for students responsible enough to handle it. The job shadow should be put into the context of academic objectives. Students should ask how much reading, math, science, and communication skill is required in the job they are shadowing. Teachers can say things such as, "School-based learning is about the world. Here is an opportunity to test your learning *in* the world, find out what you know and don't know, and tap into some real excitement about what you might be able to accomplish as an adult." When the shadow experience and its educational context have been conveyed successfully, students are ready to embark on their first contact with job shadow hosts.

Students rehearse a script for making contact with the employer (see Appendix 6.4), then call and set up the time and meeting for their job shadow. This is great rehearsal for cold calls that they may have to make later in life when they pursue employment.

At this point, if the student has not already engaged in some study of the pathway and the specifics of this job shadow opportunity within the pathway, that study should commence. Students should understand what the career pathways are, and how the students fit into them. Once a job shadow is arranged, the U.S. Department of Education's 16 career pathways can be introduced; students can fine-tune their job shadow selection and study the field in more detail.

During the actual job shadow, all students will interview their host using the questions in Appendix 6.5 and the students' own industry-specific questions. The students should pick four questions from the list in Appendix 6.5 and develop three of their own. Provide students with a clipboard, pens, and enough blank paper (or palm-sized computers) for the interview. Before the job shadow, students should practice taking notes from a live interview; some students may perform better with a hand-held tape or digital recorder from which they can later transcribe. If so, the host should be aware of the recording. Upon return, students write a report based on the job shadow interview. As part of their report, they include a Job Shadow Evaluation and Next Steps form (Appendix 6.6). A copy of this form can be shared with employers to help them improve the experience and also to see that they are having a real impact on students. Preferably the students send a thank-you note to the employer that not only shows their gratitude for the opportunity, but refers substantively to the experience, and is specific about what was learned and how it will help them develop their career and academic learning.

WHY JOB SHADOWING IS IMPORTANT

Many students will not wait until their junior year in high school for a relevant, community-based experience. Most students who are going to drop out do so before the 10th grade. The transition from middle or junior high to high school is a critical one where many are lost, if not immediately, then soon thereafter. Thus, a dynamic job shadowing program provides substantive experiences that will connect otherwise disenfranchised students, students who do not believe that there is a viable and legitimate future for them. Many youths will at an early age think that they are either going to be wildly famous and successful, or else on the lowest rung of the career ladder, or else involved in crime. The job of educators is to open up the great middle and the tremendous number of options for all students, without eliminating the highest aspirations, because that is where most of us will be living.

As another example, for a young woman to decide to defer pregnancy until after high school or college, she needs the inspiration of a rewarding career well before her high school junior year, which is the optimum time for a student developing a good career plan to do an internship. A youth who is contemplating crime is less likely to steal from someone who has sponsored that youth on a job shadow, and more likely to think that he or she just might be able to earn what he or she wants. The student with a disability can begin to see the relativity of environments, and that accommodations and good job matching could result in a gainful career, especially if that student meets and witnesses a few of the many successful employees with disabilities. And for the high-achieving student, as well as others, job shadows provide an opportunity to add meaning and focus to a high school education.

Middle school and high school need to be about something, and need not be a darkening experience of more and more limits. Rather, an exciting high school experience is one that becomes a succession of opening doors and expanding options. Job shadows are one of the most powerful ways to lay the groundwork for such expansion.

APPENDIX 6.1

Job Shadow
Employer Registration

Business/Organization _____ Contact _____

Address _____

Phone _____ Fax _____ E-mail _____

Student should call _____ at this number _____ at these times _____

Career Pathway: ____ Arts, Humanities, Communication, and Media

                       ____ Business and Marketing

                       ____ Health and Human Services

                       ____ Science, Engineering, and Industry

Describe what your organization does: _____

_____

_____

Schedule job shadows during these hours (3 to 6 hours, include lunch if possible): _____

_____

Appropriate dress in your organization is _____

Activities for student participation include _____

_____

We can host _____ job shadows every semester (September–January and February–June) for _____ students each time. (We recommend a minimum of 3, and a maximum of 15.)

For more information and to revise information on this form, contact:

H. Caulfield
Sealand Public Schools
Sealand, KS
455/555-1832
hcaulfield@sealand.org

APPENDIX 6.2
Job Shadow Guidelines for Employers

What will the student gain?

In a 3- to 6-hour experience with one individual in your organization, a student will do the following:

- See what that person does and who they are: the good, the bad, and the ugly; the fun and the not so fun.
- Begin to decide whether to pursue a career in this field.
- Practice communication skills and reduce the barrier between school culture and the adult world.
- See the connection between school, work, and achieving goals.

What will your organization gain?

By having a student spend time in your organization, you will do the following:

- Contribute to the career exploration for a student.
- Help students decide and learn who they are and how they fit in.
- Promote the image of your organization, its contributions, and the value of your field.
- See improved morale as employees increase the meaningfulness of their work by sharing.

What do we need from you?

- Let the student observe your organization exactly how it normally operates. Change nothing.
- Explain what is happening and the overall rationales of daily operation.
- Give the student a variety of tasks to complete.
- Explain how quality is measured and how it matters.
- Explain the interdependency of your organization to its broader industry.
- Answer the student's questions.
- Have the host, if possible, take the student to lunch to share more informally how she or he came to pursue this line of work.
- If the student seems overly quiet or unresponsive, be patient; some students take considerable time to become comfortable in a new environment.
- Provide the student with some of the ways to continue pursuing knowledge or a career in this field.

APPENDIX 6.3

Job Shadow Evaluation for Employers

(Complete a separate form for each student who came to do a job shadow.)

Name of Organization _____ Hosting Employee _____

Name of Student _____ Date of Job Shadow _____

	Strongly Agree			Strongly Disagree
School personnel provided good support and made the job shadow easy for me to do.	4	3	2	1
Student did a good job of making arrangements.	4	3	2	1
Student arrived on time.	4	3	2	1
Student dressed appropriately.	4	3	2	1
Student asked good questions, listened well, and took notes.	4	3	2	1
Student showed sincere interest in the organization.	4	3	2	1
Student was able to learn at least one new task while shadowing.	4	3	2	1
I would enjoy a chance to get to know this student better.	4	3	2	1

Other comments on the experience with this particular student: _____

_____

_____

Other comments on how the school staff coordinated the experience and provided you with

the information you needed to host a quality job shadow: _____

_____

_____

Other comments on how the program could be improved: _____

_____

_____

APPENDIX 6.4

Student Telephone Procedures and Script for Job Shadow

1. Call the contact person given to you by your teacher or the job shadow coordinator. Have paper and pencil ready.

2. Call during business hours.

3. Ask for the contact person. If she or he is not available, ask for a time when you can call back.

4. When you reach the contact person, say, **"Hello, my name is _____ and I am a student at _____ School. I'm participating in our job shadowing program, and I was told that you would be able to host me there. I've been learning some things about your field, and I'm interested in learning more. When would be a good time for me to come out? For me, I need to do this during these times _____, and have this completed by _____."**

5. When you have made the arrangements and written them down, thank the person: **"I appreciate your time and I appreciate this opportunity to learn."**

6. Ask, **"Is there anything I need to know before I come out there, like what I should wear, or something I need to learn before arriving?"**

7. Confirm the time, date, and exactly where in the building you will be meeting the person. Leave the name of your teacher or coordinator, and a phone number where they can be reached in case there are any changes in the arrangements. Then say thanks and close the conversation.

APPENDIX 6.5

Job Shadow Interview Questions for Students

Circle four questions you definitely want to ask.

1. What is the main work of this organization?

2. What is your part in that main work?

3. How did you come to be working here, doing this?

4. What is the favorite part of your job?

5. What is the least favorite part of your job?

6. What salary range can a person in this field expect to earn?

7. What was your education like? What did it have to do with working here?

8. What makes this organization different from others that do the same work?

9. Where will this organization be in 5 years? Where will you be in 5 years?

10. What is it like being supervised?

11. What is it like supervising others?

12. Do you prefer to work with other people, with things, with data, or with ideas?

13. What should I do if I want to pursue a career in this field?

14. What is a typical day here like?

15. Can you describe the skills I would need to work here? Consider skills in the following areas:

    - math
    - reading and writing
    - communication
    - information technology
    - social skills
    - using resources
    - decision making
    - understanding systems
    - being personally responsible

Now write three original questions of your own.

16. _____

17. _____

18. _____

APPENDIX 6.6

Job Shadow Evaluation and Next Steps for Students

	Strongly Agree			Strongly Disagree
I learned a lot about this organization.	4	3	2	1
I learned more about what I need to know to pursue a career in this field.	4	3	2	1
I enjoyed meeting the people who work there.	4	3	2	1
This experience helped me connect school to my future.	4	3	2	1
I would like to go back to this same place for another visit.	4	3	2	1
I would like to do more job shadows.	4	3	2	1

In this field, I would now like to do a job shadow. (Where?) _____

_____

In another field, I would now like to do a job shadow. (Where?) _____

_____

What did you like most about the person or persons you met? _____

_____

What did you like most about the organization? What did you like least? _____

_____

Describe what next steps you would take to pursue a career in this field. _____

_____

To what other students in your class would you recommend this job shadow? Why?
What kind of person would enjoy a career in this field or a job in this organization?

_____

_____

_____

AFTERWORD: KEEPING THE CHANGE

Shepherd Siegel, Robert Gaylord-Ross, and William Halloran ■

As in many areas of education and society, the fight to gain rights for the few most in need has set the trend for the many. School-to-work transition was first introduced in federal legislation in the Education of the Handicapped Act Amendments of 1983, P.L. 98-199. The amendments drew specific attention to the need to improve the scope and quality of transition services. The U.S. Department of Education's Office of Special Education and Rehabilitative Services defined the critical components of transition planning and put new demonstration programs into place throughout the country. The components of transition include the following:

1. Effective high school programs that prepare students to study, work, and live in the community

2. A broad range of adult service programs that can meet the various support needs of individuals with disabilities in employment and community settings

3. Comprehensive and cooperative transition planning between education and community service agencies for the purpose of developing needed services for high school graduates and for those who leave school

Since the enactment of federal legislation, we have seen a national school-to-career movement that has adopted these principles for all students.

We adapted these critical components into Career Ladders during its conceptualization and development in the 1980s. Career Ladders was distinguished by its overriding principle—services are shaped by the needs of the youths being served.

The research and demonstration efforts supported by the federal discretionary grants program stimulated the development of other new and unique approaches throughout the country. These programs demonstrated that public education can assist youths with a variety of disabilities and levels of impairments in making the adjustment to adult life in their communities. They set in place interagency cooperation between school and adult programs. They also provided instructional support systems to ensure that an individual with disabilities could succeed in real work settings. School-to-career initiatives like the Urban/ Rural Opportunities, Youth Opportunities, and Rewarding Youth Achievement grants have attempted to replicate the model for other populations facing tough circumstances: poverty, immigrant status, drug dependency, sparse employment environments, and so on.

Studies of program effectiveness have shown that three essential components are necessary for a program to succeed. First, families of youths need to be included as partners in the development and implementation of purposeful activities that maximize independence. Career Ladders' design and the findings of its follow-up studies support the efficacy of this feature. The family is a major facilitator of transition. Second, transition programs like Career Ladders must be community based. That is, authentic transition cannot be taught in the classroom, and opportunities to experience and succeed in employment and other aspects of community life must be provided. The third component, one also found in Career Ladders, is the need for working partnerships with employers to ensure that the efforts of the schools are consistent with employers' needs. Programs that prepare youths for employment should include measurement of employers' and coworkers' satisfaction. Additional strengths of successful programs include effective and systematic coordination of agencies, organizations, and individuals from a broad array of disciplines and professional fields.

Given the economic need for well-trained workers, there is obviously some discrepancy between the workers U.S. schools are turning out and extant personnel needs. Besides graduating (or losing) students who are often semiliterate, schools find that many of these youths lack the motivation to work. Although numerous entry-level jobs may be available, many disenfranchised youths size these up as low-paying, dead-end jobs that have little potential for career enhancement. In fact, these jobs, which have substantially expanded in an increasingly service-oriented economy, have been filled largely by part-time workers such as homemakers, high school students, adult immigrant newcomers, and senior citizens. Their low pay and lack of benefits cannot support the head of a household. More important, these entry-level positions do not often lead to career advancement. They are dead-end slots.

An effective and responsible career preparation program needs to orient and train individuals for employment opportunities that incorporate upward mobility. The program described in this book evolved around the notion of such career ladders. It was believed that Career Ladders staff could penetrate the business community and identify positions with career ladder potential. The staff therefore sought and engaged a number of companies of substance that could understand and help advance this vision. Students received on-the-job training in these companies, and this training often led to permanent employment. Positions typically had the potential for upward mobility in terms of job classification, salary, and benefits. In some cases, graduates were counseled to take an

entry-level job with less career potential, but as a stepping-stone to a subsequent position in another company with greater promise. (See Siegel, Avoke, Paul, Robert, & Gaylord-Ross, 1991, and Siegel, Robert, Waxman, & Gaylord-Ross, 1992, for details on Career Ladders interns' career outcomes.) Because Career Ladders transition specialists worked directly with the graduates according to the principle of ongoing availability of service, the transition specialists could guide graduates through their career. Furthermore, the students were told of, or brought into contact with, former participants in the program who were now succeeding in impressive positions. Such role modeling by competent individuals with similar backgrounds has proved to have a powerful psychological effect.

In the past, vocational education in general, and placement programs in particular, have often been posited as being at odds with basic academic instruction. Although we view this conflict as unfortunate and avoidable, it is useful to describe its characteristics. In its most adversarial and pejorative form, vocational education is viewed as removing lesser students from academic instruction and preparing them for unknown or outmoded positions—trading lower class students into lower class jobs.

Because career and technical education programs are disproportionately populated by minority students, there have been accusations that vocational education is racist in this tracking of students into low expectations and watered-down courses of study. In addition, the past decade has seen a growing demand for basic academics and a new academic standards movement. States have identified academic core curricula and absolute standards that must be met for students to graduate. Narrow interpretations have viewed vocational offerings as being outside the core curriculum. In some instances vocational courses have been reduced or eliminated to make way for expanded academic coursework.

A more mature view of career and technical education can lead to its effective synthesis with academic instruction. In fact, career and technical education should be defined as one instructional strategy within an array of effective teaching and learning methods. It should certainly not define itself as a related service and assume second-class status among the curricular offerings. Work experience may place considerable demands on youths.

In fact, in our experiences we have often seen students who might otherwise have dropped out of school altogether, perform academic tasks (e.g., math, writing) in a more spirited manner in work settings than in the classroom. Many career and technical education programs have begun to systematically cross-reference core academic curricular competencies with competencies performed in vocational activities. Thus, the student can receive justifiable academic credit for vocational experiences. Such syntheses of academic and vocational curricula are important and must be expanded in future endeavors. And the question of why a particular academic competency or standard is essential should always be asked.

Career Ladders has assumed a method that efficiently coordinates traditional academic and vocational coursework. A student receives a balance of such work in the 11th and 12th grades. Upon leaving school, the individual confers with the transition specialist about continuing education and permanent employment. Although some graduates choose one or the other, a number of persons prefer to work and continue their education, for example, at a community college. Thus, the graduates balance academic and vocational activities in adult life as well. Ultimately, a curricular agenda that is focused on citizenship (Siegel & Sleeter, 1991), where students learn to own, care for, and serve their communities, will resolve the false conflict between the agendas of vocational and academic education. Excellence in the education of youth for citizenship in a democracy will resolve both the academic and employment ills of our citizenry.

FEDERAL GRANTS AND LOCAL PROGRAMMING

The initial rapid growth of Career Ladders was primarily supported by a model transition federal grant from the U.S. Department of Education. Since the inception of the transition initiative, the federal government has funded a number of similar model programs. This secondary transition network of model programs first attempted to show that successful transition models could be implemented. Success was defined as generating effective interagency relationships that seamlessly serve the individual from secondary to postschool living, placing the individual into permanent competitive employment, and constructing a quality of life and related services that encourage the person to flourish independently in the least restrictive environment. A second goal was to have the model projects serve as seeds to germinate the growth of similar transition programs in that particular region and throughout the country. Model projects receive visitors to their sites and disseminate information at professional meetings; they publish articles, manuals, and books. Thus, programs like Career Ladders are intended to model exemplary practice and result in an expanding, if not statutory, implementation of the transition concept.

Model programs do not always achieve this dissemination function. Some programs, in fact, do not last beyond the life of the 3-year federal grant. That is, the external federal money dries up and local agencies do not have the fiscal wherewithal or ideological resolve to continue the program.

Career Ladders has had a more successful experience in engaging local agency support. Historically, the program began as a high school senior work experience program. A teacher was funded by the San Francisco Unified School District and in-kind coordination was provided by San Francisco State University. The federal grant expanded staff and services to include vocational services for graduates through transition specialists. This expansion, particularly at the postschool level, was further supplemented by local funding from the California Department of Rehabilitation. In addition, Career Ladders expanded downward through the 10th and 11th grades as the school district provided more dollars to fund community-based instructors. The current fiscal support mechanism for Career Ladders evolved from priorities developed by the State of California. The Department of Rehabilitation initially funded over 20 cooperative transition programs throughout the state. Successful Career Ladders activities encouraged the selection of San Francisco as one of these sites. Thus, ongoing local funding for transition activities had been assured by state and local educational and rehabilitation agencies.

Subsequently, a federal multidistrict outreach grant to Career Ladders made it possible for about 25 school districts nationwide to replicate the model. As one might expect, the community classroom and employment skills workshop components were more easily replicated; until 2001, no project was able to fully put the principles of Career Ladders postsecondary services into play. Five of the replication projects were in King County, Washington, and of them, Seattle was operated by Seattle Public Schools' Department of School to Work, serving about 30% students with disabilities. This ratio created an atmosphere akin to other regular education programs, and the students responded very well to the mainstreamed look and feel of the program.

In 2001, the Career Ladders Postsecondary Project, again with funding from the U.S. Department of Education's Office of Special Education Programs, was initiated with the Seattle Public Schools. This time, the clear intent was to implement Career Ladders' postsecondary principles of peer support, ongoing availability of services, continuous cyclical triage, and cohorts in an active demonstration that would hopefully influence policy by 2004.

BLUEPRINTS AND HOPES FOR THE FUTURE

The history and experience of Career Ladders paints an optimistic and idealistic picture for the future. The success it has achieved and the enlightened response it has engendered from the local and state leadership would certainly seem to bode well. But there have been inevitable conflicts as well. Certain aspects of the program's principles—the degree of attention afforded each intern, the ongoing availability of services, the development of sustaining peer support—strained or challenged the existing system beyond the level its resources, regulations, and resolve could attain. Within a year after the San Francisco Unified School District adopted the program, the intensity of the employment skills workshop decreased, and the availability of ongoing services became greatly constrained. Clearly, for substantive innovation to gain footing in this realm requires change on more than one level.

Urie Bronfenbrenner (1979) discussed human development as occurring in four different arenas. *Microsystems* are the smallest and most closed relationships and include the isolated interaction be-

tween teacher and student. *Mesosystems* include the multiple interactions among people who have overlapping contact with each other, much like Hobbs's (1982) ecosystematic approach to supporting troubled and troubling children. *Exosystems* are those whose events have an impact on people, although there is no direct or ongoing contact between the actor and the affected, such as legislative action. Finally, the *macrosystem* is the entire cultural milieu that can pervade all the other systems and create a social ambiance and atmosphere conducive (or resistant) to change.

This volume has dealt primarily with micro- and mesosystematic events and has offered a model for effecting change at that level. That is, given the freedom and latitude that was afforded Career Ladders staff through the license of a federal model demonstration project, a significant alteration in the mode of vocational services was suggested, demonstrated, and validated. In many ways, it is a reform of vocational services parallel to changes in pre- and perinatal and Head Start service proposed by Lisbeth Schorr (1988). Career Ladders is based on the same principles of reasonably sized caseloads and opportunities for long-term relationships to develop. But for either model to precipitate any significant impact, exo- and macrosystematic change must occur subsequent or parallel to local demonstration.

With exosystematic change, even more liberal deregulatory projects must be given legal sanction to allow the further testing and implementation of the Career Ladders model (or other innovative, principle-based approaches). Some reforms that would open the door for a dedicated cadre of service delivery professionals would include (a) experimental criteria for case closure and case reopening with adult service agencies that are more meaningful than 60 successful days on the job or full unemployment; (b) a cohort approach to caseloads (see Chapter 4); (c) alternative criteria to IQ testing (or race, or poverty, or geography, etc.) for need and eligibility of services; and (d) reform of Social Security benefits (see Conley, Noble, & Elder, 1986; Elder, Conley, & Noble, 1986). We hope that future waves of federal initiatives will provide some of these opportunities. Although the original Career Ladders program was designed for students with disabilities, the time is now overdue for a generic youth employment system that trains its staff to handle all variety of special circumstances, and students with all but the most severe disabilities could be competently served. Vocational rehabilitation's regular enforcement of an order of selection policy (whereby only those with the most severe disabilities are served), plus abuse of the special education system, have sent this message loud and clear.

SOCIAL CHANGES NECESSARY TO EXPAND AND IMPROVE SERVICES

In the 1990s we witnessed the legislative changes that have moved transition services from privilege to entitlement for youth with disabilities. Career Ladders and numerous other exemplary demonstration projects have provided significant direction to the field as the need for transition services becomes recognized. Development and improvement in transition programs and services have been enhanced through the identification and replication of effective practices. However, among successful efforts there are components that connect to unique local characteristics. Often, attempts to replicate successful programs do not take this into account. Successful programs use the resources of their community and therefore develop a strong sense of local ownership. The more this sense of ownership is dispersed among agencies, organizations, and individuals, the greater the likelihood of shared community commitment to the goal of successful adult life outcomes for students. Thus there is an interdependency of permission and constraint that ricochets between exo- and meso-systematic progress.

SECONDARY CURRICULUM REFORM: COMPLETING THE INITIAL TRANSITION

Transition should be perceived as a *rite* of passage and a *right* of passage for all youths leaving public school programs. If we believe it is a right, we must advocate a major change in educational practices for youths. We must care more about the quality of life they are capable of attaining beyond high school than about the uniform standards they must meet in order to pass through the public educational system; these goals are not necessarily synonymous. The goal of school-to-career transition programs should be to prepare individuals to study, work, *and* live in their communities. This major change in focus will expand the role of education—for those students who need it—from preparing them for transition to making the initial placement in appropriate community settings with sufficient time for follow-along before school exit. The measure of effectiveness of secondary programs should be not only employment, but also the quality of community life experienced after exiting school.

Career Ladders is aligned with the reforms that are currently under way to improve the outcomes for individuals making the transition from school to the community. The ordering principle of Career Ladders—services that are shaped by the needs of the youths served—must be the bottom line that holds us accountable, and must not conflict with arbitrary academic standards. The contexts, services, and tools embodied in the six principles of Career Ladders combined with the enthusiasm of its implementation present a unique formula for pursuing the reforms necessary to enable youths to become well-adjusted, suitably employed members of our communities.

The final layer of change, then, is macrosystematic. It is a change in the way our entire society views its responsibility to the post–high school outcomes of its youth. Ultimately, the success of the service changes proposed in this book is conditional upon that macrosystematic, culture-sized change. Quality education costs much more money than we currently spend on it, as does quality adult service (Kozol, 1991). Underlying the basic needs of education, training, placement, and support lies the universal need for more authentic and meaningful relationships and lives. When this need finds its way into the mainstream—when it is something adult citizens charge our systems with providing to all students—and is articulated in a fashion that stimulates a culture-wide change in values, then education will no longer be labeled as either academic or career. Instead, it will be defined simply as serving the transition to full participation in a democratic society. This service will be readily available to those who need it, and will not be squandered on those who do not. It will serve the desire for excellence that resides in all citizens and will transform work, study, social integration, and the evolution of all our institutions into tools for making meaningful, connected, and satisfying lives for all.

REFERENCES

Allen, R., Krause, R., & Hawkins, M. (2002). *CareerTalk, a special edition of SkillTalk*. Bellevue, WA: Performance Spectrum.

Americans with Disabilities Act of 1990, 42 U.S.C. § 12101 *et seq.*

Anema, D., & Lefkowitz, W. (1996). *Don't get fired! How to keep a job*. Lebanon, IN: Globe Fearon Pearson Learning Group.

Bissonnette, D. (1994). *Beyond traditional job development: The art of creating opportunity*. Chatsworth, CA: Milt Wright and Associates.

Bronfenbrenner, U. (1979). *The ecology of human development: Experiments by nature and design*. Cambridge, MA: Harvard University Press.

California State Department of Education. (1986). *Work-Ability job development manual*. Sacramento: Author.

Civil Rights Act of 1964, 42 U.S.C. § 1971 *et seq.*

Clark, G. (1979). *Career education for the handicapped child in the elementary classroom*. Denver, CO: Love.

Clark, G., & Kolstoe, O. P. (1990). *Career development and transition education for adolescents with disabilities*. Boston: Allyn & Bacon.

Conley, R. W., Noble, J. H., Jr., & Elder, J. K. (1986). Problems with the service system. In W. E. Kiernan & J. A. Stark (Eds.), *Pathways to employment for adults with developmental disabilities* (pp. 67–83). Baltimore: Brookes.

DeStefano, L., & Snauwaert, D. (1989). *A value-critical approach to transition policy analysis*. Secondary Transition Intervention Effectiveness Institute. Champaign: University of Illinois.

Edgerton, R. B. (1967). *The cloak of competence: Stigma in the lives of the retarded*. Berkeley: University of California.

Education for All Handicapped Children Act of 1975, 20 U.S.C. § 1400 *et seq.*

Education of the Handicapped Act Amendments of 1983, 20 U.S.C. § 1400 *et seq.*

Elder, J. K., Conley, R. W., & Noble, J. H., Jr. (1986). The service system. In W. E. Kiernan & J. A. Stark (Eds.), *Pathways to employment for adults with developmental disabilities* (pp. 53–66). Baltimore: Brookes.

Fair Labor Standards Act of 1938, 29 U.S.C. § 201 *et seq.*

Gibbs, J. (2001). *Tribes: A new way of learning and being together*. Windsor, CA: CenterSource.

Goldstein, A. P., & McGinnis, E. (1997). *Skillstreaming the adolescent*. Champaign, IL: Research Press.

Hazel, J. S., Schumaker, J. B., Sherman, J. A., & Sheldon-Wildgen, J. S. (1981). *ASSET: A social skills program for adolescents* [Videotape series]. Champaign, IL: Research Press.

Hobbs, N. (1982). *The troubled and troubling child*. San Francisco: Jossey-Bass.

Individuals with Disabilities Education Act of 1990, 20 U.S.C. § 1400 *et seq.*

Irvin, L. (1988). Vocational assessment in school and rehabilitation programs. In R. Gaylord-Ross (Ed.), *Vocational education for persons with handicaps* (pp. 111–141). Palo Alto, CA: Mayfield.

Kozol, J. (1991). *Savage inequalities: Children in America's schools*. New York: Crown.

Redl, F., & Wineman, D. (1951). *Children who hate*. New York: Free Press.

Rimmer, J. (2001). *Seattle Public Schools' profile of the graduate*. Unpublished manuscript.

Seattle Public Schools. (n.d.). Seattle Public Schools Academic Standards. Retrieved July 22, 2002, from http://www.seattleschools.org/area/acastan/index.xml

Schorr, L., with Schorr, D. (1988). *Within our reach: Breaking the cycle of disadvantage*. New York: Doubleday.

Siegel, S. (1988). Career Ladders: Implementing Re-ED principles in vocational settings. *Behavioral Disorders, 14*(1), 16–26.

Siegel, S., Avoke, S. K., Paul, P., Robert, M., & Gaylord-Ross, R. (1991). A second look at the adult lives of participants in Career Ladders. *Journal of Vocational Rehabilitation, 1*(4), 9–24.

Siegel, S., & Gaylord-Ross, R. (1991). Factors associated with job success among youths with learning disabilities. *Journal of Learning Disabilities, 24*(1), 40–47.

Siegel, S., Robert, M., Waxman, M., & Gaylord-Ross, R. (1992). A follow-along study of participants in a longitudinal transition program for youths with mild disabilities. *Exceptional Children, 58*(4), 346–356.

Siegel, S., & Sleeter, C. E. (1991). Transforming transition: Next stages for the school-to-work transition movement. *Career Development for Exceptional Individuals, 14*(1), 27–41.

Simon, S. B., Howe, L. W., & Kirschenbaum, H. (1995). *Values clarification: A handbook of practical strategies for teachers and students*. New York: Warner.

Stodden, R. A., & Boone, R. (1987). Assessing transition services for handicapped youth: A cooperative interagency approach. *Exceptional Children, 53*(6), 537–545.

Stodden, R. A., & Ianacone, R. (1981). Career/vocational assessment of the special needs individual: A conceptual model. *Exceptional Children, 47*, 600–609.

Varenhorst, B. B. (in press). *Peer-to-peer asset building*. Minneapolis, MN: Search Institute.

Wagner, M., & Shaver, D. (1989). *Educational programs and achievements of secondary special education students: Findings from the National Longitudinal Transition Study*. Menlo Park, CA: Stanford Research Institute.

Wilson, W. J. (1987). *The truly disadvantaged*. Chicago: University of Chicago Press.

Workforce Investment Act of 1998, 20 U.S.C. § 9201 *et seq.*

INDEX

Academic standards, 18, 19–22, 24, 190
Active listening, 75
ADA. *See* Americans with Disabilities Act (ADA)
Adult service agencies
    conflict with transition services, 125, 127–128
    coordination between, 125–127
    quota-oriented policies, 121, 128–129, 137
    transition specialist role, 78, 118–119, 121
Advocacy, strategic, 127
Allen, Ralph, 60
Americans with Disabilities Act (ADA), 12, 144
Anema, Durlynn, 60
Animal, Color, Water, White Room exercise, 68–69
Applications, job, 79, 100–101
Appointment calendars, 92
Assessments, educational/vocational, 126–127, 192
Attendance. *See also* Punctuality
    data collection and, 22
    emphasis on, 24, 64
    lesson plans, 68
    policies, 15, 38
Availability of ongoing services
    about, 6
    cyclical triage, 129–134
    intern success and, 117
    youth appreciation of, 119

Benefactor relationships. *See* Mentoring structures
Beyond Traditional Job Development: The Art of Creating Opportunity
        (Bissonnette), 137
Bissonnette, Denise, 137
Boone, R., 116
Brochures, 160, 165–168
Bronfenbrenner, Urie, 192
Burnout, 128, 136
Business proposals, 160, 170–175

Calendars, appointment, 92
Capitalism, 85
careerclusters.org, 179
Career development services. *See* Transition services
Career Ladders program. *See also* Community classrooms,
        Employment skills workshops, Postsecondary services
    admission standards, 11–12
    graduates, 7, 84, 91, 117, 120
    main components, 13
    pilot studies, 9, 14, 115
    policies, 14, 15, 25, 38, 70
    principles, 3–7, 10, 11
    success rates, 2, 7–8, 137
Career pathways, 178–179

Career Talk (Allen, Krause, & Hawkins), 60
Careers. *See* Employment
Caseload management, 132–136
Case studies, 40–43, 139–143
Character traits
    motivation, 4, 25–26, 71–72, 190
    pride, 88–89
    punctuality, 10, 15, 22, 24
    responsibility, 69–70
    stamina and determination, 71–72
Coding systems, 120, 131–132
Cohort service delivery model, 128–134
Community classrooms. *See also* Employment skills workshops,
        Postsecondary services
    defined, 9
    motivational issues, 25–26
    objectives for interns, 18, 22–23, 24, 45–46
    on-site instructor timeline, 55–56
    orientation phase, 12–14
    performance evaluations, 23–24, 45–46, 54
    phase flowchart, 27
    program phase, 16–27
    recruitment phase, 10–12
    transfers, 26
    unpaid trial period, 14, 25, 70
Community engagement, 118, 163–168, 193–194
Compensation policies, 14, 25, 70
Confidentiality, 66, 120
Conversation building exercises, 70, 85–86, 108
Counseling, 122–123
Counseling Checklist, 39
Counselor–Job Seeker agreement, 96
Crocodile Creek exercise, 80, 102–104
Curricula, school, 190–191, 193–194
Customer service, 83
Cyclical triage, 129–134

Data collection
    forms, 22, 47–53, 155–156
    job search and, 24
    journal keeping, 24, 51, 137–138
    objectives and, 22–23
    value of, 4, 18, 138–139
Decision Agent exercise, 82
Delivery models, service. *See* Service delivery models
Directions
    following, 74, 82, 111–112
    giving, 113
Disabilities
    accommodation for, 17, 131, 144
    benefits of employing youth with, 162

disclosure during interview, 12
service delivery reform and, 129
Disabilities Education Act, 12
Diversified occupations teachers. *See* On-Site Instructors
Don't Get Fired! How to Keep a Job (Anema & Lefkowitz), 60

Ecosystematic intervention, 124, 192
Edgerton, R. B., 127
Educational assessments, 126–127, 192
Employer-pleasing behaviors. *See* Job-keeping skills
Employment. *See also* entries beginning with "job"
career options exploration, 177–189
developing intern opportunities, 157–162
realities of the work world, 90
school curricula and, 190–191
value of, 7–8, 25
Employment skills workshops. *See also* Community classrooms,
Postsecondary services
closing rituals, 93
Counselor–Job Seeker agreement, 96
course objectives, 59–60
curriculum strands, 62
defined, 57
instructor–intern relationship, 61–62
lesson plans. *See* Lesson plans
on-site instructor role, 74
purpose, 57–58
pyramid of transition skills, 13, 58, 67
recommended materials, 60–61
transition specialist role, 69, 78, 119
Exercises
Animal, Color, Water, White Room, 68–69
conversation building, 70, 85–86, 108
Crocodile Creek, 80, 102–104
Decision Agent, 82
Having a Conversation exercise, 70
"I" statements, 70, 72, 94
Pioneer, Warrior, Hero, 69
problem solving, 70
values ranking, 82

Families
as job search resource, 77, 162
on-site instructor calls to, 17, 25
role in program, 5, 12–14, 33, 189–190
Feedback
negative, 85–86, 90, 109–110
positive, 73, 108
Floundering period, 117, 130
Funding
government grants, 191–192
pilot studies, 115
quota-oriented policies and, 121, 128–129
reform proposals, 118

Gaylord-Ross, Robert, 197
Gender considerations, 134
Gibbs, Jeanne, 60
Goal setting, 117
Goldstein, Arnold, 60
Government grants, 191–192
Greener, Karen, 197

Halloran, William, 197
Handoff phase, 116, 118

Having a Conversation exercise, 70
Hawkins, Marty, 60
Hobbies, 89
Hobbs, N., 192
Howe, Leland, 60

Ianacone, R., 116
Independent living skills, 123
Individualized programs, 3–4, 115, 129
Individualized Transition Plans (ITPs), 125
Instructions
following, 74, 82, 111–112
giving, 113
Instructors, on-site. *See* On-site instructors
Integration of youth. *See* Transition services
Interagency articulation, 125–127
Interpersonal Growth. *See* Social skills
Interviews
disability disclosure, 12
lesson plans, 73, 77–78, 82, 84, 91
notification paperwork, 31–32
rating sheets, 98
in recruitment phase, 11
typical questions, 97
Introduction letter, 169
Irvin, L., 116
"I" statements, 70, 72, 94
ITPs. *See* Individualized Transition Plans (ITPs)

Job applications, 79, 100–101
Job coaches. *See* On-site instructors
Job descriptions, 34–37, 119–120
Job development
cultivating employer relationship, 163
importance of, 137
marketing and sales aspect, 157–162
tools, 160, 165–175
Job-keeping skills
data collection and, 23
defined, 62
lesson plans, 65–71, 74–75, 78–80, 82–83, 85, 87–89, 92
overview, 63
Job Placement Record, 151
Jobs. *See* Employment
Job search skills
about, 26–27, 62
contact sheet, 99
data collection and, 24
lesson plans, 73–74, 76–84, 87–91
overview, 63
transition specialist role, 124–125
Job shadowing, 177–189
Job skills
defined, 62
lesson plans, 64–68, 74, 86–87, 91
overview, 63
Journal keeping, 24, 51, 137–138

Kirschenbaum, Howard, 60
Krause, Roberta, 60

Lefkowitz, William, 60
Lesson plans
job-keeping skills, 65–71, 74–75, 78–80, 82–83, 85, 87–89, 92
job search skills, 73–74, 76–84, 87–91
job skills, 64–68, 74, 86–87, 91

overview, 63
    personal growth, 66, 68–70, 72–75, 82–83, 94, 102–104
    social skills, 69, 75–76, 81, 84–86, 107–113
Letter of introduction, 169
Lights and Action, 40–43

Management issues, staff, 132–136
Marketing and job development
    brochure, 160, 165–168
    business proposal, 160, 170–175
    letter of introduction, 169
    sales skills importance, 157–162
McGinnis, Ellen, 60
Measuring performance. *See* Data collection
Mentoring structures
    about, 6–7
    coworkers, 15, 164
    job shadowing, 177–189
    on-site instructors. *See* On-site instructors
    transition specialists. *See* Transition specialists
Meyer, Gary, 197
Motivation, 4, 25–26, 71–72, 190

Negative feedback, 85–86, 90, 109–110

Office of Special Education and Rehabilitative Services
        (OSERS), 115
One-stop centers, 58, 145–146
On-site instructors
    case study evaluation by, 40–43
    community classroom timeline, 55–56
    counseling checklist, 39
    employment skills workshops role, 74
    family contacts, 17, 25
    job description, 34
    orientation phase role, 12–14
    program phase role, 16–18, 22–27
    recruitment phase role, 10–12
Open-ended questions, 74–75

Pay policies, 14, 25, 70
Peer group support, 6–7
Peer-to-Peer Asset Building (Varenhorst), 61
Performance evaluations, 23–24, 45–46, 54
Performance measurement. *See* Data collection
Personal Growth
    defined, 62
    lesson plans, 66, 68–70, 72–75, 82–83, 94, 102–104
    overview, 63
Personalized services, 3–4, 115, 129
Pilot studies, 9, 14, 115
Pioneer, Warrior, Hero exercise, 69
Policies
    attendance, 15, 38
    paid/unpaid work, 14, 25, 70
    quota-oriented, 121, 128–129, 137
Positive feedback, 73, 108
Postsecondary services. *See also* Community classrooms,
        Employment skills workshops
    cohort service delivery model, 128–134
    conflict resolution, 126
    delivery model conflicts, 125, 127–128
    ecosystematic intervention, 124, 192
    education/training support, 117, 121–124
    follow-up contact, 120–121
    handoff phase, 118

Individualized Transition Plans, 125
    interagency articulation, 125–127
    program features, 116–118
    summary of services, 147
    tracking forms, 152
    transition specialist role. *See* Transition specialists
Pride, 88–89
Principles of Career Ladders, 3–7, 10, 11
Problem-solving exercises, 70
Program manager job description, 35
Project coordinator job description, 37
Punctuality, 10, 15, 22, 24
Pyramid of transition skills, 13, 58, 67

Questions, open-ended, 74–75
Quota-oriented services, 121, 128–129, 137

Recruitment of interns, 10–12
Reeducation of Emotionally Disturbed Youth (Re-ED), 5
Referral paperwork, 29–30
Reform proposals
    funding policies, 118
    school curricula changes, 193–194
    service delivery models, 128–134, 192–193
Responsibility, 69–70
Resumes, 73–74, 80–81, 105–106
Robert, Matt, 197
Rotation of job tasks, 26
Rules. *See* Policies

Sales skills importance, 157–162
School curricula, 190–191, 193–194
Seattle Public Schools academic standards, 18–22
Service delivery models
    adult. *See* Adult service agencies
    cohort, 128–134
    social, 125, 127–134, 192–193
Services, ongoing availability of. *See* Availability of ongoing services
Shadowing, job, 177–189
Siegel, Shepard, 197
Simon, Sidney, 60
Skills
    independent living, 123
    job-keeping skills. *See* Job-keeping skills
    job search. *See* Job search skills
    on-the-job. *See* Job skills
    sales and marketing, 157–162
    social skills. *See* Social skills
    transition pyramid, 13, 58, 67
*Skillstreaming the Adolescent: New Strategies and Perspectives for
        Teaching Prosocial Skills* (Goldstein & McGinnis), 60
Social skills
    assessment, on-site, 22–23, 44
    defined, 62
    lesson plans, 69, 75–76, 81, 84–86, 107–113
    overview, 63
    transition specialist role, 123–124
Soft skills. *See* Job-keeping skills
Staff
    burnout, 128, 134
    caseload meetings, 132–135
    job descriptions, 34–37, 119–120
    management issues, 132–136
    team building importance, 116
Stamina and determination, 71–72
Stodden, R. A., 116

Team building, 116
Termination, 74
Time management, 136
Tracking. *See* Data collection
Transfers, 26
Transition services. *See also* Community classrooms, Employment
   skills workshops, Postsecondary services
   conflict with adult agencies, 125, 127–128
   defined, 2, 115
   features, 116–118
   need for, 2–3, 7–8
   principles, 3–7, 10, 11
Transition skills pyramid, 13, 58, 67
Transition specialists
   adult service agency liaison, 78, 118–119, 121
   caseload management, 132–136
   case study, 139–143
   duties, 117, 123–124, 124–125, 149, 153
   intern relationship importance, 115–119, 143, 146
   job description, 36, 119–120
   pregraduation contact, 27, 69, 78, 119, 125
   self-tracking charts, 148
   summary of services, 147

Travel time, 136
Triage, cyclical, 129–134
Triage chart, 150
Tribes: A New Way of Learning and Being Together (Gibbs), 60

Unions, 161
Unpaid work, 14, 25, 70
U.S. Office of Special Education and Rehabilitative Services
   (OSERS), 115

Values Clarification (Simon, Howe, & Kirschenbaum), 60
Values-ranking exercise, 82
Varenhorst, Barbara, 61
Vocational assessments, 126–127, 192

Wilson, W. J., 117
Work-based learning programs. *See* Community classrooms
Work demands. *See* Job skills
Workforce Investment Act, 145

Youth services. *See* Transition services

ABOUT THE AUTHORS

Shepherd Siegel, PhD, was a rock and jazz musician before embarking on a career as an educator in vocational and special education. Working with the authors of this book, he helped to establish the first Career Ladders program in San Francisco in 1985. Since then he helped with the first replications of Marriott's Bridges program, and led the King County Vocational/Special Education Cooperative. Since 1996, he has led the school-to-career initiative for Seattle Public Schools. He is currently at work on a book about play, and how it, and the creative impulse, could transform our society.

Matt Robert, MS, CCC–SLP, worked with Career Ladders from 1986 to 1992. He initially helped to develop the role of the transition specialist, and subsequently became a vocational rehabilitation counselor with the California State Department of Rehabilitation, specializing in the high school transition caseload. He has since worked with the program from time to time on a consulting basis, assisting with program evaluation. He currently works as a speech–language pathologist helping to develop literacy skills in students with language-based learning disabilities at a private school in the greater Boston area. He lives with his wife in Jamaica Plain, Massachusetts. Unbeknownst to too many, he plays fantastic jazz guitar.

Karen Greener helped establish the first Career Ladders program in San Francisco. She then went on to direct San Francisco's IAM CARES nonprofit employment agency for people with disabilities. She has also served people with HIV/AIDS, and welfare-to-work clients in this capacity. Karen has used much of the Career Ladder model in diverse programs and in teaching job search skills to clients. More recently, Karen returned to the San Francisco Unified School District to run transition programs districtwide. She now serves all students with disabilities, preemployment through postsecondary education and everything in between. Karen has two beautiful daughters and has been married more than 17 years, and is now living the good life in Marin County.

Gary Meyer was a failure in school, due to having a learning disability before anybody knew what one was. He dropped out of high school in his junior year, graduating much later and then going on to college. He started working as a truck driver for a nationwide multimedia company and retired as vice president of that company at age 45. He then opened a real estate office that went on to become the leading company in the San Francisco area. One of his three children was born with a learning disability, but through a lot of effort on his and his daughter's part, today she is a well-balanced young woman who works in day care. Gary has been on both sides of the issue of employing people facing challenges, and he knows that winning—for the company and the employee—is the necessary option.

William Halloran, PhD, has been with the U.S. Department of Education, Office of Special Education Programs, for more than 25 years. His work focuses on research activities involving training and employment of individuals with disabilities. He played a key role in the mandate to provide school-to-career transition services through the Individualized Education Plan (IEP) process. Prior to his government position he was special education teacher in Connecticut and a special education administrator with the Vermont State Department of Education. Dr. Halloran also served as a Fulbright Scholar in India.

Robert Gaylord-Ross, PhD, was a scholar devoted to his family, and a better father because of his integrity as a scholar. His honesty, respect, and acceptance of other people were fundamental to his success as a leader and to his successes on the basketball courts of South Berkeley. Robert was deeply and passionately committed to social equity and justice. Robert's values derived from his connectedness with people. His life was intertwined with the lives of working-class people, people of color, and people with disabilities. He naturally found the ideals of equity and opportunity to express the needs and goals of the people he spent time with and cared about. Before he died in 1990, Robert Gaylord-Ross was a full professor of special education at San Francisco State University and Vanderbilt University.